Building Cross-Platform Desktop Applications with Electron

Create impressive cross-platform desktop applications with Electron and Node

Muhammed Jasim

BIRMINGHAM - MUMBAI

Building Cross-Platform Desktop Applications with Electron

Copyright © 2017 Packt Publishing

All rights reserved. No part of this book may be reproduced, stored in a retrieval system, or transmitted in any form or by any means, without the prior written permission of the publisher, except in the case of brief quotations embedded in critical articles or reviews.

Every effort has been made in the preparation of this book to ensure the accuracy of the information presented. However, the information contained in this book is sold without warranty, either express or implied. Neither the author, nor Packt Publishing, and its dealers and distributors will be held liable for any damages caused or alleged to be caused directly or indirectly by this book.

Packt Publishing has endeavored to provide trademark information about all of the companies and products mentioned in this book by the appropriate use of capitals. However, Packt Publishing cannot guarantee the accuracy of this information.

First published: April 2017

Production reference: 2020118

Published by Packt Publishing Ltd.
Livery Place
35 Livery Street
Birmingham
B3 2PB, UK.
ISBN 978-1-78646-412-5

www.packtpub.com

Credits

Author
Muhammed Jasim

Reviewer
Andrea Parodi

Commissioning Editor
Ashwin Nair

Acquisition Editor
Shweta Pant

Content Development Editor
Mohammed Yusuf Imaratwale

Technical Editor
Pranav Kukreti

Copy Editor
Dhanya Baburaj

Project Coordinator
Devanshi Doshi

Proofreader
Safis Editing

Indexer
Mariammal Chettiyar

Graphics
Jason Monteiro

Production Coordinator
Nilesh Mohite

About the Author

Muhammed Jasim has been involved in enterprise web application projects for more than 8 years. He started his software development career working with the Microsoft .NET platform and is currently working as a full stack developer for JavaScript applications. Throughout his career, he has developed many projects using a wide range of technologies and frameworks in both .NET and Node.js platforms. Currently, he is working for a Dubai-based airline company and is focused on the full-stack JavaScript application development.

I would like to thank my wife, Fathima, for her love, kindness, and support she has shown during the period of writing it has taken me to finalize this book. I would also like to thank my parents for their endless love and support.

About the Reviewer

Andrea Parodi has been working as a professional software developer for more than 20 years. He has mastered many languages and technologies that he encountered in his career.

During the last years, he used JavaScript and the web platform to develop mobile applications for a big Italian software house.

During these years, he start contributing to the open source Electron community, publishing libraries in GitHub.

> *I wish to thank my wife, Tatiana, who has helped me to review this book with her patience and her precious suggestions.*

www.PacktPub.com

For support files and downloads related to your book, please visit www.PacktPub.com.

Did you know that Packt offers eBook versions of every book published, with PDF and ePub files available? You can upgrade to the eBook version at www.PacktPub.com and as a print book customer, you are entitled to a discount on the eBook copy. Get in touch with us at service@packtpub.com for more details.

At www.PacktPub.com, you can also read a collection of free technical articles, sign up for a range of free newsletters and receive exclusive discounts and offers on Packt books and eBooks.

https://www.packtpub.com/mapt

Get the most in-demand software skills with Mapt. Mapt gives you full access to all Packt books and video courses, as well as industry-leading tools to help you plan your personal development and advance your career.

Why subscribe?

- Fully searchable across every book published by Packt
- Copy and paste, print, and bookmark content
- On demand and accessible via a web browser

Customer Feedback

Thanks for purchasing this Packt book. At Packt, quality is at the heart of our editorial process. To help us improve, please leave us an honest review on this book's Amazon page at https://www.amazon.com/dp/1786464128.

If you'd like to join our team of regular reviewers, you can e-mail us at customerreviews@packtpub.com. We award our regular reviewers with free eBooks and videos in exchange for their valuable feedback. Help us be relentless in improving our products!

Table of Contents

Preface — 1
Chapter 1: Introducing Electron — 7
  Why desktop applications? — 8
  History of Electron — 9
  Introducing Electron — 10
    Why should I use Electron? — 10
    Leveraging your existing skill set — 11
    Goodbye sandbox security model — 11
  Accessing operating system APIs — 12
    Unlimited access to Node.js and NPM — 12
    What do I need to know? — 12
    Who uses Electron? — 13
  Building a hello world application using Electron — 15
    Installing Node.js — 15
      Mac — 15
      Linux - Ubuntu — 16
    Installing Electron — 16
    Writing the application — 17
    Running the application — 20
    Using Node.js inside the web pages — 21
      How does Electron work? — 26
    The browser/main process — 28
    The renderer process — 28
    Communication between renderer and browser — 28
  Summary — 29
Chapter 2: Building Your First Electron Application — 31
  Introducing the sample application — 32
    The technical stack — 32
      Angular 2 — 33
      TypeScript — 33
      Facebook Graph API — 34
      Visual Studio code — 34
      Bootstrap and Photon kit — 35
      Webpack — 35
    Bootstrapping the application — 35

Organizing files and directories	37
Setting up the development environment	**38**
Running the initial application	39
Integrating Angular with Electron	40
Configuring module bundler - webpack	41
Configuring loaders	43
Webpack plugins	44
Bootstrapping Angular with Electron	47
Configuring dev server	52
Adding a menu bar to the application	53
Adding a context menu to the renderer process	55
Styling the application using Bootstrap	56
Summary	**57**
Chapter 3: Tooling and Debugging	**59**
Debugging an Electron application	**60**
Debugging the main process	61
Debugging with Visual Studio Code	**61**
Setting up the launch configuration	61
Debugging renderer processes	64
Adding Chrome Developer Tools extensions	65
Loading the developer tools extension manually	66
Monitoring the application with Devtron	68
Integrating task runners with VS Code	70
Boosting development workflow	71
Adding hot module replacement	72
Integrating webpack dev server into the Electron shell	73
Adding keyboard shortcuts to the application	74
Controlling Electron behavior using environment variables	76
Monitoring power state changes	77
Submitting crash reports to the server	77
Capturing the desktop using Electron API	78
Summary	**79**
Chapter 4: Using Angular 2 with Electron	**81**
Introducing the Facebook Graph API	**82**
Setting up the Facebook application	82
Configuring the Facebook SDK	83
Creating the service	83
Configuring Angular router	85

Login to the Facebook API	87
Getting user profile	91
Creating the profile component	98
Creating a tab component	100
Implementing oAuth authentication with Electron	101
Summary	106
Chapter 5: Crafting User Interface	**107**
Introducing Photon kit	108
Laying out the application	108
The frameless window	108
Draggable regions	109
Laying out the application	109
Sidebars	111
Photon components	111
Bars	112
Toolbar and Actions	112
Tabs	113
Navs	113
Tables	114
Building a user interface with React desktop	116
React desktop	122
Buttons	123
Windows	124
Segmented Control	125
NavPane	127
The list view	128
Awesome Electron	130
Summary	130
Chapter 6: Using Node.js with Electron	**131**
Managing data stores	132
Using the Node MySQL driver	133
Installing dependencies	134
Creating a database service	134
Accessing hardware	142
Creating a native add-on	144
Using TypeScript and ES2015 with Electron	147
Summary	150
Chapter 7: Deep Dive into Electron API - 1	**151**
Inter-process communication with IPC module	152

IPCRenderer	152
IPCMain	154
Passing callbacks to the main process	157
Sharing variables between modules	158
Defining custom protocols	158
Sessions and cookies	161
Session	163
Intercepting content download	164
Emulating network using session API	165
Intercepting permission requests	166
Managing file download	167
Native system dialogs	169
Generic dialog boxes	172
Working with clipboard	174
Managing display and power sleep mode	176
Monitoring power changes	177
Networking from the main process	179
Managing web requests	181
Summary	184

Chapter 8: Exploring Electron API - 2 — 185

Managing the web page using webContents	186
Managing the page navigation	187
Authenticating the web view requests	188
Capturing the page snapshot	189
Emulating device viewport inside the web view	190
Printing and saving the web pages	191
Embedding guest content using WebView tag	194
Extended Node.js process	196
Customizing the browser window	198
Managing multiple windows	199
Loading POST requests	200
Listening for APPCOMMANDs on a Windows platform	201
Offscreen rendering	202
Working with the shell	203
Controlling the application life cycle using app module	204
Setting up the default protocol client	204
Managing the recent document list	204
Summary	205

Chapter 9: Integrating with Desktop Environments — 207
Introduction to desktop integration — 208
Handling desktop notifications — 209
Managing task list, recent documents, and the dock menu — 211
Linux Unity launcher shortcuts — 214
Custom macOS dock menu — 215
Thumbnail toolbars — 218
Managing display properties — 219
Dealing with tray icons — 226
Managing application logs — 227
Running Electron application as Windows service — 231
Running Electron application as Linux daemons — 236
Universal Windows platform — 237
Developing with WinRT — 238
Using notification API — 240
Packaging for Windows store in appx format — 243
Summary — 244

Chapter 10: Dealing with Web Standards — 245
Service workers — 246
What is a service worker? — 246
The service worker life cycle — 246
Managing the service workers in Electron — 247
Creating HTTPS server — 249
Adding a JSON service — 252
Creating the service worker — 253
Managing the cache version — 256
Customizing the notification — 258
Storing database locally — 260
Summary — 261

Chapter 11: Testing Electron Application — 263
Introduction to JavaScript testing — 264
Introduction to Spectron — 266
Accessing the Electron API — 269
Testing DOM tree — 270
Exploring Spectron API — 273
Accessing the webContents API — 275
Accessing the process object — 276
Accessing the renderer process logs — 276
Using ESNext in test cases — 277

Using Chai as Promised	278
Summary	280
Chapter 12: Packaging and Distributing the Application	**281**
Building and packaging the Electron application	282
Packaging the Electron into asar archive	284
Generating the asar archive	284
Rebranding the application	286
Using Electron builder	287
Automating the build process	289
Creating the native installer	293
Programmatic Usage	303
Publishing the artifacts	303
Auto updating the application	305
Submitting to the App Store	308
Windows App Store submission guide	308
Mac App Store submission guide	309
Continuous Integration	311
Summary	313
Index	**315**

Preface

This book guides readers through building desktop applications that runs on Windows, Mac, and Linux platforms using the GitHub Electron framework. The book describes how to use your existing web development skills to build a cross-platform desktop application using HTML, CSS, and JavaScript.

Electron is one of the most popular frameworks for creating cross-platform desktop applications using JavaScript and Node.js. It's built on top of the Google's chromium project. Nowadays, it's getting more popular and companies and developers are using it for their production applications.

In this book, we'll talk through everything from installing tools, writing the application, and using various third-party tools and frameworks along with Electron.

What this book covers

Chapter 1, *Introducing Electron,* gives a basic overview about Electron and explains the internals of the Electron. Here, we will be seeing how Electron works and the architecture of the Electron.

Chapter 2, *Building Your First Electron Application,* discusses the step-by-step guide to develop an Electron application. It covers the steps to create a simple application from environmental setup to running the application.

Chapter 3, *Tooling and Debugging,* is all about tooling and debugging the application. It gives a detailed idea about debugging the application using various tools and IDEs that are available today.

Chapter 4, *Using Angular 2 with Electron,* explains using Angular 2 and TypeScript for creating the user interface for Electron application. The chapter will also discuss some other new technologies that are trending today. It will provide you with a detailed idea about using modern frontend frameworks and technologies with your Electron application.

Chapter 5, *Crafting User Interface,* showcases creating user interfaces for Electron applications. We will be covering various UI frameworks and some of the Electron-based UI frameworks, such as Photon, in this chapter. The chapter will be also covering how to use the popular React framework to craft your user interface for an Electron application.

Chapter 6, *Using Node.js with Electron*, teaches you how to use the Node.js context that is available inside the Electron in your project. This will be providing you with a complete guide to use the Node.js APIs inside an Electron application.

Chapter 7, *Deep Dive into Electron API - 1*, gives a detailed idea about various Electron APIs. We will be covering Electron APIs such as Clipboard, Process, Shell, Image, File, Dialog, Accelerator, and Session. This chapter will also cover some advanced topics, such as request intercepting and custom protocol implementation.

Chapter 8, *Exploring Electron API – 2*, continues exploring various Electron APIs. This will cover some of the advanced features, such as webContents API, which is used to control the rendering process, possible Chrome command-line switches, and the download API, among other things.

Chapter 9, *Integrating with Desktop Environments*, shows that different operating systems provide different features for integrating desktop applications into their desktop environments. This chapter explains how to integrate our application into those desktop environments with Electron APIs.

Chapter 10, *Dealing with Web Standards*, focuses on how various web standards can be integrated with Electron. This will cover topics such as caching network resources using a service worker, using local storage, and persisting data using IndexedDB.

Chapter 11, *Testing Electron Application*, informs that testing is an important aspect of the software application development process. This chapter covers testing your Electron application. The chapter also covers how to use popular JavaScript testing frameworks and, also, how to use those frameworks inside the Electron application.

Chapter 12, *Packaging and Distributing the Application*, explains how to package the application for final production. We will cover various libraries to package and distribute our application. This section will describe how to move to native packaging for each platform, how to enable autoupdating for the application in case of new changes, creating ASAR packages, creating installers for each platform, and guidelines to submit to various stores.

What you need for this book

- A text editor to edit and create HTML, CSS, and JavaScript files; you can use your preferred editor.
- Node.js should be installed in your system, at least 4.x or later version should be installed. It is preferable to have at least 6.x and later version.

- A package manager such as npm or yarn; npm will be installed by default when you install Node.js.
- (Optional) Git client should be installed on your computer if you would like to check out the recipe source code directly from our Git repository.

Who this book is for

If you are a developer familiar with HTML, CSS, and JavaScript, and you wish to develop a desktop application using these technologies, then this book is for you. This book is also targeting experienced JavaScript developers with a basic understanding of frontend development and Node.js development. This book is also suitable for frontend/web developers who want to develop a desktop application using the same technologies they are using for web development.

Conventions

In this book, you will find a number of text styles that distinguish between different kinds of information. Here are some examples of these styles and an explanation of their meaning.

Code words in text, database table names, folder names, filenames, file extensions, pathnames, dummy URLs, user input, and Twitter handles are shown as follows: "Electron then loads the HTML page using the `loadurl` function."

A block of code is set as follows:

```
{
    "name"    : "your-app",
    "version" : "0.1.0",
    "main"    : "main.js"
}
```

Any command-line input or output is written as follows:

```
curl -sL https://deb.nodesource.com/setup_7.x | sudo -E bash -
  sudo apt-get install -y nodejs
```

New terms and **important words** are shown in bold. Words that you see on the screen, for example, in menus or dialog boxes, appear in the text surrounded by quotes, or like this: "Just hit the **Download** button and click **OK**."

Warnings or important notes appear in a box like this.

Tips and tricks appear like this.

Reader feedback

Feedback from our readers is always welcome. Let us know what you think about this book—what you liked or disliked. Reader feedback is important for us, as it helps us develop titles that you will really get the most out of.

To send us general feedback, simply e-mail feedback@packtpub.com, and mention the book's title in the subject of your message.

If there is a topic that you have expertise in and you are interested in either writing or contributing to a book, see our author guide at www.packtpub.com/authors.

Customer support

Now that you are the proud owner of a Packt book, we have a number of things to help you to get the most from your purchase.

Downloading the example code

You can download the example code files for this book from your account at http://www.packtpub.com. If you purchased this book elsewhere, you can visit http://www.packtpub.com/support and register to have the files e-mailed directly to you.

You can download the code files by following these steps:

1. Log in or register to our website using your e-mail address and password.
2. Hover the mouse pointer on the **SUPPORT** tab at the top.
3. Click on **Code Downloads & Errata**.
4. Enter the name of the book in the **Search** box.
5. Select the book for which you're looking to download the code files.
6. Choose from the drop-down menu where you purchased this book from.
7. Click on **Code Download**.

You can also download the code files by clicking on the **Code Files** button on the book's webpage at the Packt Publishing website. This page can be accessed by entering the book's name in the **Search** box. Please note that you need to be logged in to your Packt account.

Once the file is downloaded, please make sure that you unzip or extract the folder using the latest version of:

- WinRAR / 7-Zip for Windows
- Zipeg / iZip / UnRarX for Mac
- 7-Zip / PeaZip for Linux

The code bundle for the book is also hosted on GitHub at `https://github.com/PacktPublishing/Building-Cross-Platform-Desktop-Applications-with-Electron`. We also have other code bundles from our rich catalog of books and videos available at `https://github.com/PacktPublishing/`. Check them out!

Downloading the color images of this book

We also provide you with a PDF file that has color images of the screenshots/diagrams used in this book. The color images will help you better understand the changes in the output. You can download this file from `https://www.packtpub.com/sites/default/files/downloads/BuildingCross-PlatformDesktopApplicationswithElectron_ColorImages.pdf`.

Errata

Although we have taken every care to ensure the accuracy of our content, mistakes do happen. If you find a mistake in one of our books—maybe a mistake in the text or the code—we would be grateful if you could report this to us. By doing so, you can save other readers from frustration and help us improve subsequent versions of this book. If you find any errata, please report them by visiting http://www.packtpub.com/submit-errata, selecting your book, clicking on the **Errata Submission Form** link, and entering the details of your errata. Once your errata are verified, your submission will be accepted and the errata will be uploaded to our website or added to any list of existing errata under the Errata section of that title.

To view the previously submitted errata, go to https://www.packtpub.com/books/content/support and enter the name of the book in the search field. The required information will appear under the **Errata** section.

Piracy

Piracy of copyrighted material on the Internet is an ongoing problem across all media. At Packt, we take the protection of our copyright and licenses very seriously. If you come across any illegal copies of our works in any form on the Internet, please provide us with the location address or website name immediately so that we can pursue a remedy.

Please contact us at copyright@packtpub.com with a link to the suspected pirated material.

We appreciate your help in protecting our authors and our ability to bring you valuable content.

Questions

If you have a problem with any aspect of this book, you can contact us at questions@packtpub.com, and we will do our best to address the problem.

1
Introducing Electron

Node.js is an open source cross-platform runtime environment for developing server-side web applications using JavaScript. It uses Google's V8 engine to interpret JavaScript. A variety of web frameworks such as Express and Hapi is available in Node.js. Nowadays, it's very commonly used for tooling purposes on a normal software development cycle. For example, most of the client-side JavaScript frameworks use Node.js to automate various development processes such as build, minify JavaScript, compile source code, and so on. But most people have a false impression that node is all about web applications and for command-line utilities. But the truth is we can use Node.js for almost everything that is possible with other programming languages and platforms.

In this book, we will be discussing how to use Node.js to build desktop applications that run on all major operating systems. You may be wondering about this combination--JavaScript and desktop applications. You may be using this type of application in your daily life. Have you ever used Slack at work? Or are you using GitHub Atom editor or Microsoft Visual Studio Code for editing your source code? Then you have used a Node.js based desktop application. These are some of the classic examples of Node.js based desktop applications.

There are two main choices available for building desktop applications using Node.js and web technologies:

- NW.js (formerly known as node-WebKit)
- Electron (formerly known as atom shell)

Both of these frameworks are open source and supported by major companies such as Intel and GitHub. Both have larger communities around them. In this book, we will be exploring building desktop applications using the GitHub Electron framework. Let's look into the internals and architecture of Electron before we get started with application development. In this chapter, we will be discussing the following points:

- Brief history and introduction of Electron
- Advantages of Electron over traditional desktop applications
- Building a hello world application using Electron
- Integrating a Node.js environment into web pages using Electron
- Architecture and internal of Electron

Why desktop applications?

The software development has changed tremendously over the past few years. At the beginning of the last decade, most software was available as desktop applications. But over time that began to change and the Web became dominant. The advent of Ajax again pushed the Web to a new era of software. Everything became distributed over the Internet. Cloud computing IOT pushed software technology to the next level and it spread over multiple devices.

So, do we really need to develop desktop applications? We cannot completely get rid of desktop applications. Even if the world is moving towards cloud and web technologies, there are some situations in which we need desktop applications:

- When data security is essential and it cannot be compromised by exposing over the Internet, desktop applications are the best choice
- When your application wants to access the operating system components and underlying hardware
- When you want to develop applications for various tooling purposes such as IDE, editors, and so on

So, there are still some situations in which only desktop applications are needed. But building an application that works on multiple operating systems is always challenging. Also, you can't afford to develop a desktop application that works on a single platform these days. And developing for each platform needs a lot of effort and technical knowledge in each platform which is more challenging. Here comes the possibility of cross-platform applications.

Cross-platform applications are not a new concept. Most of the modern programming languages work on all three major platforms. There are various frameworks available to create desktop applications using these languages. But for web developers, this would be a barrier to develop a desktop application in these languages as they have to learn these languages and its APIs.

Electron offers web developers a way to build desktop applications with the same skill set they are using for web development. Moreover that, the application could work across Windows, Mac, and Linux. This overcame the barrier that developers had faced to develop the desktop application. Also, they could reuse the same code base and skills for all three platforms. This is a massive advantage over other cross-platform application development frameworks. In addition to that, the popularity of Node.js leverages developers thousands of open source libraries to build their application with. This provides developers with a much faster timeline to desktop application development than traditional ways of development.

History of Electron

The history of Node.js desktop applications starts back in 2011 with Roger Wang, the creator of NW.JS. He started the node-webkit project as a simple Node.js module that can create a browser window using WebKit--the browser engine used by Safari. The main advantage of the node-webkit module was that you can use Node.js APIs inside the webpage. But this implementation relied on the WebKit library, which lacked lots of modern browser features. Later, Roger improved the node-webkit by replacing WebKit with the **chromium embedded framework** (**CEF**). CEF is also an open source project that facilitates embedded browser use cases in third-party applications.

In 2012, Intel (where Roger Wang was working) recruited Cheng Zhao, a Chinese student, as an intern to work on the node-webkit project. But instead of improving the current implementation he started by rewriting everything based on chromium's content shell, which is a minimal browser implementation inside the chromium project. He kept working with Roger at Intel for node-webkit until v0.3.6. In the meantime, GitHub was developing their atom editor. Cheng ended his internship with Intel and joined GitHub to work on Electron. After the efforts to migrate atom to node-webkit failed, they decided to write a new shell with fundamental architectural changes from node-webkit. The new shell was named atom-shell. Later, it was renamed to Electron.

Introducing Electron

The electron is a runtime that allows you to develop desktop applications using HTML, CSS, and JavaScript. It is an open source framework developed by GitHub. Previously called atom shell, it was originally built for atom editor (a very popular code editor from GitHub) to handle chromium to Node.js event loop integration and native API. Basically, it works by combining the chromium content framework and Node.js together in a single framework. You could see it as a variant of Node.js runtime that is focused on desktop application instead of web servers. This does not mean that Electron is a JavaScript binding for native platform API and GUI libraries. Your application will run in a minimum chromium browser, which is controlled by Node.js runtime and JavaScript.

The interesting part is that you can have the full power of both chromium and Node.js together in the same application. Usually, web browsers use sandboxed security models that block web pages from accessing operating system components. You are very limited with web applications in terms of native-operating system API access. On the other hand, Node.js provides native-operating, system-level access, but it does not provide a way to create graphical user interfaces for your application.

The electron really shines here by combining both frameworks together in a single shell. It's not a complex framework at all. You don't have to learn a lot of conventions in order to start application development with Electron. It's very easy to structure an application using Electron as there is no complex tooling required to set it up. We will be discussing some best practices and tips throughout this book.

Why should I use Electron?

We need to be very conscious about how we write the code when we are developing web applications because whatever we are writing is supposed to be executed on a user's computer or devices. Users could be using a wide range of browsers from the latest modern Chrome or Firefox to old legacy Internet Explorer. So, we will not have any idea of where the application will be rendered. This will end up in writing code that supports from outdated Internet Explorer to modern browsers, and you will not have the flexibility to use modern features and solutions that are available in modern browsers because of cross browser compatibility.

Suppose you are developing a cross-platform desktop application using QT or Java. In order to run your application users still, need to install the same or higher version of Java or any other SDK and environment setup that you used to develop the application. There will also be operating system requirements in order to install these frameworks.

When we build our application with Electron, we are packaging a particular version of chromium and Node.js along with our application. You will have the freedom to use cutting edge platform features that are supported by chromium and Node.js as you are shipping the same version of chromium and Node.js that you are using for development. Electron always keeps up to date with chromium and node versions. The chromium used inside Electron is always two weeks behind the latest stable chromium version. It typically includes the latest version of the node and v8 engine. Let's look at some other benefits of Electron.

Leveraging your existing skill set

Nowadays, most programmers have much more experience in developing web applications than desktop applications. Even if we would like to add the ability to add the desktop application development into our toolset, it's too costly for us in terms of time and effort. We would have to invest in learning a new programming language to get it done, which is not a simple thing. Electron helps you in this situation by using your existing skill set. You don't have to learn anything other than web technologies such as HTML, CSS, and JavaScript.

Goodbye sandbox security model

Traditional web applications are more limited in terms of native operating system API access. As web applications are distributed over servers and clients browsers render the web pages in separate processes that do not have access to the native operating system resources and APIs. At least, it's well defined by the browser what these processes can access and what they cannot access.

In Chrome, each tab is rendered in its own process. The chromium sandbox model encapsulates processes inside a very restrictive environment. This restricts the processes from accessing the native APIs. But for a desktop application, it's essential to access native operating system APIs. To provide native access the Electron team modified chromium as well as Node.js built-in and third-party modules. In Electron, the chromium sandbox protection can be disabled so that any application running inside Electron is given unfiltered access to the operating system.

Accessing operating system APIs

Electron applications are a lot like any other desktop application. It sits inside the user's filesystem and you can access it from the Windows start menu or Mac's dock menu. It can trigger any operating system events such as opening the file dialog. Additionally, Electron can present some of the operating system user interface components inside the application such as creating an operating system based menus and context menus. The electron also provides a lot of APIs to access the operating system features, such as:

- Adding menus to the application window
- Adding context menus to the application
- Sending the notifications to the user using operating system notifications system
- Adding items to the recent items list
- Custom dock menu and user tasks
- Progress bar in the taskbar

Unlimited access to Node.js and NPM

Electron provides direct access to Node.js APIs as well as NPM modules from web pages inside the application. Unlike normal web pages, the entire Node.js runtime is available inside your application. This enables you to use custom node modules and third-party modules without any additional effort. You can also use compiled Node.js native modules, which are usually written in C or C++.

What do I need to know?

If you are a web developer then you already know how to develop an Electron application. You don't need any experience in developing desktop applications. You should be comfortable with HTML, CSS, and JavaScript. It's helpful if you know the basics of Node.js and how the module system works in Node.js.

Who uses Electron?

Major companies and developers are already using Electron for their application development. You can find a long list of applications on the Electron showcase page (http://electron.atom.io/apps). There is also a community effort called awesome Electron (https://github.com/sindresorhus/awesome-electron/blob/master/readme.md) where you can get a list of apps with Electron. Awesome Electron not only lists apps but also a lot of resources and library information is available on that page.

It was originally developed as the foundation for the atom editor. Later, a lot of companies started using it for their production applications. Facebook has released a package for atom editor called Nuclide, which is heavily based on Electron:

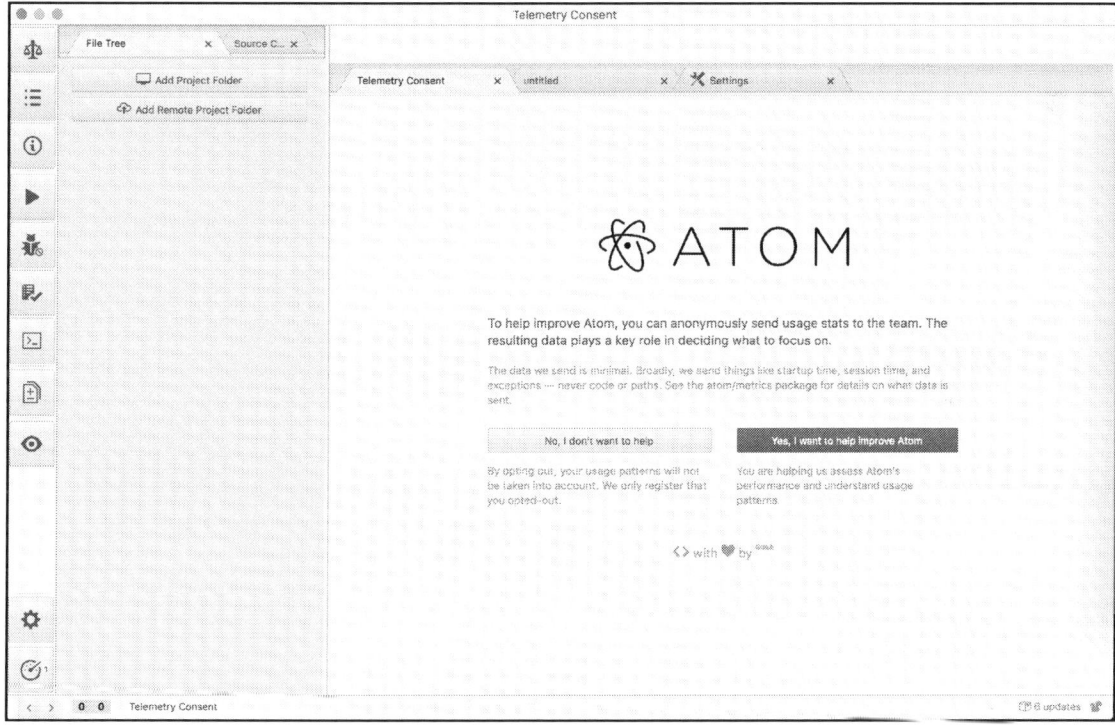

Screenshot of GitHub Atom editor

Introducing Electron

In 2015 Microsoft released a source code editor for Windows, Mac, and Linux. This is also based on Electron. It uses Visual Studio Online Monaco editor for creating its editor interface:

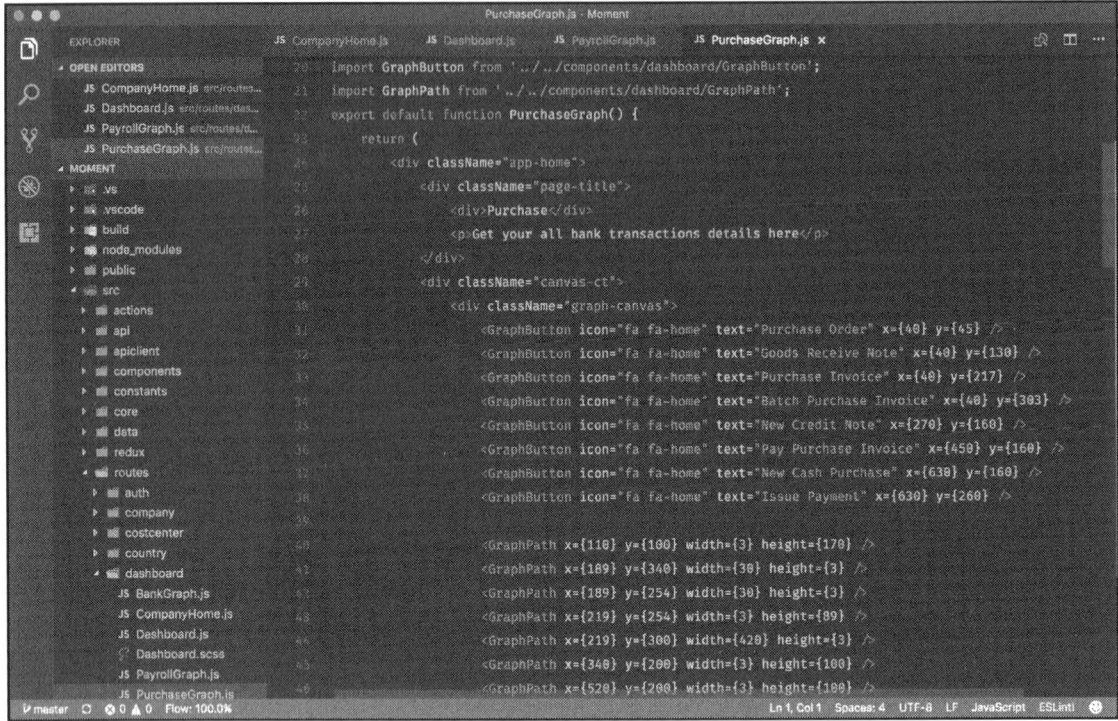

Microsoft Visual Studio code

We can have a lot of other examples on Electron-based applications. Nowadays most companies prefer it as their primary desktop application development platform. Here are some popular applications based on Electron:

- **Slack**: It's a cloud-based team collaboration tool. It's completely based on web technologies such as React, Redux, ES6/7, and Node.js.
- **Nyla's n1**: An open source e-mail client that boasts a great level of flexibility, expandability, and configuration. It's built with Electron and React js. You can find its source code on GitHub (https://github.com/nylas/N1).

- **Wordpress.com**: Popular content management system, WordPress uses Electron for their desktop version. It's an open source project and it is available on GitHub (https://github.com/Automattic/wp-desktop).
- **Pixate**: It's a mobile app prototyping tool from Google.

Building a hello world application using Electron

Let's check how to build a simple application with Electron, which will give you a better understanding of how the Electron application works. You should have Node.js installed on your machine to start Electron application development. You can check whether Node.js is installed or not by opening your terminal/command line prompt and entering the following command:

```
node -v
```

This should give you Node.js version installed on your computer.

Installing Node.js

The best way to install Node.js is using the installer. You can visit www.nodejs.org to download the installer for your operating system. There are a couple of other ways to install Node.js.

Mac

Installing Node.js and NPM is pretty straightforward using HomeBrew. You can find more about installing HomeBrew on http://brew.sh/. Once you have brew installed on your Mac, open the terminal and type the following:

```
brew install node
```

Homebrew downloads some files and installs them. And that's it.

Linux - Ubuntu

The Node.js for Linux-based distribution is available from the NodeSource (http://nodesource.com), Debian, and Ubuntu binary repository. Type the following command in your terminal to install Node.js on your machine:

```
curl -sL https://deb.nodesource.com/setup_6.x | sudo -E bash -
sudo apt-get install -y nodejs
```

Alternatively, for Node.JS v7:

```
curl -sL https://deb.nodesource.com/setup_7.x | sudo -E bash -
sudo apt-get install -y nodejs
```

To compile and install the native add-ons from npm you may also need to install build tools:

```
Sudo apt-get install -y build-essential
```

Now we should have both Node.js and npm working. You can verify this by entering the `node -v` command and `npm -v` command in your terminal.

Installing Electron

Once you have node and npm installed, then you need to install Electron. Basically, Electron is an npm module that contains precompiled versions of Electron. You can install Electron using npm by issuing the following command in your terminal or command line prompt:

```
npm install -g electron
```

The command is pretty straightforward. It says npm to install Electron module into global npm repository by specifying -g flag. In npm there are two ways to install the module:

- **Globally**: this installs the module in the global directory, usually inside the user's profile directory. Just like a global variable, these modules are accessible across the operating system.

- **Locally**: local modules can be installed with the same command, but without the -g flag. The modules will be installed into the current directory. Its scope is limited to the current directory.

Writing the application

Structuring an Electron application is very simple. In this example, we need to create only three files to build the application. Create project structure in your current working directory as follows:

```
app
 |- index.html
 |- main.js
 |- package.json
```

You can generate `package.json` using the following command:

npm init

`package.json` holds various metadata relevant to the project. This file is used to give the information to Node.js, npm, and Electron that helps to identify the project as well as the dependencies used inside the project. `package.json` in our hello world application might look like the following:

```
{
  "name"    : "your-app",
  "version" : "0.1.0",
  "main"    : "main.js"
}
```

The filename specified by the main field in `package.json` is the entry point for our application. This script should create the windows and handle the system events. If the main field is not present in `package.json` then Electron will attempt to load an `index.js` file.

Introducing Electron

 You can find two example folders inside the code bundle. The first one contains the hello-world electron example that is what we are describing here. The second example contains a simple mark-down viewer that will be discussed in next section of this chapter.

Create the `main.js` file, which is responsible for loading the main window with the following content:

```
const { app, BrowserWindow } = require('electron');

let win = null;

// index.html file path
const appUrl = `file://${__dirname}/index.html`;

/**
 * Create Electron Browser window instance
 * @return {BrowserWindow} win
 */
function createElectronShell() {
  // Initializes the new browser window
  win = new BrowserWindow({ width: 800, height: 600 });
  // Load the html file into the browser window
  win.loadURL(appUrl);
  // Release the variable reference when the window is closed
  win.on('closed', () => {
    win = null;
  });
  // Opens the chrome devtool
  win.webContents.openDevTools();
}

/**
 * Create the BrowserWindow instance and open the the main application window
 * when Electron's app module emits the ready event.
 */
app.on('ready', createElectronShell);

/**
 * The app module should exit when all the windows are closed.
 * The app.quit method should be explicitly called except on Mac machine
 */
app.on('window-all closed', () => {
  if(process.platform !== 'darwin') app.quit();
});
```

[18]

```
/**
 * Re-activate the main window when the application in bringing forward to
the
 * foreground. On mac machine the instance should be created each time when
the
 * application activate event emits
 */
app.on('activate', () => {
  if(win== null) createElectronShell();
});
```

In the preceding code, the first line imports app and browser window modules to the application. The app module is responsible for managing the life cycle of your application. The `BrowserWindow` module creates and manages the application window.

The electron then loads the HTML page using the `loadurl` function. This example loads the HTML page from the current directory. You can inspect your HTML page using chrome developer tools. This can be opened using the `win.webContents.openDevTools()` method.

Next create your `index.html` file inside the same directory where your `package.json` resides:

```
<html>
  <head>
    <base href="./">
    <title>Hello Electron</title>
    <meta charset="UTF-8">
    <meta name="viewport" content="width=device-width, initial-scale=1">
    <style type="text/css">
      #banner {
        font-size: 22px;
        font-weight: bold;
        font-family: Verdana;
        margin: 10px;
      }
      #shellInfo {
        margin: 10px;
        line-height: 2;
        font-size: 14px;
        font-family: verdana;
      }
    </style>
    <script>
    document.addEventListener('DOMContentLoaded', () => {
      const { node, chrome, electron } = process.versions;
```

```
            document.querySelector('#nodeVersion').innerHTML = node;
            document.querySelector('#chromeVersion).innerHTML = chrome;
            document.querySelector('#electronVersion).innerHTML = electron;
        });
        </script>
    </head>
    <body>
        <div id="banner">Electron is up and running</div>
        <div id="shellInfo">
            <div>Node : <span id="nodeVersion"></span></div>
            <div>Chrome : <span id="chromVersion"></span>div>
            <div>Electron : <span id="electronVersion"></span>div>
        </div>
    </body>
</html>
```

This is a simple HTML file that displays the version of chrome, Electron, and node. It directly accesses the Node.js process to get this information, which is available globally inside the DOM. These three files are enough to get it run in our simple application.

Running the application

Once you are done with creating your `index.html`, `package.json`, and `main.js` files you will probably want to try running the application.

If you have installed Electron globally with npm, then you will only need to run the following command from your application source directory:

`electron .`

If Electron is installed locally, then run the following command from your application source code directory:

`"./node_modules/.bin/electron" .`

The Electron command will try to load your `main.js` file and it will create a window for you. It will then load your `index.html`. You should get output as follows:

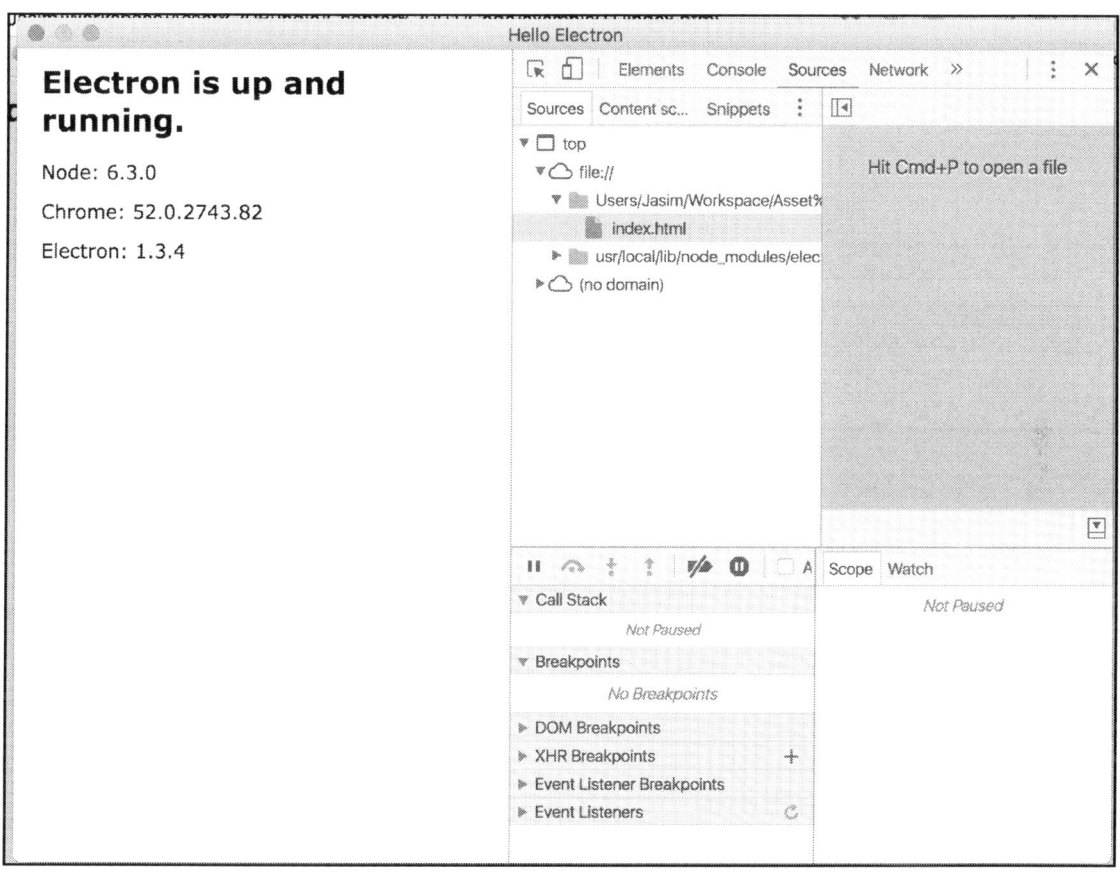

Hello world Electron Shell output

Using Node.js inside the web pages

The preceding application does nothing other than display a static file in the Electron shell. Let's add some more functionality to the application to get a much more clear idea about what Electron can do and how it works. You can get the source code for this section in `example02` folder of the chapter 01 code bundle.

Introducing Electron

As we discussed earlier, with Electron you can directly access Node.js and its modules directly from your web page. Let's expand our application to use node native file system modules to access operating systems file system. We don't have the readme file inside the application, which is essential for providing some information about the application to other developers. So let's add one `readme.md` file to the root of the application and add some dummy markdown content. If you are new to markdown, it's a lightweight markup language with plain text formatting syntax. It can be converted to HTML and many other formats.

Create a `readme.md` file with the sample content. You can get some same dummy content here from this URL: `https://raw.githubusercontent.com/electron/electron/master/README.md`. We then need to display this markdown into the HTML page by transforming the markdown to HTML.

Create a new JavaScript file named `markdown-processor.js` in the same directory where your `main.js` sits. Node.js does not support parsing markdown file natively. But there are lots of third-party libraries available over the Internet. Let's check how to install third-party node modules via npm. Install Node.js markdown parser called marked (`https://github.com/chjj/marked`) into the application via npm by entering the following command from your project directory:

```
npm install --save marked
```

Save the flag that says that this library information should be added to the `package.json` dependencies section.

Let's add some code to the `markdown-processor.js` file:

```
// imports the node js module
const fs = require('fs');
const marked = require('marked');

// read the contents of readme.md file using fs module
const content = fs.readFileSync('readme.md', 'utf-8');

// transform readme.md file's content into html using marked library
const html = marked(content);

// update the DOM with the transformed html. Even if this is a node context
// we have the access to the browser DOM
document.getElementById('viewer').innerHTML = html;
```

The preceding code is pretty much straightforward. The first two lines use the require function to load the external modules into the current scope. It's like importing some other classes and methods in Java or C#. We use Node's `fs` module, which gives a wrapper around the standard POSIX function to read the content `readme.md` file. All the methods inside the `fs` module have synchronous and asynchronous versions. Usually, when working with Node.js in server environments it's always recommended to use an asynchronous version of `fs` module methods as multiple users need to access the resources concurrently. But here in case of Electron, you can simply use asynchronous or synchronous as we are not targeting multi user experience on the desktop client system Here we use the `readFileSync` method to read file content synchronously. It then parses the content and transforms it into HTML using the *marked* library.

Until now it's just an independent module. Import it into your HTML file either using a standard script tag or using node's require function as follows:

```html
<!DOCTYPE html>
<html>
  <head>
    <meta charset="UTF-8">
    <title>Hello World!</title>
    <link rel="stylesheet" type="text/css" href="style.css" />
    <link rel="stylesheet" type="text/css" href="github-markdown.css" />
    <style type="text/css">
      #banner {
        font-size: 22px;
        font-weight: bold;
        font-family: Verdana;
        margin: 10px;
      }
      #shellInfo {
        margin: 10px;
        line-height: 2;
        font-size: 14px;
        font-family: verdana;
      }
    </style>
    <script>
      document.addEventListener('DOMContentLoaded', () => {
        const { node, chrome, electron } = process.versions;
        document.querySelector('#nodeVersion').innerHTML = node;
        document.querySelector('#chromeVersion).innerHTML = chrome;
        document.querySelector('#electronVersion).innerHTML = electron;
      });
    </script>
  </head>
```

```
<body>
  <div id="banner">Electron is up and running.</div>
  <div id="shellInfo">
    We are using node <span id="nodeVersion"></span>
    Chrome <span id="chromeVersion"></span>, and
    Electron <span id="electronVersion"></span>.
  </div>
  <div id="viewer">
  </div>

  <script type="text/javascript">
    require('./markdown-processor');
  </script>
  </body>
</html>
```

Our application is ready to display the content of the markdown file. But before running the application, let's add some style to the application. Create a file called `style.css` in the same directory with the following content:

```
body, html {
  margin: 0;
  padding: 0;
  height: 100%;
  width: 100%;
  background: #F5f5f5;
}

#viewer {
  margin: 10px auto 0 auto;
  max-width: 968px;
  background-color: #FFF;
  border: solid 1px #ECECEC;
  box-shadow: 0 0 15px 0px #ccc;
  padding: 15px;
}
```

Add the style sheet reference to the HTML file. As we are using the markdown file from the official GitHub Electron repository, let's style it using the official GitHub styles. There is an open source GitHub style sheet available for markdown files at this URL (https://github.com/sindresorhus/github-markdown-css). Let's add this CSS to the application:

```
<head>
  ...
  <link rel="stylesheet" href="style.css" />
  <link rel="stylesheet" href="github-markdown.css" />
```

```
</head>
....
```

Run the application using the following command from the current working directory:

`electron .`

You should get an output like this:

Application renders markdown to HTML

With Electron you can see how to combine the power of node and Chrome together on one page. The power of HTML and CSS allows us to create the amazing user interface. In the preceding example, we could work with native file systems directly from the DOM, which is not possible with traditional web applications. This is why Electron really shines.

How does Electron work?

The electron is based on Google's Chromium project. Chromium is an open source version of Google's Chrome web browser. Electron uses Chromium's content module to render the web pages. Chromium content modules are the core code needed to render a web page in multi process sandboxed browser. It includes all the web features (HTML renderer blink engine, v8 engine to execute JavaScript) and GPU acceleration. It does not include chrome features, that is, extension/autofill/spelling and so on. For better understanding let's look into how the chrome browser works.

Before we get into the details of the Electron architecture, let's check out the multi-process architecture of chromium because Electron uses a simplified version of Chromium's multi process architecture. Modern operating systems are robust because they put an application into different processes that are separated by each other. A crash in one application does not have any impact on another application and it will not affect the integrity of the operating system. In a similar way, Google Chrome uses a separate process for each tab to protect overall bugs and glitches from the rendering engine. It also restricts access from each rendering process to others and to the rest of the system. So basically the Chrome browser runs two types of processes. The main process runs the UI and plugin process and tabs specific processes which render the web page. The following figure shows how the multi process architecture works in Electron. The main process can start multiple renderer processes with different URLs loaded into it:

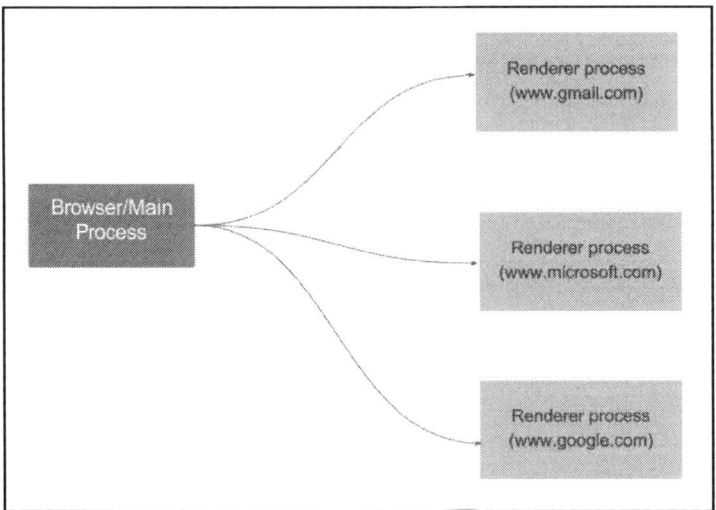

As I mentioned earlier, Electron uses a simplified version of this multi process architecture. It consists of three main parts:

- **Browser**: This is responsible for business logic and data access. It works on its own process called the main process. It creates the browser window and corresponding modules to render the web pages. In our application, `main.js` is running in this process, which creates the main window.
- **Renderer**: This is responsible for rendering each web page. Each web page renders on its own thread.
- **Modules** that bridge browser and renderer and control application life cycle:

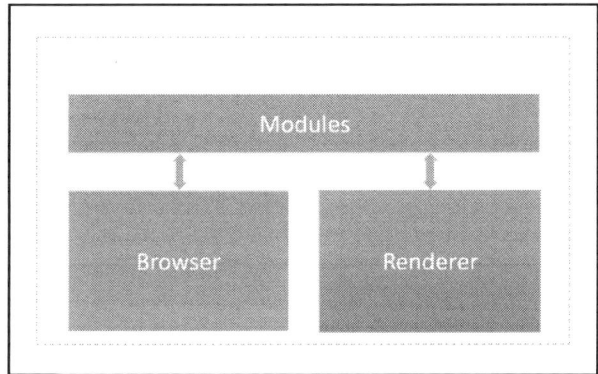

If you look at our preceding example, `main.js` is responsible for creating windows and managing the application state. It creates a window by instantiating a browser window object. This `main.js` is running in the **Main** process. The **Main** process creates a web page by creating a `BrowserWindow` object. Each `BrowserWindow` runs the web page in its own separate renderer process. These renderer processes will be terminated when the corresponding `BrowserWindow` object is destroyed.

The main process is responsible for managing all the web pages and its renderer processes. Each renderer process is isolated and cares only about the web page running in it:

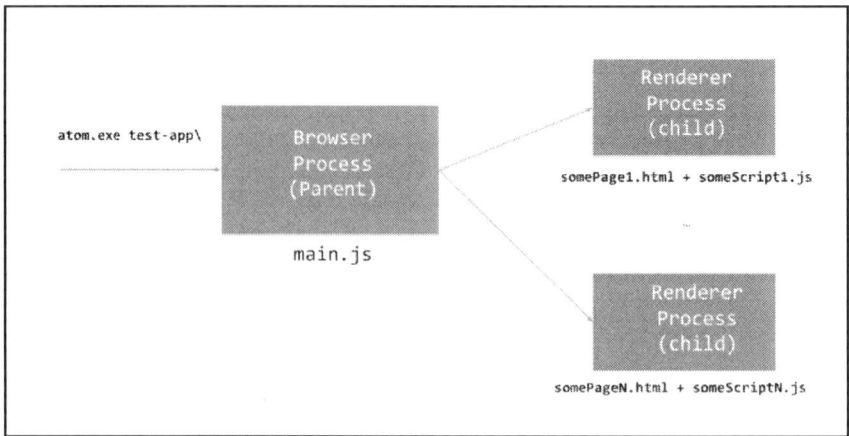

As I mentioned earlier, in Electron there are two types of processes that control the entire application.

The browser/main process

The main process is responsible for responding to applications life cycle events, starting and quitting the application. Normally, the web browsers render each page inside a sandboxed environment. Because of these sandboxed environments, the web pages are not allowed to access the native resources. But in the case of Electron, it provides the Node.js execution context inside the renderer process, which allows you the lower level operating system interactions from your web pages rendered in the Electron shell.

The renderer process

The renderer process is responsible for loading the web pages to display the graphical user interface. Each process can load and execute additional JavaScript files in the same process. Unlike Chromium, Electron renderer processes enable us to use some Node.js APIs directly from web pages. Each renderer process is isolated and each process cares only about the page running in it.

Communication between renderer and browser

Browser and renderer are separately running processes that communicate using special APIs called chromium inter process communication (Chromium IPC). The Electron team has built a simplified API called ipc on top of it. Sharing the state between these processes has to go through the `ipcmain` and `ipcrenderer` module. The JavaScript context in each of these processes is kept different. Electron transmits the data between these modules in an explicit fashion. `ipcMain` and `ipcRenderer` modules are basically event emitters that handle the communication between main processes and other renders processes.

Summary

In this chapter, we introduced Electron and discussed how it allows developers to build desktop applications using web technologies. We discussed some of the example implementations that are used for production use. We also looked at how to integrate the Electron with underlying platform features and APIs. We then created a tiny sample application to understand the structure of a basic Electron application. Finally, we looked at how Electron works under the hood by discussing chromium architecture, chromium content shell, multi process architecture, and inter process communication. Now we have a brief idea about Electron and its architecture. In the next chapter, we will be discussing using Electron in a real-world scenario. We will also discuss integrating Electron with front end frameworks.

2
Building Your First Electron Application

The previous chapter provided an introduction to Electron and covered various topics including a detailed view of the framework itself, the history of Electron, the architecture of Electron and some real-world examples of Electron use in production. We also looked at how to create a basic hello world application using Electron. Now we are ready to build more complex applications with real-world scenarios. The rest of this book is structured around the construction of a sample application that presents how to use Electron in real-life projects. The rest of this book is structured around some real-world examples on the electron and node JS that presents how to use Electron for your real-life projects.

Over the next three chapters, we will be creating a simple social media application client. This will help us to demonstrate the use of Electron APIs as well as to cover scenarios such as operating system access from Electron pages, remote API access using Node.js from a typical desktop environment, using local desktop based authentication, and so on. This chapter will demonstrate how to set up an Electron application with Angular 2 as the front end framework. Even though we are discussing Angular as a front end framework, any of the available front-end frameworks can be used instead of the Angular. Setting up an Electron application is simple, but when it comes with modern frontend frameworks, the process includes various tools and frameworks to get it run the first time. The majority of this chapter looks at Angular 2 and its setup with Electron. We will also discuss the following points:

- The problem domain and the technical stack used in the sample application
- Architecture and folder structure of the sample application
- Brief about development tools and the IDE used to develop the application
- Automated build process using popular task runners

- Configuring a module bundler to run the Angular 2 application
- Configuring and running the sample application skeleton using Webpack and Angular 2
- Creating and using an operating system-based user interface component, such as the menubar, using Electron

Introducing the sample application

We are going to create a sample social media client application to showcase the Electron features in the most advantageous environment. This application will be a desktop client that uses Facebook APIs. So basically, we will be implementing a limited set of Facebook features in this application. The backend data is supposed to be consumed from the Facebook Graph API which is the primary way that data is retrieved from or posted to Facebook. This sample application can be used to get your Facebook newsfeed, post stories and images to your Facebook wall, get your Friends list and manage your Friends, and so on. As we are developing a sample application, we will be implementing only a limited set of functionalities from Facebook. We will start the application bootstrapping process in this chapter, and in later chapters we will also look at how to integrate this sample application into our desktop environment by providing some nice desktop features like notifications, background tasks and live tile views on the Windows taskbar.

The technical stack

Even though this book primarily focuses on developing a desktop application using Electron, it's arguably hard for a developer to build a JavaScript application without using some frameworks. Nowadays there are number of JavaScript frameworks that are available for both client-side and server-side. It's very hard to choose between these frameworks as the JavaScript ecosystem grows day by day. Here also, we need to have a framework in our stack to build the application with less effort. Also, bear in mind that Electron does not need any frameworks. It can work together with any framework to build a desktop application. Some of the front end frameworks has already been integrated with Electron and these libraries are available over the Internet.

One of the great examples of this type of integration is the React desktop, which integrates Facebook react with Electron. In this book, we will explore how to wire up a social media app using Angular 2 and Electron. As Electron renders the user interface as web pages, any front-end frameworks could be used with Electron. So, the details described here could be easily adapted to make use of others. Let's have a look at the tools and technologies that we are going to use to build our sample application.

Angular 2

As a number of frameworks are available, it's a little confusing for a frontend developer to choose between them for front-end development. We will be using Google's ever-popular web development framework Angular for our application. This should be easy for you if have worked with Angular 2 before. You can skip a lot of development setup-related stuff if you have previous experience on Angular 2. However, no prior knowledge on Angular 2 is required to follow the example in this book. We will go through all the steps to set up an Angular application with Electron in this chapter and the following chapters too. However, Angular is not the only framework that can be used with Electron. Any front-end framework can be used to build the user interface. If you are proficient in React, Ember or Vue, you could use either with Electron.

The process of developing a desktop application with Electron and Angular is almost the same as developing for the web with the same technologies. We don't have to master any additional conventions to develop for the desktop using Electron and Angular.

TypeScript

TypeScript is the superset of JavaScript developed by Microsoft. It adds optional static typing and class-based object-oriented programming to the language. Unlike JavaScript, it gives static code analyzing features when used with TypeScript-enabled IDEs like Visual Studio code. The browser cannot run the TypeScript file directly inside your web pages. Instead, you need to compile it into JavaScript to execute it inside web pages. You can get the TypeScript compiler, called tsc, along with your TypeScript installation, which compiles the TypeScript to JavaScript.

Building Your First Electron Application

As you probably know, Angular 2 is written in TypeScript. We use TypeScript because Angular 2 recommends it for development, but it's not mandatory to use TypeScript. You could even use ES2015 or ES5. There are some benefits of using TypeScript:

- It provides static type checking which reduces development time errors.
- It gives more language features than ECMA script 2015/2016.
- We use Angular 2 to build the user interface for our application. TypeScript is recommended over JavaScript for Angular 2.

We will be using Typescript to write the user-interface related code which is used by Angular.

Facebook Graph API

The Graph API is the primary way that data is retrieved from or posted to Facebook. It is a low-level HTTP-based API that you can use to query data, post new stories, and a variety of other actions that an app might want to do. We will be using this API heavily to get the Facebook data into the client application. These API requests are composed using the browser's built-in Ajax capabilities and also some third-party node modules like request JS. You can get more details about the Facebook Graph API at `https://developers.facebook.com/docs/graph-api/reference/user/friends/`.

Visual Studio code

Visual Studio code is a source code editor from Microsoft. It is built on top of Electron. The entire editor is written in JavaScript and TypeScript. It provides a simple and streamlined experience of code editor which is what developers need for their development cycle. It gives first class support to edit and debug the JavaScript-based application. It also gives comprehensive language support for JavaScript, TypeScript, and thus for Angular 2. Throughout this book, we will be discussing various tips and tricks that can be useful when developing an application using VS code. But VS code is not the only editor available to develop an Angular 2/Electron application. You can use any other IDEs or editors that support TypeScript and JavaScript: Atom, Sublime, and Bracket are some other examples. I prefer VS code because it has built-in support for Node.js debugging, support for automated task management, Angular 2 templating support, and much more.

Grab the latest version of Visual Studio code for your platform from: `https://code.visualstudio.com/`.

Bootstrap and Photon kit

Angular itself doesn't provide a user interface library. It also does not force you to use any particular framework or component library. It's up to you to choose the framework to build the user interface. To make a social media application, we will use the famous Twitter bootstrap framework and Photon kit, a popular Electron-based UI library. PhotonKit is a component library similar to bootstrap. These components are designed for desktop-like user interfaces to be used in frameworks like Electron and nwjs. It provides a native like look and feel for your component. You can even use this library for your web applications as it's simply developed on HTML and CSS.

Webpack

Managing JavaScript modules and assets manually is not practical in a large JavaScript application as there may be hundreds of modules present inside the application. We should use module bundler to bundle the JavaScript application. System JS with Browserify, Webpack, and Rollup are some of the best choices for module bundler. A server-side node application or a pure Electron based application does not need to bundle the assets into a single file if you are not using any of the latest language features that node does not supports, as Node.js runtime knows how to load the dependencies. However, in our sample application, we are creating the user interface using Angular, and it is supposed to be rendered in a browser window provided by Electron. So we need to bundle our Angular applications for a better user experience.

In this book, we use the Webpack to bundle our source code into manageable chunks. Basically, it takes code modules with dependencies and generates static assets representing those modules. webpack not only creates an application bundle but also automate lots of other tasks, from linting to bundling, for our Angular application. We will look at how to use it with Electron shortly in this chapter.

Bootstrapping the application

We have made some important decisions about the technical stack and tools to be used while building our sample social media client. Now let's kick start our development process. Here we will start building the application from scratch and we don't want to use any of the boilerplate code available online. The main reason behind this decision is that it will help you to create, not only an Electron application but also to integrate any other front end frameworks with Electron other than Angular 2.

Building Your First Electron Application

Creating an application from scratch will provide a better understanding of the nuts and bolts of Electron and its internals. The recommended way to develop an Angular application is to use Angular CLI as it provides complete workflow and boilerplate code for the development process.

We have already discussed how to build a simple Electron application in the previous chapter. We initialize our node project using the `npm init` command. The command will ask you for some metadata information for your application. When your terminal prompts for a name, give the application name that you want. It will then ask you for a version number and some other information. Give the proper values for your terminal prompts. Now npm has initialized our node project and you can find the `package.json` file in your project directory. Install the Electron distribution using `npm install` command. Refer to the previous chapter on how to install it using npm. The following screenshot shows the npm prompt that asks you to fill the metadata information for your application at the `npm init` command:

```
name: (Electron) electron
version: (1.0.0)
description:
entry point: (index.js)
test command:
git repository:
keywords:
author:
license: (ISC)
About to write to /Users/Jasim/Workspace/EK Workspace/Electron/package.json:

{
  "name": "electron",
  "version": "1.0.0",
  "description": "",
  "main": "index.js",
  "scripts": {
    "test": "echo \"Error: no test specified\" && exit 1"
  },
  "author": "",
  "license": "ISC"
}
```

Organizing files and directories

There are many ways to organize our application. The electron does not restrict you to follow any specific structure. Our sample application structure is as displayed in the following image:

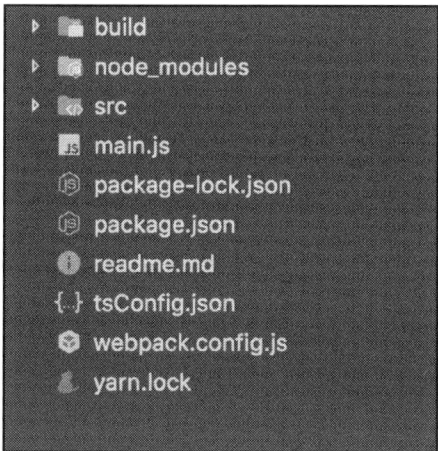

As you can see in this structure, the `src` folder contains the Angular application source code and the `main.js` file is the entry point for the Electron shell.

Our sample application contains the following folders and files:

- `src`: `src` folder contains our application's front-end source code. We will have our Angular 2 application source in this folder.
- `build`: Application bundles that are compiled using webpack will be placed in this directory. The production version will be based on this directory. We will have the packaged Angular 2 application and other JavaScript files inside this folder along with static assets.
- `webpack.config.js`: The configuration for Webpack to bundle the Angular application should be written in this file.
- `main.js`: This is the entry point for the Electron shell. We had already checked the content of this file in the previous chapter. The `main.js` will be almost similar to what we developed in the previous chapter.

Setting up the development environment

For a painless development cycle, we need to use the best tools and libraries available. This section describes the setting up of the development environment. The primary requirement is that Node.js is installed on your computer. We have already discussed Node.js and npm in the previous chapter so I assume that you have already installed Node.js and Electron in your machine.

Kickstart the application development by creating the directory structure discussed in above section. We have already initialized Node.js project inside the current directory using npm, and Electron is installed. Refer to the previous chapter to get more details about these steps.

Install Electron into the project by using the `npm install --save electron` command. This will create the `node_modules` folder automatically in your project.

Once the application skeleton is ready, open the `package.json` manifest file from the root of the project. The content should look like following:

```
{
  "name": "electron-app",
  "version": "1.0.0",
  "description": "",
  "dependencies": {
    "electron": "^1.7.5"
  },
  "devDependencies": {},
  "scripts": {
    "test": "echo "Error: no test specified" && exit 1"
  },
  "author": "",
  "license": "ISC"
}
```

Running the initial application

The previous chapter was discussed creating a hello world application. The same code can be used to kickstart the electron shell. Create the `main.js` file at the root of the project folder and copy the following code to it. The code is similar to the previous chapter except the HTML file's path is changed to the build folder which supposed to have `index.html` once the webpack bundling happens:

```javascript
const { app, BrowserWindow } = require('electron');

let win;

// index.html file path - This should be from the webpack build path
const appUrl = `file://${__dirname}/build/index.html`;

/**
 * Create Electron Browser window instance
 * @return {BrowserWindow} win
 */
function createElectronShell() {
  // Initializes the new browser window
  win = new BrowserWindow({ width: 800, height: 600 });
  // Load the html file into the browser window
  win.loadURL(appUrl);
  // Release the variable reference when the window is closed
  win.on('closed', () => {
    win = null
  });
  // Opens the chrome devtool
  win.webContents.openDevTools();
}

/**
 * Create the BrowserWindow instance and open the the main application
 * window when Electron's app module emits the ready event.
 */
app.on('ready', createElectronShell);

/**
 * The app module should exit when all the windows are closed.
 * The app.quit method should be explicitely called except on Mac machine
 */
app.on('window-all-closed', () => {
  if(process.platform !== 'darwin') app.quit();
});
```

Building Your First Electron Application

```
/**
 * Re-activate the main window when the application in bringing forward to
 * the foreground. On mac machine the instance should be created each time
 * when the application activate event emits
 */
app.on('activate', () => {
  if(win== null) createElectronShell();
});
```

The above is similar to the code described in the previous chapter, except we have changed the index.html path. You can place the same HTML from the previous example into the build folder to run the application.

Integrating Angular with Electron

Creating an Angular application is easy with Angular CLI. Angular CLI is the command-line utility to create and manage the Angular application. This tool is provided by the Angular team. Even though the recommended way to develop the Angular application is to use the CLI, here we are not going to use it. Instead, we will be manually crafting the application using Webpack. The use of Webpack is only to bundle the Angular application. The rest of this chapter will be about integrating Angular with Electron. We have already talked about Electron architecture. The architecture looks like the following diagram when the application is finished. The renderer process will use the Angular applications which will be rendering the user interfaces and interacting with the main process and Node.js runtime.

As a first step, let's initialize an Angular 2 project inside our Electron application:

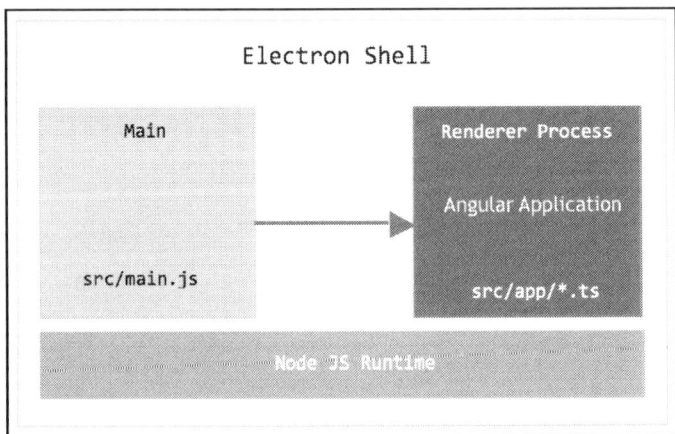

Configuring module bundler - webpack

Configuring the module bundler is the first step to getting started with an Angular 2 application. Webpack is a powerful and popular module bundler. The term bundle means a JavaScript file that incorporates the assets that belong together and should serve to clients in response to a single file request. A bundle can include almost any kind of file including JavaScript, CSS, and HTML.

Webpack works by scanning your source code to check all the `import` statements used inside the application. It then generates a dependency graph before bundling your source code. It can process the JavaScript natively. But, to include other types of files inside the bundle, you need to use Webpack loaders. The Webpack loader knows how to process the file and transform it into JavaScript bundles.

For example, you can use `awesome-typescript-loader` to transform the TypeScript code into the JavaScript so that you don't have to manually compile your source code to run it. The webpack will take care of everything from compiling to bundling all your TypeScript code into a single source code bundle. Usually, we need to have a series of actions to be completed in order to get an application bundle. We need to have separate tasks to do each and every step, from linting to bundling. When using `webpack`, we don't have to worry about all these steps to run the code.

The webpack can be installed through npm:

```
npm install -g webpack
```

Now the `webpack` command is available in your path and we can start using it. We need to have `webpack` installed locally in the project:

```
npm install --save-dev webpack
    OR
yarn add --dev webpack
```

`webpack` works heavily based on the configuration object. We need to have this configuration file inside our project to start working with `webpack`. Let's start feeding webpack with proper configurations. Create the configuration file and name it `webpack.config.js`. The `webpack` configuration is a simple JavaScript object as follows:

```
var path = require('path');
var webpack = require('webpack');
```

```
// Webpack configuration
module.exports = {

};
```

We need to define an entry point for webpack to get started with bundling. webpack looks for this entry point to build the dependency graph. It does not restrict you to a single entry point. You can have multiple entry points in the application which helps you split your code into multiple bundles. A common use case on multiple bundles is when you want to split the code between vendor specific code to actual application source code. In this case, all the third-party source code can be bundled into a separate JavaScript file, while your actual source will be in a different bundle. Defining an entry point is simple, as follows:

```
var path = require('path');
var webpack = require('webpack');

// Webpack configuration
module.exports = {
  // The base directory for resolving entry points
  context: __dirname,

  // Source map configuration
  devtool: 'inline-source-map',

  // Entry points for the application
  entry: {
    app: './src/app.ts',
    vendor: './src/vendor.ts',
    polyfill: './src/polyfill.ts'
  }
};
```

Here we define three entry points. webpack will create three bundles from the entry point configuration. The app will contain our actual application code. The third-party libraries will be bundled into vendor and polyfill contains polyfill to patch the Electron renderer with newest features. We don't have to include our Electron entry point--the `main.js` file - into the webpack configuration file as it's running in a separate process to the Angular application. We will create this `app.ts` file shortly when we bootstrap the Angular application.

We need to tell webpack where to put the output bundle. Update the `webpack.config.js` file as follows to configure the output path:

```
var path = require('path');
var webpack = require('webpack');

// Webpack configuration
module.exports = {
  //...
  output: {
    path: path.resolve(__dirname, './build'),
    publicPath: __dirname + '/build',
    filename: '[name].js',
    sourceMapFilename: '[name].js.map',
    chunkFilename: '[id].chunk.js'
  },
  resolve: {
    extensions: ['.js', '.ts', '.css', '.html'],
    modules: ['./src', 'node_modules']
  }
};
```

Output options tell webpack how to write the compiled output to disk. The filename specifies the name of each output file on disk. The `path` option determines the location on disk the files are written. `[name]` in the filename option will be replaced by name of the chunk (entry point name). The `publicPath` specifies the public URL address of the output files when referenced in a browser. `resolve.extensions` is an array of extensions that should be used to resolve the modules.

Configuring loaders

Loaders allow you to preprocess files as you require or import them. Loaders can transform files from a different language like TypeScript to JavaScript. It even allows you to import the CSS or SASS files right in your JavaScript files. To tell webpack to transform specific modules with loader, you need to configure it in the webpack config file. These loaders are not included in the webpack itself. You should install loaders as you need to use them. Update your webpack config files and add the loaders as follows:

```
var path = require('path');
var webpack = require('webpack');

// Webpack configuration
module.exports = {
  // ....
```

```
    module: {
      rules: [
        {
          test: /\.ts$/,
          loader: ['awesome-typescript-loader', 'angular2-template-loader']',
          exclude: [/node_modules/]
        },
        {
          test: /\.json$/,
          loader: 'json-loader'
        },
        {
          test: /\.html$/,
          loader: 'raw-loader'
        },
        {
          test: /\.(png|jpe?g|gif|svg|woff|woff2|ttf|eot|ico)$/,
          loader: 'file-loader?name=dist/[name]-[hash].[ext]'
        },
        {
          test: /\.css$/,
          use: ExtractTextPlugin.extract({
            fallback: "style-loader",
            use: "css-loader"
          })
        }
      ]
    }
};
```

The previous configuration instructs webpack to use the specified loaders when importing that type of file. But these loaders should be installed separately using npm from the project root directory:

```
npm install --save-dev angular2-template-loader awesome-typescript-loader
css-loader file-loader html-loader raw-loader style-loader typescript
webpack webpack-target-electron-renderer
```

You also use yarn instead of npm. Change your command as follows if you are using yarn:

```
yarn add --dev angular2-template-loader awesome-typescript-loader css-
loader file-loader html-loader raw-loader style-loader typescript webpack
webpack-target-electron-renderer
```

Webpack plugins

The webpack build pipeline uses well-defined phases and we can hook custom script into this build pipeline. These scripts/plugins can interrupt the actual build process and can change the output behavior. For example, adding `webpack.optimize.UglifyJsPlugin()` into the pipeline will minify the bundle output. You can add custom plugins into the webpack config object by adding them into the plugins array. Here we need to add two `plugins extract-text-webpack-plugin` and `html-webpack-plugin`. Install the npm dependencies:

```
npm install --save-dev html-webpack-plugin extract-text-webpack-plugin
```

You can use yarn as follows instead of npm:

```
yarn add --dev html-webpack-plugin extract-text-webpack-plugin
```

Update the webpack config files to add the plugins:

```
var path = require('path');
var webpack = require('webpack');
var HtmlWebpackPlugin = require('html-webpack-plugin');
var ExtractTextPlugin = require('extract-text-webpack-plugin');

// Webpack Configuration
module.exports = {
  // ....
  plugins: [
    new HtmlWebpackPlugin({ template: './src/index.html' }),
    new ExtractTextPlugin('style.css')
  ]
};
```

The `html-webpack-plugin` is very useful for the creation of HTML files on-the-fly to serve your webpack bundles. When working with the file name with hashes on the webpack bundle, this plugin can save your life as maintaining the hashes in your HTML is tedious: the plugin will take care of creating the HTML for you and will include the hashed bundles automatically into the generated HTML. You can also provide a lodash template to customize the HTML output. The `extract-text-webpack-plugin` is used to extract the CSS code into a separate file from the bundle.

Building Your First Electron Application

The final webpack configuration should look like as follows:

```
var path = require('path');
var webpack = require('webpack');
var HtmlWebpackPlugin = require('html-webpack-plugin');
var ExtractTextPlugin = require('extract-text-webpack-plugin');

// Webpack Configuration
module.exports = {

  // The base directory for resolving entry points
  context: __dirname,

  // Source map configuration
  devtool: 'inline-source-map',
  target: 'electron-main',

  // Entry points for the application
  entry: {
    polyfills: './src/polyfills.ts',
    vendor: './src/vendor.ts',
    app: './src/app.ts'
  },
  output: {
    path: path.resolve(__dirname, './build'),
    publicPath: __dirname + '/build',
    filename: '[name].js',
    sourceMapFilename: '[name].js.map',
    chunkFilename: '[id].chunk.js'
  },

  resolve: {
    extensions: ['.js', '.ts', '.css', '.html'],
    modules: ['./src', 'node_modules']
  },
  module: {
    rules: [
      {
        test: /\.ts$/,
        loader: ['awesome-typescript-loader', 'angular2-template-loader'],
        exclude: [/node_modules/]
      },
      {
        test: /\.json$/,
        loader: 'json-loader'
      },
      {
        test: /\.html$/,
```

```
        loader: 'raw-loader'
      },
      {
        test: /\.(png|jpe?g|gif|svg|woff|woff2|ttf|eot|ico)$/,
        loader: 'file-loader?name=dist/[name]-[hash].[ext]'
      },
      {
        test: /\.css$/,
        use: ExtractTextPlugin.extract({ fallback: "style-loader", use:
"css-loader" })
      }
    ]
  },

  // we need this due to problems with es6-shim
  node: {
    global: true,
    progress: false,
    crypto: 'empty',
    module: false,
    clearImmediate: false,
    setImmediate: false,
    __dirname: false,
    __filename: false
  },

  plugins: [
    new HtmlWebpackPlugin({ template: './src/index.html' }),
    new ExtractTextPlugin("style.css")
  ]
};
```

Bootstrapping Angular with Electron

We have configured the webpack in previous section, but, we have not yet started working with the Angular part. Install the Angular dependencies to get started with Angular. Angular is scattered around multiple libraries so you need to install the following libraries to work with Angular:

npm install --save @angular/common @angular/compiler @angular/core @angular/forms @angular/http @angular/platform-browser @angular/platform-browser-dynamic @angular/router core-js reflect-metadata rxjs systemjs zone.js

Use the following command if you are using yarn:

```
yarn add  @angular/common @angular/compiler @angular/core @angular/forms
@angular/http @angular/platform-browser @angular/platform-browser-dynamic
@angular/router core-js reflect-metadata rxjs systemjs zone.js
```

webpack compiles the TypeScript files by looking into a TypeScript configuration file called `tsconfig.json`. The `tsconfig.json` file in the root of the project tells the TypeScript compiler that it's a TypeScript project. It gives the configuration to the compiler, like root files and other compiler options required to compile the project.

Create the `tsconfig.json` file with the following content in the project root to feed webpack:

```
{
  "compilerOptions": {
    "target": "es5",
    "module": "commonjs",
    "moduleResolution": "node",
    "sourceMap": true,
    "emitDecoratorMetadata": true,
    "experimentalDecorators": true,
    "removeComments": false,
    "noImplicitAny": true,
    "supressImplicitAnyIndexErrors": true,
    "lib" : [
      "es2016",
      "dom"
    ],
    "exclude": [
      "node_modules"
    ]
  }
}
```

Read more about the `tsconfig` option on TypeScript website (https://www.typescriptlang.org/docs/handbook/tsconfig-json.html).

When working with external JavaScript libraries with TypeScript, you will need to use a declaration/definition file(`.d.ts`) to describe the shape of that library. The TypeScript compiler looks for these declaration files to get metadata about a JavaScript library before compiling the source code. All the libraries installed on top is having the Typescript definition files inside the library itself. So we don't have to install them separately and the Typescript compiler can locate them from `node_modules` folder.

But some of the modules do not contain it natively inside the library. We need to install them separately. Use the following command to install missing type definition files into the project.

```
npm install --save-dev @types/core-js @types/electron @types/node

Or the following command if you are using yarn:
yarn add --dev @types/core-js @types/electron @types/node
```

We are done with setting up the application. Let's add some code to it and start our Electron client.

webpack starts the bundling process from entry points configured in the webpack configuration object. So, let's create that entry points first. Create the vendor.ts file inside the src folder to import the vendor modules that we need:

```
// Angular 2
import '@angular/platform-browser';
import '@angular/platform-browser-dynamic';
import '@angular/core';
import '@angular/common';
import '@angular/http';
import '@angular/router';

// RxJS
import 'rxjs';

// Other vendors for example jQuery, Lodash or Bootstrap
// You can also import js, ts, css, sass, etc.
```

You can import all the third-party libraries here, so that webpack will bundle them against the vendor entry point.

Create our last entry point for webpack where the real application starts to execute. Paste the following content into src/app.ts:

```
import { platformBrowserDynamic } from '@angular/platform-browser-dynamic';
import { enableProdMode } from '@angular/core';
import { AppModule } from './app/app.module';

if (process.env.ENV === 'production') {
  enableProdMode();
}

platformBrowserDynamic().bootstrapModule(AppModule);
```

[49]

webpack treats this as the entry point for our Angular application, which will be rendered using Electron's renderer process. Now declare your Angular module in the `src/app.module.ts` file. You can find more about Angular modules and its responsibilities at: https://angular.io/docs/ts/latest/guide/ngmodule.html:

```
import { NgModule } from '@angular/core';
import { BrowserModule }  from '@angular/platform-browser';
import { AppComponent } from './app.component';

@NgModule({
  imports: [
    BrowserModule
  ],
  declarations: [
    AppComponent
  ],
  bootstrap: [
    AppComponent
  ]
})
export class AppModule { }
```

Our application component `src/app.component.ts` should look like following:

```
import { Component } from '@angular/core';
import * as os from 'os';
import './style.css'

@Component({
  selector: 'electron-app',
  template: `
    <div id="shellInfo">
      <h1> Angular Bootstrapped </h1>
      <div id="processInfo">
        <table>
          <tr>
            <td>Node Version</td>
            <td>{{nodeVersion}}</td>
          </tr>
          <tr>
            <td>Platform</td>
            <td>{{platform}}</td>
          </tr>
          <tr>
            <td>Home Directory</td>
            <td>{{homedir}}</td>
          </tr>
```

```
        </table>
      </div>
    </div>
  `
})
export class AppComponent {
  public platform = os.platform();
  public homedir = os.homedir();
  public nodeVersion = process.versions.node;
}
```

`AppComponent` renders the Angular application into the renderer. This code just displays the version of node, chrome, and Electron using Angular. Rewrite your HTML file inside `src/app/index.html` so that webpack can inject the compiled bundles before loading into Electron:

```
<!DOCTYPE html>
<html>
  <head>
    <base href="/">
    <title>Hello Electron - Angular</title>
    <meta charset="UTF-8">
    <meta name="viewport" content="width=device-width, initial-scale=1">
  </head>
  <body>
    <electron-app>Loading...</electron-app>
  </body>
</html>
```

Our app is ready to run now. We need to tell webpack to compile it before running the application. Compile the source code using webpack with the following command:

webpack --watch

Once this runs successfully, you can find the compiled output in the `build` folder. To run the application, use the electron command like we did in the previous chapter:

electron .

Configuring dev server

Webpack provides a Node.js based development server called `webpack-dev-server`. Using the this can be helpful at the development stage because it emits the webpack compiled output whenever you change your source code. Modern development features, like live reload and hot module replacement, are not possible when you load the page with the file protocol. `webpack-dev-server` gives first class support for these features by using plugins. It's not mandatory to have it in our workflow. If you would like to configure it, follow these steps also in addition to the above steps.

Install `webpack-dev-server` server using `npm`, project `npm` dependencies:

```
npm install --save-dev webpack-dev-server
```

Open the webpack configuration file and add the following entry to enable the webpack development server inside the application:

```
devServer: {
  historyApiFallback: true,
  contentBase: './src',
  publicPath: '/build'
},
```

Run the webpack development server using the following command:

```
webpack-dev-server --inline --progress --port 3000 --config
devutils/webpack/webpack.config.js --watch
```

`webpack-dev-server` executes webpack in the background and emits a new bundle whenever you have a change in your source code inside the `src` folder. As we've discussed before, `webpack-dev-server` is a node-based server and you can access the output on a configured port, in this case, port `3000`. You need to change the HTML file path into the webpack server URL. In this case, it should be `http://localhost:3000/`

Our Electron application is now integrated with Angular and it's ready to run. Run the application using the Gulp `run-electron` command and you should be getting the Angular component rendered on the Electron web view.

The following diagram shows how the Electron works with Angular 2 and webpack when using the webpack dev server:

Chapter 2

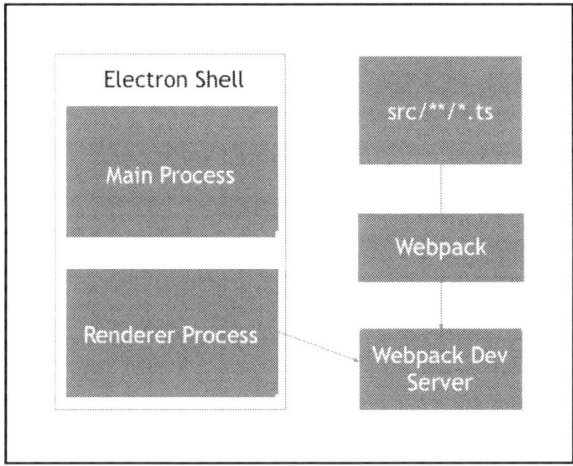

This workflow is only applicable for development. In production, we will not have a node server or development server running along with Electron. The compiled output will be rendered in production using the file protocol. If you look at the previous figure, we are not rendering the local file as we were doing in the previous chapter. Instead, we asked Electron to render the output coming from webpack-dev-server. The development server knows how to manage the application bundle for each change.

 **Note**: If you are developing a desktop application with some other front end framework, like React, you can reuse the similar steps and code with webpack. Only the frontend framework code needs to be changed according to the framework you are using.

Adding a menu bar to the application

You must have a menu bar for a desktop application. As we are dealing with HTML and CSS, it's easy to create a menu based on HTML and CSS. However, here, in order to understand Electron's ability to use the native operating system components, let's create it the Electron way. This uses a native operating system component.

Electron provides two classes to create menus: Menu and MenuItem. Each menu consists of multiple menu items and each menu item can have a sub menu. The menu class is only available in the main process. So, this will be rendered along with your Electron window.

Building Your First Electron Application

Open the `main.js` file inside `src` folder and update the code as shown in the following:

```
const { app, BrowserWindow, Menu } = require('electron');

const template = [{
  label: 'File',
  submenu: [
    {
      // similar to role: 'reload'. The code is just for demo
      // purpose. For reloading the window content in menu used
      // the role reload.
      label: 'Reload',
      accelerator: 'CmdOrCtrl+R',
      click (item, focusedWindow) {
        if (focusedWindow)
          focusedWindow.reload()
      },
    },
    {
      // This section can be replaced with role: toggledevtools
      //as there is a role available to do the same.
      label: 'Toggle Developer Tools',
      accelerator: process.platform === 'darwin' ?
      'Alt+Command+I' : 'Ctrl+Shift+I',
      click (item, focusedWindow) {
        if (focusedWindow)
          focusedWindow.webContents.toggleDevTools()
      }
    },
    {
      type: 'separator'
    },
    {
      role: 'resetzoom'
    },
    {
      role: 'zoomin'
    }
  ]
}];

function createWindow() {
  //...
  // Initializes the Menubar from the template
  const menu = Menu.buildFromTemplate(template);
  Menu.setApplicationMenu(menu);
}
```

Each item in the template array serves as the constructor parameter for the `MenuItem class.role` string. Define the action of the menu item; when specified the click property will be ignored. You can attach an event handler to the menu item by specifying the click function explicitly. The Type option can be used to specify the type of menu item: possible values are normal, separator, submenu, checkbox, or radio.

Adding a context menu to the renderer process

To access the menu module from the renderer process you need to use a remote module. So, to create a menu or context menu inside your angular component. Open the `app.component.ts` file and update the code with the following content:

```typescript
import { Component, OnInit } from '@angular/core';
import * as os from 'os';
import { remote } from 'electron';
const { Menu, MenuItem } = remote;
import './style.css';

@Component({
  selector: 'electron-app',
  template: ``
})
export class AppComponent implements OnInit {
  public platform = os.platform();
  public homedir = os.homedir();
  public nodeVersion = process.versions.node;

  public ngOnInit() {
    const menu = new Menu();
    menu.append(new MenuItem({
      label: 'MenuItem1',
      click() {
        console.log('item 1 clicked');
      }
    }));
    menu.append(new MenuItem({ type: 'separator' }));
    menu.append(new MenuItem({ label: 'MenuItem2',
      type: 'checkbox', checked: true
    }));
    window.addEventListener('contextmenu', (e) => {
      e.preventDefault();
      menu.popup(remote.getCurrentWindow());
    }, false);
  }
}
```

Styling the application using Bootstrap

Styling the application is essential, and using any standard CSS frameworks is important to reduce the boilerplate. In this application, we are going to use the Twitter bootstrap, a very popular CSS framework. There are a lot of Angular 2 integrations available for bootstrapping, but we'll use it directly without using any other third-party libraries.

Install Bootstrap using `npm`:

```
npm install --save bootstrap
```

Open `vendor.ts` inside and add an import at the end of the file to include the library in the application as follows:

```
import 'bootstrap/dist/bootstrap.css';
```

Restart the webpack, or it will automatically detect the changes and re-bundle if you run it with the `--watch` flag. Now you are ready to use the Twitter bootstrap framework.

Now the bootstrap will be bundled into your application bundle and you can use it in your Angular application and the rendered web page. The final output should look like the following screenshot. As this is a hello world Electron application using Angular 2, we haven't discussed anything details about the Electron APIs in this chapter:

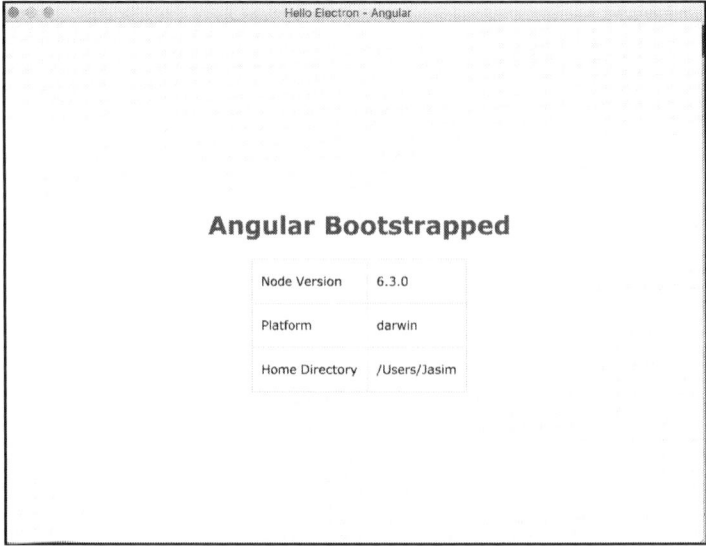

Summary

We discussed how to create an Electron application using Angular 2 from scratch. We started by discussing our sample application and went through the technical stack that we are using in this book. We then successfully ran the Electron application using Angular 2 in the renderer process. Most of this chapter discussed the setting up and running of an Angular application. Though this book is about Electron it's essential to use one front end framework with Electron when developing large-scale applications. We have one more chapter focused on front end technology, and this will focus on developing a user interface for our application. There are some points to be noted when using Electron with front end frameworks:

- Always use the best available tools and frameworks as Electron won't restrict you on the choice of framework.
- Use any of the module bundlers if you are using Angular 2, React, or any other libraries.
- Serve the file to Electron from a local web server at the development stage. This will solve a lot of tooling issues like live reloading, hot module replacement, and so on. Using file protocol cannot provide a solution for all these. When you package your app, you use file protocol so that your app does not need a web server running internally in the application.

Towards the end of this chapter, we looked at the implementation of a native menu and context menu with Electron. In the next chapter, we will be looking at debugging Electron applications and the integration of various tools that will help us to simplify development workflows.

3
Tooling and Debugging

Detecting and finding bugs is an important aspect of programming. It needs a lot of metadata information--what the bug or fault is, where it has occurred, how it was caused, and so on. After developing a program, the next step is to test the program to find out whether the program works and produces the output as desired. In real situations, we frequently test the program against each functionality soon after the development of that piece of code. Usually, there can be different types of errors, and bugs can be figured out at this stage that need to be fixed before proceeding further on to development. This is where we need to debug the application. It's a step-by-step process of finding bugs or errors in a program. This process will reduce the error count, and the quality can be increased in the development stage itself.

But this is not a manual process, and we need to have some tools that we can use to figure out the cause of bugs through debugging. Usually, IDEs can be used to debug the application. There are multiple tools available for debugging the Electron application. Debugging an Electron application is little bit different than debugging other languages or normal JavaScript applications because, as we discussed in previous chapters, the Electron application is running on different processes, and each process runs independently of the others, so we have to debug each process separately.

In this chapter, we will be discussing the tooling and debugging of Electron applications. We need to have a clear idea about debugging before we develop an entire application. So before continuing on to development, we will look at the following points in detail in this chapter:

- Debugging an Electron application's main process using Visual Studio Code and Chrome Developer Tools
- Debugging Electron renderer processes using Chrome Developer Tools
- Integrating task runners and tools into the VS Code editor and Electron shell for a better development experience

- Implementing live reload and hot module replacement for Electron renderer processes at the development stage
- Getting familiar with **Devtron**--A popular debugging tool for Electron
- Adding third-party extensions to Electron's Chrome Developer Tools
- Brief about various Electron APIs that can be used for tooling purposes

Debugging an Electron application

Debugging Electron applications is very similar to debugging JavaScript code for web applications. But here we need to take care of different types of Electron processes. The main process and renderer process (or the rendered web page) should be debugged separately as these processes are running separately. In the following sections, we will look at how to debug both of these processes. We have a couple of options to debug the application. This chapter will provide you with step-by-step instructions to fix development bugs easily with debuggers.

Nowadays, most editors provide great debugging support for Node.js applications. In addition, node binaries provide built-in support for debugging the application via Chrome Developer Tools. Electron can also make use of these tools to debug the application. This section will provide you with step-by-step explanations on how to use Visual Studio Code and Chrome Developer Tools to debug both the main process and renderer processes in an Electron application. You can use either Visual Studio Code or Chrome Developer Tools to debug the application. We will also discuss some other tools that can make a developer's life easier when working with Electron.

There is no recommended way to debug an Electron application, but debugging renderer processes always works well with Chrome Developer Tools inside browser windows, which renders your web page and provides the basic user interface for your Electron shell windows. Also, for main processes, debugging inside VS Code looks more promising than integrating into the developer tools.

Debugging the main process

The developer tools inside the browser window can only debug the renderer process or the scripts present inside your web page. To debug the main process, Electron provides some flags to enable developer tools to debug the scripts from the main process. But other than developer tools, Visual Studio provides built-in support for debugging the main process scripts from Electron. Visual Studio can hook into Electron's debug mode once the application is running with debug mode enabled. Use the following command-line switches to debug Electron's main process:

```
--inspect=[port]
```

When this switch is used for executing the application, Electron will listen for v8 debugger protocol messages on the configured port. The default port is 5858. The following switch is the same as `--inspect`, but it tells the debugger to pause on the first line soon after the execution:

```
--inspect-brk=[port]
```

To debug the application that we created in our previous chapter, you should change the run command as follows to enable the debug mode in Electron:

```
electron main.js --inspect
```

Now the v8 engine will start to listen for the debugger protocol message on port 5858.

Debugging with Visual Studio Code

Debugging Node.js applications is built into the VS Code and it helps to accelerate the edit, compile, and debug loops. Since Electron is powered by the same Node.js infrastructure, we can use VS Code's Node.js debugging capabilities to debug and analyze our Electron application source code. Visual Studio Code provides a way to launch and debug the application from within the editor using launch configurations. Launch configurations are simple JSON files that are expected to be present inside the `.vscode` folder inside your project root. VS Code also provides a way to integrate your task runners directly into the editor. The task runners mostly run from the command line and perform the automation outside the editor where you will be doing most of your developments, so integrating automated tasks into VS Code is very helpful as we are able to execute the task and analyze the results from within VS Code. You don't have to switch between environments to get something done in your development cycle.

Tooling and Debugging

Setting up the launch configuration

To bring up the debug view, click on the Debugging icon in the view bar at the left-hand side of VS Code. VS Code depends on the launch configuration file for debugging the application. It is a JSON file named `launch.json` and it should be present under the `.vscode` directory inside the project workspace. VS Code will take care of generating the launch configuration file. Click on the configure gear icon on the debug view top bar, choose your debug environment (in our case, it's Node.js), and VS Code will generate a `launch.json` file under the `.vscode` directory:

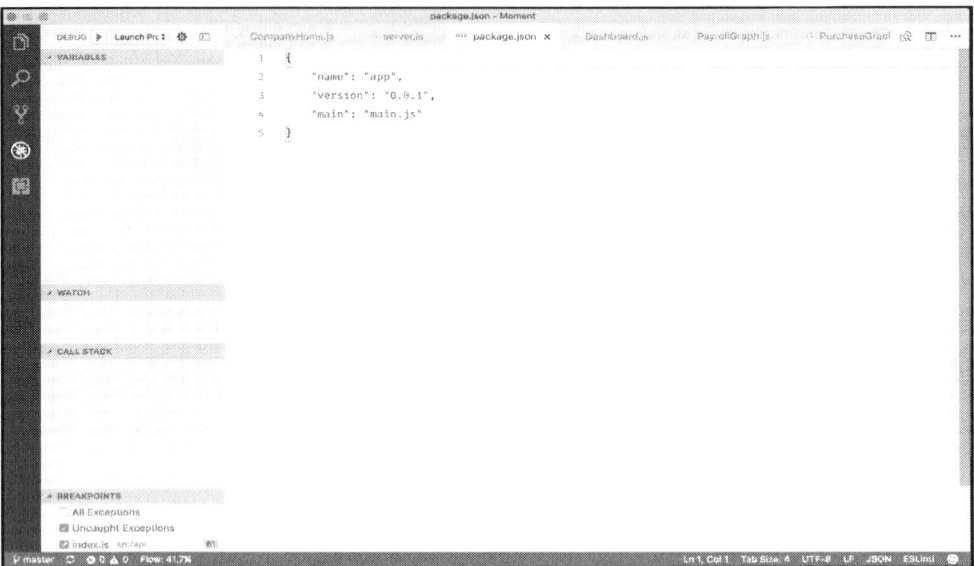

The generated launch configuration is supposed to run the Node.js application. So we need to change the configuration file so that VS Code will execute the Electron shell and load the Angular application into it:

```
{
  "version": "0.2.0",
  "configurations": [
    {
      "name": "Launch Electron",
      "type": "node",
      "request": "launch",
      "program": "${workspaceRoot}/main.js",
      "stopOnEntry": false,
      "args": [],
      "cwd": "${workspaceRoot}",
```

```
      "preLaunchTask": null,
      "runtimeExecutable": "${workspaceRoot}/node_modules/.bin/electron",
      "runtimeArgs": [
        ".",
        "--inspect"
        "--enable-logging",
        "--nolazy"
      ],
      "env": {
        "NODE_ENV": "development"
      },
      "console": "internalConsole",
      "sourceMaps": false
    }
  ]
}
```

The runTimeExecutable should point to the electron binary. You should be passing your local electron binary path like ./node_modules/.bin/electron even if you have the electron available in your global path. The VS code debugger won't work with your global electron executable.

Once you have the launch.json file edited as shown in the preceding snippet, you can find three configurations in your VS Code debug view:

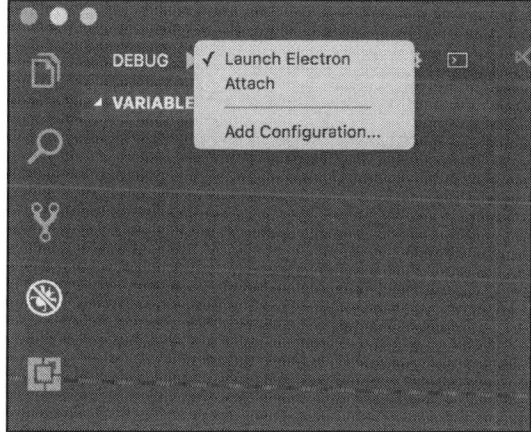

Tooling and Debugging

Now you can select the launch configuration and press the **Run** button to launch Electron with various configurations. Select **Launch Electron** configuration and click on the **Run** button; the Electron shell should start executing now. Let's dig into the details of the launch configuration file:

- `name`: Configuration name used to identify you in Visual Studio Code
- `type`: Configuration type, for Electron and it's node
- `request`: Defines whether the application will be launched (launch), or if it will be attached to another process (attach)
- `program`: Your app entry point--the same as `main` in `package.json`
- `args`: Array of arguments to pass to the program
- `cwd`: Path to the program being debugged
- `runtimeExecutable`: Path to the Electron executable
- `runtimeArgs`: Array of arguments that we will pass to Electron
- `env`: Collection of environment variables

The request configuration tells VS Code either to launch the application or to attach to the currently executing process for debugging. The second set of configurations attach VS Code into the already running debugger instance. To debug Electron using VS Code, you need to run the Electron in debug mode first:

```
electron main.js --inspect
```

You can start debugging by clicking the launch button or by pressing the *F5* button. Set some breakpoints in `main.js`, and start debugging in debug view. You should be able to hit the breakpoints.

Debugging renderer processes

Debugging a web page rendered inside the Electron shell is comparatively easier than debugging the main process. The process is similar to debugging JavaScript code in regular web pages. As we discussed before, developer tools can be opened using the following code inside your main process:

```
browserWindow.openDevTools();
```

Working with developer tools should be easy for you if you have a web development background. Start putting the break points inside your source code, you can find them under the source tab.

Adding Chrome Developer Tools extensions

Electron supports Chrome Developer Tools extensions, which can be used to extend the ability of developer tools. Most of the modern JavaScript frameworks provide Chrome Developer Tools extensions to inspect and analyze the component tree and the application state. The Angular team also provides a developer tools extension called Augury, which helps developers to visualize the Angular application through component trees and visual debugging tools. Inspecting the Angular component is essential when developing large scale applications using Angular 2, or even when using popular front end frameworks. With Augury, you can get immediate insight into the application structure, component tree, change detection, and application state management.

Using Chrome extensions such as Augury is important when developing with front end frameworks such as Angular 2. If you are planning to not use Angular 2 for your user interface in web pages with Electron, choose the right extension that supports the framework you are using. For example, the React team provides React developer tools to analyze and inspect the react component tree. Similarly, Ember also provides developer tools if you want to work with Ember in your Electron web pages

Developer tools extensions can be loaded into Electron either manually or using a third-party tool called `electron-devtools-installer`, which installs the extension directly from the Chrome web store. Using `electron-devtools-installer` is the easy way to install Chrome extensions into Electron. You don't have to mess with downloading extensions and finding the extension folder and configuring it in Electron. In this section, we will install the Augury Chrome extension into Electron using Electron extension installer and manually install `electron-devtools-installer` using `npm`:

```
npm install --save-dev electron-devtools-installer
```

Then add the following script into your `main.js` file:

```
const { default: installExtension } = require('electron-devtools-installer')

function createElectronShell() {
  //...
  installExtension('elgalmkoelokbchhkhacckoklkejnhcd')
    .then((name) => console.log(`Added Extension:  ${name}`))
    .catch((err) => console.log('An error occurred: ', err));
}
```

Technically, we can use whatever extension we want. Find the Chrome extension ID of the extension that you want to install and call the following function from your main process script--in our case, that is main.js:

```
installExtension('YOUR_ID_HERE').
```

The electron-devtools-installer provides a few popular extension IDs inside the package that can be used to easily import the plugin as your application's devtools extension. The following code demonstrates using these values inside your application:

```
const {
  default: installExtension,
  ANGULARJS_BATARANG,
  VUEJS_DEVTOOLS,
  REACT_DEVELOPER_TOOLS
} = require('electron-devtools-installer');
```

Loading the developer tools extension manually

To load the extension manually, install the Chrome extension in your Chrome browser and then locate its filesystem path. Once you find the location, load the extension by calling the following method inside the main process (main.js):

```
let win
function createElectronShell() {
  win = new BrowserWindow({ width: 800, height: 600 });

  // Add the dev tools extension.
  // Call the function once you initialize the BrowserWindow object.
  BrowserWindow.addDevToolsExtension(extensionPath)
}
```

To install Augury, follow these steps:

- Install the Augury extension in your Chrome browser from chrome web store.
- Open the extensions page in your Chrome browser and find the extension ID. If you can't find the extension ID then ensure the developer mode checkbox is checked. The extensions page can be accessed through the `Chrome://extensions` URL. The extension ID is a hash string, and it should be something similar to `elgalmkoelokbchhkhacckoklkejnhcd`.
- Find out the extension folder in your system. The extension path depends on your operating system:
    - On Windows, usually, it's under the

        `%LOCALAPPDATA%\Google Chrome\User\Data\Default\Extensions`

        folder.
    - On Linux, it could be the `~/.config/google-Chrome/Default/Extensions` folder.
    - On Mac OS, it is the `~/Library/Application Support/Google/Chrome/Default/Extensions` directory:
        - The extension can be found inside the folder with the extension ID as its name.
        - Pass the location of the extension to the `BrowserWindow.addDevToolsExtension` method. For Augury, it should be as follows:

            ```
            let win;
            function createElectronShell() {
              win = new BrowserWindow({ width: 800, height: 600 });
              // Give the extension path here. Here is the Mac version of Path
              const extensionPath = '/Library/Application Support/Google/Chrome/Default/Extensions/elgalmkoelokbchhkhacckoklkejnhcd/1_14_0';
              // Add the dev tools extension
              BrowserWindow.addDevToolsExtension(extensionPath)
            }
            ```

Tooling and Debugging

You should check the version of the extension and append to the path string as shown previously. You should get the Augury extension in your Electron's Chrome Developer Tools:

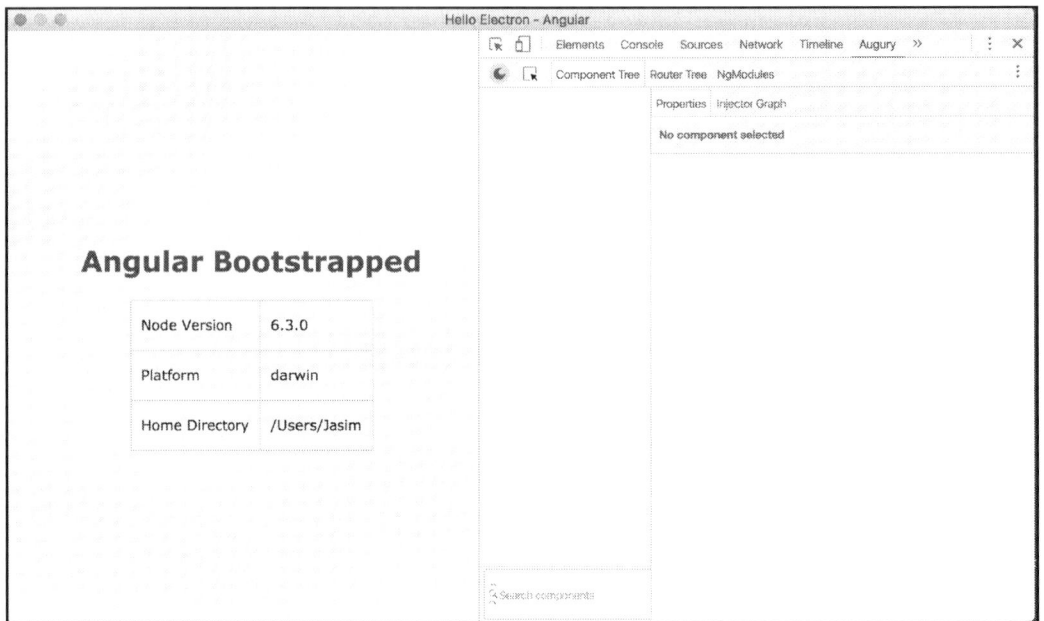

 The `BrowserWindow.addDevToolsExtension` method cannot be called before the `ready` event of the app module is emitted.

Monitoring the application with Devtron

Devtron is an open source Electron developer tools extension that helps you to inspect, monitor, and debug the application. This is a useful tool that can be used along with VS Code to monitor the application. Other than debugging, it provides some useful features that help us to monitor various aspects of the application. Some of the unique features of Devtron are:

- **App linter**: Checks the application for possible issues and missing functionalities
- **Require graph**: This helps to visualize internal and external library dependencies in both main and renderer processes

- **IPC monitor**: Tracks all the messages sent and received between the processes using IPC modules
- **Event inspector**: Shows the events and listeners that are registered in your application on the core Electron APIs, such as the window, the app, and the processes

Installing Devtron can be done using `npm`:

```
npm install --save-dev devtron
```

Open your `main.js` file and add the following code to install the devtron into the application:

```
let win;
function createElectronShell() {
  win = new BrowserWindow({ width: 800, height: 600 });
  win.loadURL(appURL);

  // Add this line once you initialize the BrowserWindow and
  // load the web page into the BrowserWindow
  require('devtron').install();
}
```

You should then see a Devtron tab added:

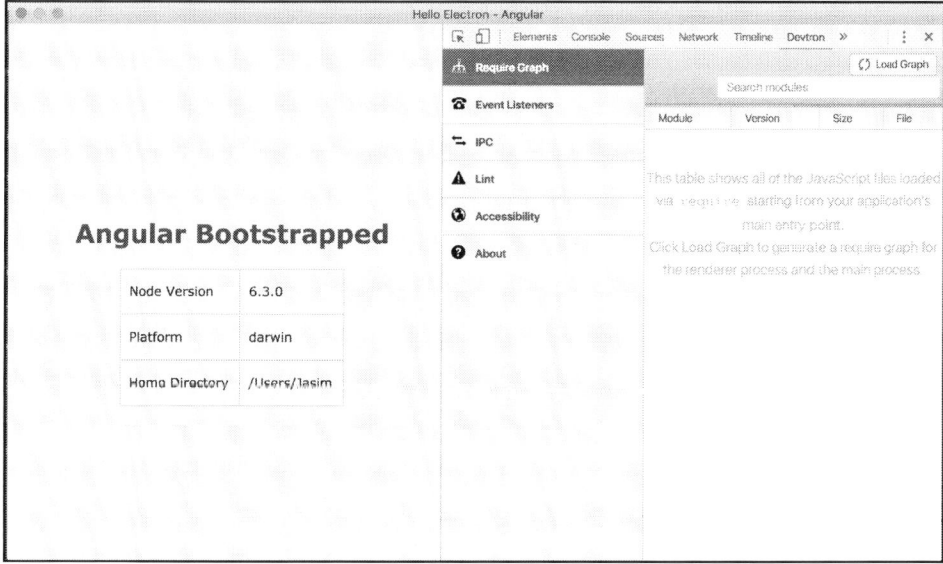

Integrating task runners with VS Code

There are lots of tools available to automate the tasks inside software development loops. These tools mostly run from command-line terminals outside the editor. It's very helpful if we can execute these tasks and analyze them from within the Visual Studio Code. VS Code provides ways to integrate these tasks into the editor itself. You can define custom tasks inside your workspace task.json file.

To generate this JSON file, press *command + shift + P* on Mac or *Ctrl + Shift + P* on Windows. Select the **Configure Task Runner** option and you will see a list of task runner templates. Choose **Others** from the list. You should now see a task.json file inside the .vscode folder inside your workspace:

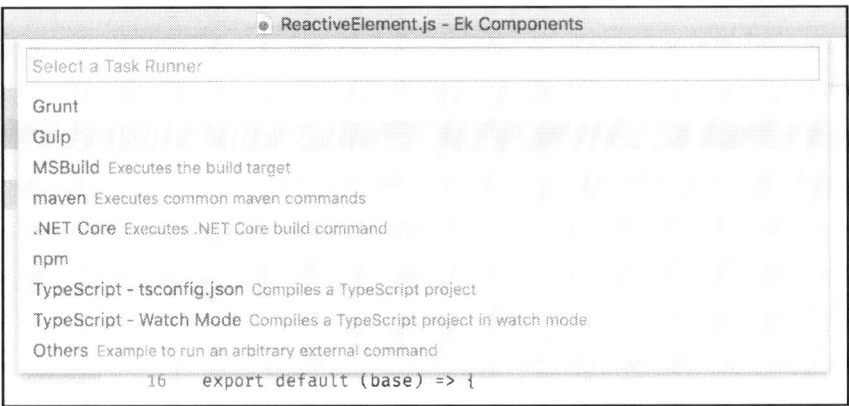

The following content should be there in the file:

```
{
  "version": "2.0.0",
  "tasks": [{
    "taskName": "build",
    "command": "npm run build",
    "type": "shell"
  },
  {
    "taskName": "watch",
    "command": "npm run watch",
    "type": "shell"
  },
  {
    "taskName": "start",
    "command": "npm run start",
```

```
    "type": "shell",
    "problemMatcher": []
  }]
}
```

Once you have configured the VS Code with tasks, you can execute the configured tasks from within the editor itself. Press *command + shift + P* on Mac or *Ctrl + Shift + P* on Windows and then type and select the run task from the list. You should get the list of configured tasks. Select the task you want to execute:

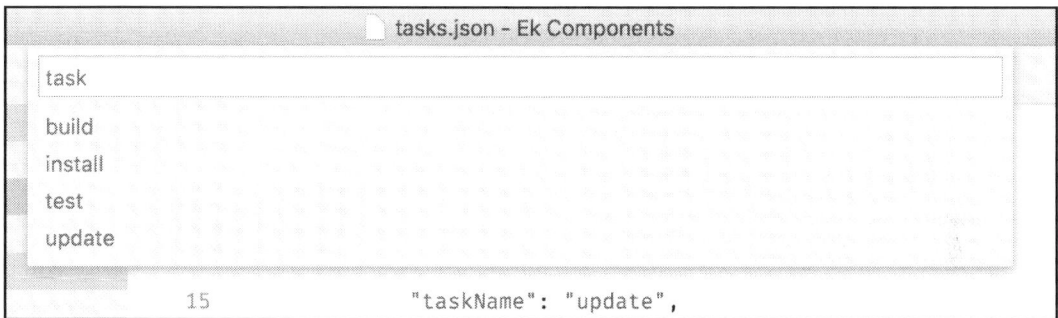

Boosting development workflow

In previous sections, we have discussed using VS Code, Devtron, and Chrome Developer Tools for debugging the Electron application. We have already set up Gulp and webpack to leverage the full power of front end workflow in Electron-based desktop applications in the previous chapter. We used webpack to run and bundle the Angular 2 applications, which render the actual application user interface. The rest of this chapter discusses integrating these tools into the VS Code editor and Electron shell themselves. We will also check out some of the Electron APIs that can be used to reduce development efforts.

Adding hot module replacement

Hot module replacement is a way of exchanging code modules in a running application. It's a time-consuming effort to build the application and reload the browser for output every time you change your source code. As a solution, there is a live reload, which reloads the page whenever you make some changes in your source code. Browser sync is an example for the live reloading tool. But still, in a large-scale application that contains hundreds of modules, it's still not a good idea to reload the page every time you change the source code, for multiple reasons:

- Page reload resets your state, so you need to do the same actions to get back your previous state
- Application bundles may take some time to load with all the assets, which is time-consuming

HMR provides a better solution for these problems. We use webpack here to enable the HMR. Webpack adds a small HMR runtime to the bundle during the build process that then runs inside your application. When the build completes, webpack will watch your source code for any changes. If it detects some changes, webpack rebuilds only the changed module, and the HMR runtime will update the changed module inside the running application. In this way, our application will never reload, and the state won't be reset to get the new changes inside the application. Angular 2 applications may contain hundreds of modules. In our example, it is also built on top of multiple modules, so this feature is good to have in our stack.

The simple way to enable hot module replacement is to specify `--hot` on the command line with `webpack-dev-server`. This adds `HotModuleReplacementPlugin` to the webpack configuration file at runtime. Once it's enabled in the application, you should see the following messages in Electron's Chrome Dev Tools console:

```
[HMR] Waiting for update signal from WDS...
[WDS] Hot Module Replacement enabled.
```

To enable HMR in our application, launch webpack dev server by entering the following command in your terminal:

```
webpack-dev-server --inline --hot
```

Integrating webpack dev server into the Electron shell

In the previous chapter, we ran the Electron application and Angular application separately. The Angular application is served using webpack dev server, and Electron accessed it through the dev server port. This approach gives us the leveraged to have all the useful features that webpack provides. But it's a good idea to integrate webpack dev server with Electron at development time. The production version will use the file protocol to access the application so that we don't have to run any server. When integrating, the development server should be started when Electron starts the main process. In the following code, the main process (`main.js`) checks for the environment variable, and if its value is `development` then it creates the HTTP server and loads the index HTML. Update your `main.js` file as follows to integrate the webpack dev server with the Electron main shell:

```
if(process.env.NODE_ENV == 'development') {
  const webpack = require('webpack');
  const webpackDevServer = require('webpack-dev-server');
  let config = require('./webpack.config.js');
  config.entry.app = [
    "webpack-dev-server/client? http://localhost:8080/",
    "webpack/hot/dev-server",
    "./src/app.ts"
  ];
  config.output.publicPath = '/build';
  config.plugins.push(new webpack.HotModuleReplacementPlugin());
  const compiler = webpack(config);
  const devServer = new webpackDevServer(compiler, { hot: true });
  devServer.listen(8080);

  // Change the application file path to the dev server url
  appUrl = 'http://localhost:8080/';
}
```

The preceding code does the same as we did in our last chapter using webpack. To enable Electron to use the webpack dev server, the following changes are to be added in the webpack configuration file:

- Add an entry point to the webpack configuration: `webpack/hot/dev-server`
- Add `webpack.HotModuleReplacementPlugin()` to the webpack configuration
- Add `hot: true` to the `webpack-dev-server` configuration to enable HMR on the server

Now the webpack runtime is integrated into the Electron shell at development time, so whenever you run the application, the webpack development server will build the Angular app and listen to the development port.

Adding keyboard shortcuts to the application

Keyboard shortcuts are an essential part of a better user experience. This helps users to perform valuable tasks with one key press. Attaching keyboard shortcuts to common tasks, such as opening dev tools or refreshing the page, can also be useful during development. In this section, we will see how we can improve the development cycle by using Electron's building functionality. These details are not only suitable for tooling, but they can also work with real-life scenarios in your applications.

There are two ways that we can create keyboard shortcuts:

- Using accelerators
- Using global shortcuts

We have already discussed how to create menus and menu bars for Electron applications. You can attach keyboard shortcuts to this menu action using accelerators. They can contain multiple modifiers and key codes combined by the + character. You can use the following Electron modifiers along with the key codes:

- Command (or Cmd for short)
- Control (or Ctrl for short)
- CommandOrControl (or CmdOrCtrl for short)
- Alt
- Option
- AltGr
- Shift
- Super

For example, creating a menu with acceleration should be done as follows:

```
{
  label: 'Toggle Developer Tools',
  accelerator: process.platform === 'darwin' ? 'Alt+Command+I' :
'Ctrl+Shift+I',
  click (item, focusedWindow) {
    if (focusedWindow) focusedWindow.webContents.toggleDevTools()
  }
}
```

The preceding code set the keyboard shortcut to the menu action using the accelerator.

> You need to take care of the special keys when defining the accelerators. Always try to use CommandOrControl instead of using these keys individually as the command key does not have any effect on Windows and Linux. In this way, the shortcut can be working on all the platforms. In the same manner, the *Option* key only exists on Mac OS, whereas the *Alt* key is available on all platforms, so you can use it to make the shortcut available globally on all the platforms.

globalShortcut can register or unregister an event with the operating system. You need to keep in mind that these shortcuts are global and this will work even if the app does not have keyboard focus. You should not use this module until the app module emits the ready event. A globalShortcut can be defined as follows:

```
const {app, globalShortcut} = require('electron')

app.on('ready', () => {
  const ret = globalShortcut.register('CommandOrControl+X', () => {
    console.log('CommandOrControl+X is pressed')
  })
})

app.on('will-quit', () => {
  globalShortcut.unregister('CommandOrControl+X')
})
```

You can use the globablshortcut.unregisterAll method to remove all the handlers registered inside the application. You can also check whether a shortcut is registered or not using the globalshortcut.isregistered method by passing the accelerator as a parameter:

```
globalShortcut.isRegistered(accelerator)
```

Controlling Electron behavior using environment variables

Certain Electron behaviors can be changed using environment variables. You can use the following environment variables for development and debugging purposes:

ELECTRON_RUN_AS_NODE

This starts the Electron process as a normal Node.js process:

ELECTRON_ENABLE_LOGGING

This prints Chrome's internal logging to console.

You can find a list of all available variables used in Electron in the official documentation (https://github.com/electron/electron/blob/master/docs/api/environment-variables.md).

Other than Electron, normally you can use environment variables to provide custom behaviors to the renderer process or to the main process itself. Dotenv is a popular Node.js library that loads environment variables from the .env file into node environment variables at development time. These environment variables can be used as configuration for your application. Installing dotenv can be done using npm:

```
npm install dotenv –save
```

Create an .env file in the root with the following content:

```
NODE_ENV=development
```

This file can be loaded into process.env using the following code:

```
require('dotenv').config();
```

Now the values are present inside the process.env object and they can be accessed using process.env.NODE_ENV.

Monitoring power state changes

We can monitor a power state change from our Electron application using the `powerMonitor` module. The `powerMonitor` module should only be used after the ready event is emitted by the app module. You can attach four types of events to the `powerMonitor`, which indicates the power state of your machine:

- Suspended: The event that will be emitted when the system is suspending.
- Resume: When resuming the machine.
- On-ac: When the system changes to the AC power state. This event is only available on Windows.
- On-battery: When the system changes to battery power--This event is also only available on the Windows platform:

```
const { app} , electron = require('electron')
app.on('ready', () => {
  electron.powerMonitor.on('suspend', () => {});
  electron.powerMonitor.on('resume', () => {});
});
```

The `powerMonitor` module is available only on the main process, and you should attach the event in your `main.js` or in your main process. When you want to attach some user interface with these events use IPC messaging and notify the renderer process to update the user interface according to the event. We will see how IPC messaging works in the following chapter.

Submitting crash reports to the server

Submitting crash reports to the server is an important feature that should be in the application when going to production. Electron's `crashReporter` module can be used to submit crash reports automatically to the server. But you should have a server running that accepts and processes crash reports. You can use one of the following projects to set up the server:

- Socorro: Server implementation from Mozilla that accepts breakpad crash reports (https://github.com/mozilla/socorro)
- Mini-breakpad-server: https://github.com/electron/mini-breakpad-server

Electron uses a new crashpad client on Mac OS that is different from breakpad on Windows and Linux. To enable crash collection, you are required to initialize crashpad in the main process and in each renderer process.

You can use the following code to initialize crashpad in the `main.js` file and also in your HTML file:

```
const { crashReporter } = require('electron')
crashReporter.start({
   productName:"Product Name",
   companyName: "Company Name",
   submitURL: 'https://post-url,
   autoSubmit: true
})
```

As I mentioned before, you need to add this piece of code both in your main process and renderer process. This should be called once Angular is bootstrapped in the renderer process so that the crash reports will be sent to the server from both processes.

Capturing the desktop using Electron API

This section shows how to capture screenshots and videos of Electron's screens using the built-in `desktopCapturer` module and some other third-party modules.
Internally, `desktopCapturer` uses the `navigator.webkitGetUserMedia` API to capture and manipulate media content. Capturing video can be done in your renderer process:

```
desktopCapturer.getSources({types: ['window', 'screen']}, (error, sources) => {
  if (error) throw error
    navigator.webkitGetUserMedia({
        audio: false,
        video: {
          mandatory: {
            ChromeMediaSource: 'desktop',
            ChromeMediaSourceId: sources[0].id,
            minWidth: 1280,
            maxWidth: 1280,
            minHeight: 720,
            maxHeight: 720
          }
        }
      }, function(stream) {
    document.querySelector('video').src = URL.createObjectURL(stream);
}, function(error) {
console.log(error);
})
})
```

Sources are an array source object; each source represents a screen or individual window that can be captured. The preceding example captures the video from the first screen present inside the source array and streams it into an HTML video element inside the web page. The following code can be used to take a screenshot of a current page:

```
// In your renderer process
var remote = require('electron').remote;
remote.getCurrentWindow().capturePage(function handleCapture (img) {
  remote.require('fs').writeFile(filename, img.toPng(), function() {
    console.log('Screenshot created')
  })
})
```

You can also use any of the Node.js APIs available for recording the video or taking the screenshot. We will see how we can use the media API to record and play the video using a camera or external devices in the following chapter.

Summary

In this chapter, we discussed debugging Electron applications using both Visual Studio Code and node-inspector. Most of the content in this chapter was about using various tools with Electron to reduce development effort. We then discussed installing Chrome Developer Tools extension into the Electron shell.

We will continue developing our sample application in the next chapter and onwards. Tooling and debugging is important in the development cycle, so it is necessary to have an idea about these things before we continue to the next chapter. The next chapter will discuss creating our sample application user interface and services using Angular 2. Most of the content in the next chapter will be about Angular 2 and access the Facebook Graph API using Angular 2.

4
Using Angular 2 with Electron

The user interface is the most important part of an application. Modern browsers are capable of rendering a complex user interface using HTML, CSS, and JavaScript. Also, we have a number of JavaScript frameworks available in the industry that leverage us to write complex applications in the client side itself. Most of the business logic is also moved from server to client. When it comes to the desktop application development, we have a huge number of choices, in terms of JavaScript framework, that makes our life easier when developing a complex desktop application using Electron. We have already discussed about creating a simple Electron application using Angular 2 in previous chapters. As we know, Electron does not provide a way to build a user interface on its own. Instead, we need to use HTML, CSS, and JavaScript to build the user interface. So, building an application with Electron is almost the same as building a web application, especially in terms of the user interface.

In this chapter, we will continue to develop our sample application. However, most of this chapter does not discuss Electron or its own APIs. Instead, we will discuss how we can use JavaScript frameworks along with Electron; in our case, Angular 2. If you are a web developer, the primary concern that you need to be aware of is that with Electron we will not have a server or client-server communication in most cases. Even though we can communicate with multiple servers, the desktop application works from within the client machine itself and the user interface will work accordingly. We will be covering the following points in detail in this chapter:

- Using Angular 2 with Electron
- Using the Facebook Graph API and accessing remote content from the renderer/main process

- Accessing underlying platform components from the Angular 2 components and services
- Creating a fully-fledged social media client application using all these technologies

We already have a boilerplate code ready to run as a sample hello world application. Let's continue with developing the rest of the application functionalities.

Introducing the Facebook Graph API

The Graph API is the primary way to read and write data to Facebook. It can be used in a immens variety of ways. In this chapter, we will use this API to fetch and post the user data to Facebook. You can get a better idea of how to access the remote APIs or content from Electron by using this Graph API. Basically, there are multiple ways available with an Electron application to connect to a remote endpoint or to fetch data from the remote server. When you want to fetch or post data to a remote server from your main process, you need to use any of the available HTTP client libraries available for the Node.js framework. Node's built-in HTTP module, Request JS, and isomorphic-fetch are some of the best examples of these kinds of libraries. Connecting to a remote server from a renderer process is much easier than the main process. There you can use standard fetch or `XmlHttpRequest` APIs to do your jobs. You can also make use of third-party Node.js modules, that we mentioned for using in the main process, to fetch or post data to a remote server from a renderer process.

Setting up the Facebook application

You need to have a developer account in order to access the Facebook content from your Electron application. You also need to set up a Facebook application once you have a developer account. You can find more about creating a Facebook application at this URL: (`https://developers.facebook.com/docs/apps/register`). Note down the application's ID and the password to be used in the application to access the API content.

A detailed discussion about the Facebook API and its endpoints is beyond the scope of this book. So we will be discussing only the APIs required to create our small sample application.

Configuring the Facebook SDK

Facebook provides an SDK toolkit for various platforms and languages which helps us to reduce our efforts to access its API. It also provides JavaScript SDK to use in web applications. It's a single JavaScript file that can be included using a script tag in your HTML document. But, as we are using Angular 2, we should try including it in an Angular way instead of adding a simple script tag inside the HTML, which may break the build pipeline.

Creating the service

Angular follows component-based architecture. Each application is composed of multiple interconnected components. All of these components need access to the application's data or may want to share some common functionalities. So, we need to create a reusable data service that can be used to get and post data to the Facebook server. It can be used for any other functionalities that can be shared between the components. Refer to the following link to get more details about Angular 2 services:
(`https://angular.io/docs/ts/latest/tutorial/toh-pt4.html`). Create a new source file called `fbsdk.service.ts` in the app directory with the following content:

```
import { Injectable } from '@angular/core';
@Injectable()
export class FbSdkService {
    constructor() {

    }
}
```

The Angular service is a simple class that is decorated using an injectable decorator. Angular's dependency injection system can recognize the `@Injectables` and manage the dependencies for us. The preceding code creates an empty injectable service which can be used by any other Angular component. Next, we need to add the Facebook SDK into the application and it can be done by either using script tags in an `index.html` file or can be included using JavaScript. Add the following content to the service to add the SDK:

```
import { Injectable, NgZone } from '@angular/core';

@Injectable()
export class FbsdkService {

    constructor(private zone: NgZone) {
```

```
        }
        public loadSdkAsync(callback: () => void) {
            window.fbAsyncInit = () => this.zone.run(callback);

            const s = "script";
            const id = "facebook-jssdk";
            var js: any, fjs = document.getElementsByTagName(s)[0];
            if (document.getElementById(id)) return;
            js = document.createElement(s);
            js.id = id;
            js.src = "http://connect.facebook.net/en_US/sdk.js";
            fjs.parentNode.insertBefore(js, fjs);
        }
    }
```

This method does nothing but it creates a script tag dynamically and includes the Facebook SDK asynchronously. Once it's loaded, the SDK will check for the `fbAsyncInit` method in the window object and will execute it once the SDK has loaded into the renderer process. This method can be used to initialize the Facebook SDK. If you are new to Angular 2, you may be wondering about the constructor arguments for this service. We are passing an instance of `NgZone` as a parameter for this service. Actually we don't have to worry about the initialization of `@injectable` services as Angular's built in dependency management system will take care of initializing and injecting the dependencies for us. Here, once the SDK is loaded, we trigger a callback in a separate zone. A zone is an execution context that persists across async tasks.

Open the `app.component.ts` file and attach the service into the app component. You should call the `loadSdkAsync` function from the app component and initialize the SDK as follows:

```
import { Component, OnInit } from '@angular/core';
import { FbsdkService } from './fbsdk.service';

declare var FB: any;

@Component({
    //...
    providers: [FbsdkService]
})

export class AppComponent {
    constructor(private fbSdk: FbsdkService) {
        this.fbSdk.loadSdkAsync(() => {
            FB.init({
                appId: 'your_client_id_here',
```

```
            secret: 'your_fb_app_password',
            status: false,
            xfbml: false,
            version: 'v2.8'
        });
    });
  }
}
```

All the SDK methods are available inside the FB object. Once the SDK is loaded you should initialize the application using the `FB.init` method with your application's configuration, which can be found in your developer home page.

Configuring Angular router

When the application is composed of multiple components, it's very important to have a mechanism to navigate between the components. Angular's built-in router enables navigation from one view to the next as the user performs some application tasks. It can interpret the browser URL and navigate to the corresponding client generated Angular view/component. It's important to configure the router before we start writing any other components as it's the core part to navigate between the components. Here also, we don't want to get into the details of Angular 2 routing. You can get the complete details about Angular routing in the official documentation at the following URL: (https://angular.io/docs/ts/latest/guide/router.html). Configuring the router is easy and you may follow the steps described next to configure the router in our sample application.

Add a base href to the `index.html` file as the first child inside the head section as follows:

```
<base href="/">
```

Angular does not ship the `router` module along with its code module. It's available as a separate library and you need to import it separately to use inside the application. Open the `app.module.ts` file and import the `router` module:

```
import { RouterModule }   from '@angular/router';
```

The application will have one router. The router watches for URL changes in the browser. When it detects any changes on the URL, it looks for the corresponding router from which it can display the corresponding component:

```
@NgModule({
   imports: [
      BrowserModule,
      RouterModule.forRoot([
         { path: '', component: AppComponent }
      ])
   ],
   declarations: [
      AppComponent
   ],
   bootstrap: [
      AppComponent
   ]
})
export class AppModule { }
```

The router component has no routes until we configure it in the application module. The path property specifies the path that should be triggered to display the component. In the preceding example, we use an empty path which will be rendered as the default component. You can use ** to 404 components that can be displayed when no matching route is found.

We need to provide a host component to display the configured router components. Angular provides a special component called `RouterOutlet` that displays the router components in the host view's HTML. Add the router-outlet tag into the app component's (`app.component.ts`) template:

```
<router-outlet></router-outlet>
```

Replace your entire template section with the router-outlet component. Now your `app.component.ts` template section should look like this:

```
@Component({
   selector: 'electron-app',
   template: <router-outlet></router-outlet>,
   providers: [FbsdkService]
})
```

You will get a blank page without errors once you run the application at this stage. Let's add a login screen to the application.

Login to the Facebook API

To get or post data to the server, a valid authentication token should be present inside all the requests sent to the Facebook server. Usually, we need to set up an oAuth authentication mechanism in our application to log in to remote servers such as Facebook. We will cover how to do this with Electron at the end of this chapter. But here, in the case of Facebook, the SDK provides a simple function to log in to the application which will open the Facebook login screen inside a separate window and allow the user to log in with their credentials. There are several types of authentication mechanisms available with the Facebook SDK. Here we follow a custom login process, which is described in the Facebook developer portal at:
(https://developers.facebook.com/docs/facebook-login/manually-build-a-login-flow).

Create a new component called `LoginComponent` in the `login.component.ts` file with the following content:

```
import { Component } from '@angular/core';
@Component({
    selector: 'fb-login',
    template: `<style>
      .login_btn {
        position: absolute;
        top: 45%;
        background: #4080ff;
        border-radius: 3px;
        border-color: #4080ff;
        border-width: 1px;
        color: #fff;
        display: inline-block;
        font-family: Freight Sans, 'helvetica neue',helvetica,arial,'lucida grande',sans-serif;
        font-size: 14px;
        padding: 12px 20px 10px 20px;
        left: 30%;
      }
    </style>
    <div class="container">
      <button class="login_btn" (click)="login()">Login to FaceBook</button>
      </div>
```

```
})
export class LoginComponent {
}
```

This shows a simple button and if the user is not logged in, the user should be getting this screen to enable the user to login with their Facebook credentials. Configure the router to show the login component if the user is not logged in. Change the router configuration in the `app.module.ts` file as follows:

```
import { LoginComponent } from './login.component.ts';

@NgModule({
    imports: [
        BrowserModule,
        RouterModule.forRoot([
            { path: '', component: AppComponent },
            { path: '/login', component: LoginComponent }
        ])
    ],
    declarations: [
        AppComponent,
        LoginComponent
    ],
    bootstrap: [
        AppComponent
    ]
})
export class AppModule { }
```

Now the `LoginComponent` is independent and by default `AppComponent` will be rendered to the screen. So we need to ask the Angular router to check the user authentication status before displaying `AppComponent`. The Angular router provides a `canActivate` property which provides a way to execute some logic before rendering a component. This property accepts an Angular service that implements the `CanActivate` interface from the Angular router module. Add the `LoggedInGuard` service in the `loggedinguard.service.ts` file with the following code:

```
import { Injectable } from '@angular/core';
import { CanActivate, Router, ActivatedRouteSnapshot, RouterStateSnapshot } from '@angular/router';
@Injectable()
export class LoggedInGuard implements CanActivate {
    constructor(private router: Router) {

    }
    canActivate(route: ActivatedRouteSnapshot, state: RouterStateSnapshot):
```

```
    any {
        if (state.url !== '/login') {
            FB.getLoginStatus((response: any) => {
                if (response.status !== 'connected') {
                    this.router.navigate(['/login']);
                    return false;
                }
            });
        }
        return true;
    }
}
```

Update the router configuration and add the `LoggedInGuard` service into the `CanActivate` hook:

```
@NgModule({
    imports: [
        BrowserModule,
        RouterModule.forRoot([
            { path: '', component: AppComponent, canActivate: [LoggedInGuard]
},
            { path: '/login', component: LoginComponent }
        ])
    ],
    providers: [
        LoggedInGuard
    ],
    declarations: [..],
    bootstrap: [...]
})
```

Once you run the application, you should be getting the login component instead of `AppComponent`. Open `LoginComponent` and add the `login` method as an event handler for the login button click:

```
@Component({
    selector: 'fb-login',
    template: <div class="container">
      <button class="login_btn" (click)="login()">Login to
FaceBook</button>
    </div>
})
export class LoginComponent {
```

Using Angular 2 with Electron

```
    constructor() { }

    public login() {
        FB.login();
    }
}
```

Once you click on the button, the default Facebook login window should open. You can log in with your Facebook credentials for further data retrieval. The app's login screen should look like the following:

Getting user profile

Once we are authenticated, we can retrieve the data with very simple GET requests. All the information can be retrieved from the `http://graph.facebook.com` endpoint or its sub-endpoints. In this section, let's try to get the profile information from the server. It can be retrieved from the endpoint at: `http://graph.facebook.com/me`. All nodes and edges in the Graph API can be read simply with an HTTP GET request to the relevant endpoint. But most of the API calls must be signed with an access token that we have already discussed in earlier sections. An important aspect when retrieving the data from the Graph API is that you need to specify the data fields of which you want to get the data. It's not practical to remember all the fields available with the API. For this purpose, Facebook provides a tool called GraphQL explorer, which can be used to query the data directly from the developer website. You can also use this tool/interface to test your API requests before using it in the application.

GraphQL explorer can be found at: `https://developers.facebook.com/tools/explorer`.

Let's create the application's home page interface with this functionality. We are going to create an interface with three tabs for the profile, posts, and friends. After login, the Angular router should navigate to the `HomeComponent`. We should be seeing the Angular component tree like the following. We will check each of these components in detail in the following sections:

|- AppComponent

   |- RouterOutlet

      |- HomeComponent

         |- ProfileComponent

         |- PostsListComponent

         |- FriendsListComponent

      |- LoginComponent

Create an HTML file called `home.component.html` and add the following content to create the UI:

```html
<div class="container">
    <div class="header">
        <h1>Facebook</h1>
    </div>
    <div class="cover-holder">
        <div class="cover">
            <img src="{{coverImage}}" alt="" />
        </div>
        <div class="profile-pic">
            <div class="profile-name">
                <h1>{{name}}</h1>
            </div>
        </div>
    </div>
    <div class="button-holder">
        <a href="#">Profile</a>
        <a href="#">Posts</a>
        <a href="#">Friends</a>
    </div>
    <div class="status-box"></div>
    <div class="posts-box">
        <textarea placeholder="Whats on your mind ?"></textarea>
        <a href="#" class="post-btn">Post</a>
    </div>
    <div class="post-card-holder">

    </div>
</div>
```

Now the starting components template is ready in a separate template file. Add an Angular component in `home.component.ts`:

```
Import { Component } from '@angular/core'
Import { FbsdkService } from './fbsdk.service';
@Component({
selector: 'user-home',
templateUrl: './home.component.html',
styleUrls: ['style.css'],
providers: [FbsdkService]
})
export class HomeComponent {
constructor(private fbService: FbSdkService) {
}
}
```

Update the style.css file and add the following content to it:

```
body * {
    margin: 0;
    padding: 0;
}
.container {
    width: 414px;
    margin: auto;
    min-height: 400px;
    border: 1px solid #3b5998;
    background: linear-gradient(white, #e4e8f5);
}
.header {
    height: 50px;
    width: 100%;
    background-color: #3b5998;
    border-bottom: 1px solid #29487d;
    color: #fff;
}
.profile-pic {
    width: 100%;
    background-size: 100%;
    padding: 0;
    margin: 0;
    position: absolute;
    bottom: 0;
}
.avatar {
    position: relative;
    bottom: 20px;
    height: 80px;
    width: 80px;
    border: 1px solid #ddd;
    left: 5%;
    float: left;
    display: inline-block;
}
.profile-pic img,
.avatar img {
    max-width: 100%;
    height: auto;
}
.profile-name {
    position: relative;
    height: auto;
    bottom: 0px;
```

```css
      float: left;
      display: block;
      margin-right: 20px;
      left: 8%;
      width: 68%;
 }
 .profile-name h1 {
      color: #FFF;
      font-family: 'helvetica', arial;
      font-size: 23px;
      text-shadow: 1px 1px 4px #111;
 }
 .button-holder {
      margin: auto;
      text-align: center;
      background: #FFF;
      border-bottom: 1px solid #a5aab3;
      clear: both;
      position: relative;
      margin-top: -3px !important;
      background: #ffffff;
      /* Old browsers */
      background: -moz-linear-gradient(top, #ffffff 0%, #f6f6f6 47%, #ededed 100%);
      /* FF3.6-15 */
      background: -webkit-linear-gradient(top, #ffffff 0%, #f6f6f6 47%, #ededed 100%);
      /* Chrome10-25,Safari5.1-6 */
      background: linear-gradient(to bottom, #ffffff 0%, #f6f6f6 47%, #ededed 100%);
      /* IE6-9 */
      border-top: 1px solid #f6f6f6;
 }
 .button-holder a {
      padding: 18px 20px 18px 20px;
      text-decoration: none;
      font-size: 14px;
      font-family: 'helvetica', arial;
      color: #333;
      border-radius: 3px 3px;
      width: 19.33%;
      display: inline-block;
      border-left: 1px solid #dedede;
      font-weight: bold;
 }
 .button-holder a:first-child {
      border: none !important;
 }
```

```css
.cover {
   height: auto;
   position: relative;
   background: #a5aab3;
}
.cover img {
   max-width: 100%;
   height: auto;
}
.cover-holder {
   position: relative;
   display: inline-block;
}
.posts-box {
   padding: 20px;
}
.post-card-holder {
   padding: 20px;
   clear: both;
   margin-bottom: 40px;
}
.posts-box textarea {
   background: #FFF;
   border: 1px solid #a5aab3;
   padding: 10px 10px 10px 10px;
   height: 70px;
   width: 94%;
   font-family: 'helvetica', arial;
   margin-bottom: 5px;
}
.post-btn {
   border-color: #29447e #29447e #1a356e;
   color: #fff;
   background-color: #5B74A8;
   background-image: -webkit-gradient(linear, 0 0, 0 100%, from(#637bad), to(#5872a7));
   background-image: -moz-linear-gradient(#637bad, #5872a7);
   background-image: -o-linear-gradient(#637bad, #5872a7);
   background-image: linear-gradient(#637bad, #5872a7);
   -webkit-box-shadow: 0 1px 0 rgba(0, 0, 0, 0.1), inset 0 1px 0 #8a9cc2;
   -moz-box-shadow: 0 1px 0 rgba(0, 0, 0, 0.1), inset 0 1px 0 #8a9cc2;
   box-shadow: 0 1px 0 rgba(0, 0, 0, 0.1), inset 0 1px 0 #8a9cc2;
   margin: 0;
   text-decoration: none;
   text-align: center;
   font: bold 11px/normal 'lucida grande', tahoma, verdana, arial, sans-serif;
   white-space: nowrap;
```

```css
    cursor: pointer;
    position: relative;
    z-index: 1;
    overflow: visible;
    display: inline-block;
    padding: 8px;
    float: right;
}
.post-avatar {
    float: left;
    padding: 8px;
    height: 32px;
    width: 32px;
}
.post-details {
    float: left;
    display: inline-block;
    padding: 8px;
}
span.activity {
    color: #a5aab3 !important;
    font-weight: normal !important;
    padding: 8px;
}
span.post-date {
    float: left;
    width: 100%;
    clear: both;
    margin-top: 5px;
    font-weight: normal;
    color: #a5aab3;
}
.post-text {
    clear: both;
    margin-bottom: 20px;
    display: inline-block;
    font-weight: normal;
    font-size: 13px;
    line-height: 20px;
    padding: 8px;
}
img.post-img-responsive {
    max-width: 100%;
    height: auto;
}
.header h1 {
    padding: 11px;
    font-size: 25px;
```

```
      font-family: 'helvetica', arial;
}
.post-avatar img {
   max-width: 100%;
   height: auto;
}
```

The primary user interface is ready. Add the `getProfileInfo` method to the `fbsdk` service to get the profile data from the server. As we discussed earlier, we can get the profile info from the `graph.facebook.com/me` endpoint. This endpoint accepts a parameter called fields which specifies the fields to be retrieved from the server. For example, to get your name and e-mail, you can send a GET request to the server as follows:

```
GET   graph.facebook.com
/me?
Fields=name,email
```

Update the Angular service and add the following method to it:

```
public getProfile() {
    return new Promise((resolve, reject) => {
        let fields = [
"id", "name", "email", "cover", "birthday"
        ];
        FB.api(/me?fields=${fields.toString()}, (response: any) => {
            resolve(response);
});
});
}
```

The preceding code uses the Facebook SDK's API method. We use this method instead of Angular's HTTP module because this will take care of sending an authentication token along with each request. This can also be done using Angular's HTTP module or using normal Ajax calls using `XmlHttpRequest` or `fetch`. Open your `HomeComponent`, then call the `getProfile` method on the `ngOnInit` life cycle event. `ngOnInit` is a life cycle event which will be executed when the component/directive is initialized and Angular first displays the data-bound properties. You can use this method to invoke API calls or to any other initialization process within the component:

```
export class HomeComponent implements OnInit {
    ..
ngOnInit() {
   this.fbService.getProfile().then((json: any) => {
        this.profile = json;
        this.coverImage = json.cover.source;
        this.name = json.name;
```

```
        });
    }
}
```

Run the application and you should get this output:

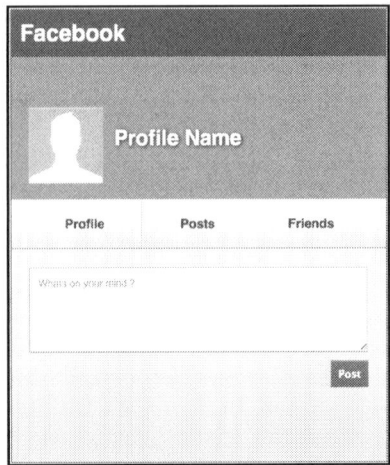

Creating the profile component

Now we have the user profile information available inside HomeComponent. Let's create another component to show the profile information as a first tab inside the application. As we are already getting the profile information when the application starts, we don't need to repeat the same inside the profile component. This data can be passed from HomeComponent to ProfileComponent as it's going to place a direct child of HomeComponent. Create a new file called profile.component.ts inside the app directory and add the following content to it:

```
import { Component, Input } from '@angular/core';
@Component({
    selector: 'user-profile',
    templateUrl: './profile.component.html'
})
export class Profile {
    @Input('data') data: any = {};
    constructor() { }
}
```

We don't need any logic to be present inside the profile component as it's intended to display the user profile information. The profile data will be passed to this component from the parent component. We use the Angular `@Input` decorator to get the data from the parent via the component's attribute. The Input decorator is used to get some data from the parent as attributes. The parameter for the decorator specifies the attribute name from which the data should be taken to this component. If you are not passing the parameter, then Angular will check for attributes with the same name as the variable name for the data. Here we pass the data as the attribute to the component and this information will be available inside the instance variable called data. Create the template for this component in a new file called `profile.component.html` inside the app folder:

```html
<div class="user-profile-info">
    <header>Basic Info</header>
    <div>
        <div class="row">
            <div class="pull-left">Mobile</div>
            <div class="pull-right">{{mobile}}</div>
        </div>

        <div class="row">
            <div class="pull-left">Birth Day</div>
            <div class="pull-right">{{data.birthday}}</div>
        </div>

        <div class="row">
            <div class="pull-left">Interested In</div>
            <div class="pull-right">{{data.interested_in.join(',')}}</div>
        </div>

        <div class="row">
            <div class="pull-left">Languages</div>
            <div class="pull-right">
                <span *ngFor="let language of data.languages">
                    {{language.name}},
                </span>
            </div>
        </div>
    </div>
</div>
```

This is a sample template for the profile component. You can enhance it with the data provided by the Graph API.

Creating a tab component

You can see multiple tabs in the preceding screenshot. One for profile, another for posts, and the last one for friends. With Angular 2, it's easy to create a tab like the user interface without using any third-party UI libraries. We don't have to manipulate DOM directly and we just need to manipulate the data to update the DOM. Let's configure the tab panel interface inside the app component before attaching the profile component to the app component. Update the App.Component.html as follows:

```
<div class="button-holder">
        <a href="#" (click)="selectedTabIndex=1">Profile</a>
        <a href="#" (click)="selectedTabIndex=2">>Posts</a>
        <a href="#" (click)="selectedTabIndex=3">>Friends</a>
</div>

<div class="posts-box">
        <textarea placeholder="Whats on your mind ?"></textarea>
        <a href="#" class="post-btn">Post</a>
</div>
<div class="container">
   <user-profile *ngIf="selectedTabIndex == 1" [data]="profile"></user-profile>
   <div *ngIf="selectedTabIndex == 2"></div>
   <div *ngIf="selectedTabIndex == 3"></div>
</div>
```

Add the selected TabIndex variable to app.component.ts as follows:

```
//..
class AppComponent {
   public selectedTabIndex = 1;
constructor() {}
}
```

So far, we have checked how to use Angular 2 with Electron to create a small social media client. We are not going to cover each and every step to create an Angular application as it's out of the scope of this book. You can easily do the rest of the application using Angular 2. The complete application source code is available at:
http://github.com/jasimea/AngularElectron.

Implementing oAuth authentication with Electron

We have checked how we can authenticate an application with the Facebook SDK. There are some other situations where we have to implement oAuth authentication, which is not a simple task. With oAuth, the authentication process will be happening at a remote URL and will be redirected to the client domain when the authentication is successful. So we need to handle redirections. Usually, it's easy with a normal web application as the server will simply redirect to the domain. But with Electron, we don't have any domain running from the local file and the server does not have any access to our local HTML file embedded inside the Electron shell. So, it's a challenge to handle this with Electron. Let's look at how we can implement oAuth authentication with Electron. As an example, let's try to log in to the GitHub API with Electron. This part is not included in the sample application but we need to have a clear idea about this type of authentication with Electron as the procedure is a little bit different from the traditional web application.

The initial step is to configure the GitHub application's credentials:

```
var options = {
    client_id: 'your_client_id',
    client_secret: 'your_client_secret',
    // Scopes limit access for OAuth tokens.
    scopes: ["user:email", "notifications"]
};
```

We need to open the resource manager's (in this case, GitHub.com) authentication page, which enables the user to authenticate with their system. Add the following to your page:

```
var authWindow = new BrowserWindow({ width: 800, height: 600, show: false, 'node-integration': false });
var githubUrl = 'https://github.com/login/oauth/authorize?';
var authUrl = githubUrl + 'client_id=' + options.client_id + '&scope=' + options.scopes;
authWindow.loadURL(authUrl);
authWindow.show();
```

Once you are logged into the website, the server will redirect the page into your domain. In this case, we need to handle the redirection manually as we are running from the local filesystem. Electron emits two events when the page is about to redirect:

```
authWindow.webContents.on('will-navigate', function (event, url) {
    handleCallback(url);
});
```

```
authWindow.webContents.on('did-get-redirect-request', function (event,
oldUrl, newUrl) {
  handleCallback(newUrl);
});
```

The remote server will pass the authentication code along with the redirected URL. You can also get the error messages with the URL if any error occurs. We need to extract the authentication code from the URL as follows:

```
function handleCallback (url) {
  var raw_code = /code=([^&]*)/.exec(url) || null;
  var code = (raw_code && raw_code.length > 1) ? raw_code[1] : null;
  var error = /\?error=(.+)$/.exec(url);

  if (code || error) {
    // Close the browser if code found or error
    authWindow.destroy();
  }

  // If there is a code, proceed to get token from github
  if (code) {
    self.requestGithubToken(options, code);
  } else if (error) {
    alert('Oops! Something went wrong and we couldn\'t' +
      'log you in using Github. Please try again.');
  }
}
```

Release the auth window object on close:

```
authWindow.on('close', function() {
    authWindow = null;
}, false);
```

Once the user is authenticated, we need to request the authentication token that should be attached with each API request sent to the server. Once the token is received, save it in a shared storage where both the main process and the renderer process have access like local storage:

```
function requestGithubToken(options, code) {
  fetch('https://github.com/login/oauth/access_token', {
      method: 'POST'
      body: {
          client_id: options.client_id,
          client_secret: options.client_secret,
          code: code,
      }
```

```
        })
        .then(function (response) {
            if (response && response.ok) {
                window.localStorage.setItem('githubtoken',
response.body.access_token);
            }
        });
}
```

If everything is implemented correctly, you can now start accessing the GitHub content. This is almost the same as any oAuth authentication provider. Even with Facebook, you can follow these steps. But Facebook provides a wrapper for this through the Facebook SDK. For our Angular application, the same code can be rewritten as an Angular service as follows:

```
import { Injectable } from '@angular/core';
import { Http, Headers } from '@angular/http';
import { Store } from '@ngrx/store';
import { AppState } from './../store/appState.store';
import { AUTH_ACTION_TYPES } from './../store/auth.store';
import { remote, BrowserWindow } from 'electron'

const options = {
    client_id: 'your_client_id',
    client_secret: 'your_client_secret',
    // Scopes limit access for OAuth tokens.
    scopes: ["user:email", "notifications"]
};
```

Update the authentication service with the following constructor. The browser window should be initialized inside the constructor. This browser window can be used to load the oAuth login page:

```
@Injectable()
export class Authentication {
    authWindow: any;
    http: Http;

    constructor(public store: Store<AppState>, http: Http) {
        this.authWindow = new BrowserWindow({ width: 800, height: 600, show: false });
    }
}
```

Add the following method into the service. Build the oAuth page login URL and load it into the `BrowserWindow`. When you log in successfully, the page will be redirected to the callback URL that you configured in your app. You need to handle it using the will-navigate event handler of the `BrowserWindow`:

```
githubHandShake() {

    // Build the OAuth consent page URL
    let githubUrl = 'https://github.com/login/oauth/authorize?';
    let authUrl = githubUrl + 'client_id=' + options.github.client_id +
'&scope=' + options.github.scopes;
    this.authWindow.loadUrl(authUrl);
    this.authWindow.show();

    // Handle the response from GitHub
    this.authWindow.webContents.on('will-navigate', (event, url) => {
      this.handleGitHubCallback(url);
    });

    this.authWindow.webContents.on('did-get-redirect-request', (event,
oldUrl, newUrl) => {
      this.handleGitHubCallback(newUrl);
    });

    // Reset the authWindow on close
    this.authWindow.on('close', function () {
      this.authWindow = null;
    }, false);
}
```

Add the following method to your service. This handles your oAuth provider callback. When the login is successful, this method asks for the authentication token which needs to be added to all your requests after the login:

```
handleGitHubCallback(url) {
    let raw_code = /code=([^&]*)/.exec(url) || null;
    let code = (raw_code && raw_code.length > 1) ? raw_code[1] : null;
    let error = /\?error=(.+)$/.exec(url);

    if (code || error) {
      // Close the browser if code found or error
      this.authWindow.destroy();
    }

    // If there is a code, proceed to get token from github
    if (code) {
      this.requestGithubToken(options.github, code);
```

```
    } else if (error) {
      alert('Oops! Something went wrong and we couldn't' +
        'log you in using Github. Please try again.');
    }
  }
```

The following code requests the token to GitHub. Add the following code into the service:

```
    requestGithubToken(githubOptions, githubCode) {
      let creds = 'client_id=' + githubOptions.client_id + '&client_secret='
+ githubOptions.client_secret + '&code=' + githubCode;

      let headers = new Headers();
      headers.append('Accept', 'application/json');

      this.http.post('https://github.com/login/oauth/access_token?' + creds,
'', { headers: headers })
        .subscribe(
        response => {
          //call the store to update the authToken
          let body_object = JSON.parse(response['_body']);
          this.requestUserData(body_object.access_token);
        },
        err => console.log(err),
        () => console.log('Authentication Complete')
        );

  }
requestUserData(token) {

    let headers = new Headers();
    headers.append('Accept', 'application/json');

    this.http.get('https://api.github.com/user?access_token=' + token, {
headers: headers })
      .subscribe(
      response => {
        //call local storage
},
      err => console.log(err),
      () => console.log('Request Complete')
      );
  }
```

[105]

Summary

In this chapter, we discussed how we can use Angular 2 to create a desktop application with Electron. There is not much difference in developing an Electron application from traditional web development in terms of the user interface. We have checked how we can connect our Electron application to a remote server to get some data. Also in the last part of the chapter, we discussed implementing oAuth authentication with Electron and handling response redirection in Electron.

So far, all we have discussed is using Angular with Electron but we have not discussed in detail any user interface libraries. In the next chapter, we will discuss some user interface libraries available for Electron. We will also check how we can use those libraries to build a native-like user interface for Electron.

5
Crafting User Interface

Hundreds of JavaScript and CSS libraries are available to build the user interface. Electron-based applications can also use all of these libraries. But Electron is supposed to run in native environments inside client machines. So it's important to provide a native-like user experience for users in terms of the look, feel, and performance. As an Electron user, the look and feel of web technologies can be easily achieved using CSS and JavaScript. Also, performance will never be an issue with Electron as it runs on top of a powerful V8 engine. There are some frameworks available to create a native-like look and feel in Electron. Actually, these frameworks can be used even with normal web applications as they're written in pure JavaScript and CSS. In this chapter, we will look into building a native-like user interface using these frameworks. In the previous chapter, we looked at how we can create an application using modern JavaScript frameworks and we created a user interface simply using HTML and CSS. Here we will be discussing how we can create a native-like user interface. We will also be discussing the following points in this chapter:

- Creating an Electron user interface with the Photon library
- Exploring components available inside the Photon library
- Using React with GitHub Electron
- Building user interface with a React desktop

We will also briefly discuss React with Electron in this chapter. You will have a better idea about developing native desktop user interfaces by the end of this chapter.

Introducing Photon kit

Photon kit is a CSS library that provides a native-like look and feels for widgets. If you have ever worked with Bootstrap, you know that the CSS frameworks are important for creating a responsive user interface. It reduces a lot of efforts by providing solutions to common problems. Photon is almost the same as Bootstrap, but it is built for Electron or any other desktop application development. It's a very lightweight framework that includes CSS styles to create both Mac and Windows native-like widgets and user interface. You can download the Photon library from: http://www.photonkit.com.

Laying out the application

Download the framework and copy the `dist` folder into the project root. You can include the style using standard link tags in your `index.html` file. Every Photon application has some basic structure. All the application elements should be wrapped by two container `div`'s with the window CSS class and `window-content` class:

```
<div class="window">
  <div class="window-content">
    <!-- The application content goes here -->
  </div>
</div>
```

Another point to note when using Photon is to disable the Electron window frame and make the window frameless if you want to use the custom window design provided by the Photon toolkit. This is because the Photon kit provides a native-like window look and feel that can be customized very easily to any extent.

The frameless window

The frameless window is a window that has no chrome. Creating a frameless window can be done easily using the `BrowserWindow` objects features. To create a frameless window, you just need to pass `frame: false` into the `BrowserWindow` object:

```
const {BrowserWindow} = require('electron')
let win = new BrowserWindow({ width: 800, height: 600, frame: false })
```

But the problem with the frameless window is that it will reduce your flexibility to interact with the window. For example, the close, minimize, and maximize buttons won't be there and you need to handle it manually. In Mac OS there is an alternative way to specify the chrome window. Instead of setting the frame equal to false, set the title bar style as hidden so that only the window title bar will be hidden and window controls will be visible:

```
const {BrowserWindow} = require('electron')
let win = new BrowserWindow({ titleBarStyle: 'hidden' })
```

Draggable regions

By default, frameless windows are non-draggable. The application needs to specify `-webkit-app-region: drag` in the CSS property to Electron which regions are draggable. The application can also use the `webkit-app-region: no-drag` CSS property to exclude the non-draggable areas from the draggable region:

```
<header style="-webkit-app-region: drag" class="toolbar toolbar-header">
</header>
```

It's always good to disable the text selection when you enable the dragging behavior into an element:

```
.titlebar {
  -webkit-user-select: none;
  -webkit-app-region: drag;
}
```

Laying out the application

For creating the layouts, we can either use Bootstrap or an advanced CSS layout such as flexbox or grid layout. Photon Kit also provides some CSS classes to layout the application. You can create a paned layout by using Photon's `pane-groups` and `pane` CSS classes:

```
<div class="window">
    <header class="toolbar toolbar-header">
      <h1> Header with actions</h1>
    </header>
    <div class="window-content">
       <div class="pane-group">
          <div class="pane-sm">
             Left side pane
          </div>
          <div class="pane">
```

Crafting User Interface

```
                Main Content Goes Here
            </div>
        </div>
    </div>
</div>
```

The preceding code will render three horizontal panes with exact width and height as follows:

Sidebars

A sidebar is useful for housing the navigation. With Photon you can add a sidebar CSS class to your pane so that the pane can be used as a sidebar:

```
<div class="pane-group">
    <div class="pane-sm sidebar">
        Here will be your sidebar content
    </div>
    <div class="pane">
        Here goes your main contents
    </div>
</div>
```

Here is the basic HTML template when using Photon kit:

```
<!DOCTYPE html>
 <html>
  <head>
    <title>Application Title</title>
    <link rel="stylesheet" type="text/css" href="./photon/css/photon.css">
  </head>

  <body>
    <div class="window">
      <header class="toolbar toolbar-header">
        <h1 class="title">Photon</h1>
      </header>
      <div class="window-content">
      </div>
      <footer class="toolbar toolbar-footer">
        <h1 class="title">Footer</h1>
      </footer>
    </div>
  </body>
</html>
```

Photon components

Photon toolkit provides only CSS-based components and we don't have to do code changes in our JavaScript source code. You can think of it as a variant of Bootstrap, but for Electron. This does not mean that you can replace Bootstrap with Photon. It's only for achieving native-like user interface. You can also use Bootstrap along with Photon or React desktop, which is another library for Electron with React. Let's look into some of the CSS components available in Photon.

Bars

Bars can be placed at the top or bottom section of the application. A bar can be used as a title bar of the application or as a footer or status bar. These can be created by adding a CSS class called `toolbar` and `toolbar-header` for the header section and toolbar-footer for the footer section.

You can use standard header and footer tags to create this type of component. The H1 tag with title class should be the child to display the header and footer text as follows:

```
<header class="toolbar toolbar-header">
  <h1 class="title">Header Text Goes Here</h1>
</header>
```

Similar way footer can be created as follows:

```
<footer class="toolbar toolbar-header">
  <h1 class="title">Header Text Goes Here</h1>
</footer>
```

Toolbar and Actions

Actions can be added to the bars either as buttons or as button groups. You can create toolbar-like actions with the following markup:

```
<header style="-webkit-app-region: drag" class="toolbar toolbar-header">
  <h1 class="title">Header with actions</h1>
  <div class="toolbar-actions">
    <div class="btn-group">
      <button class="btn btn-default">
        <span class="icon icon-home"></span>
      </button>
      <button class="btn btn-default">
        <span class="icon icon-folder"></span>
      </button>
      <button class="btn btn-default active">
        <span class="icon icon-cloud"></span>
      </button>
      <button class="btn btn-default">
        <span class="icon icon-popup"></span>
      </button>
      <button class="btn btn-default">
        <span class="icon icon-shuffle"></span>
      </button>
    </div>
```

```html
      <button class="btn btn-default">
        <span class="icon icon-home icon-text"></span>
          Filters
      </button>
      <button class="btn btn-default btn-dropdown pull-right">
        <span class="icon icon-megaphone"></span>
      </button>
</header>
```

Tabs

With Photon tab group classes, you can create a native-like tab interface easily:

```html
<div>
  <div class="tab-group">
    <div class="tab-item active">
      <span class="icon icon-cancel icon-close-tab"></span>
        Tab - 1
    </div>
    <div class="tab-item">
      <span class="icon icon-cancel icon-close-tab"></span>
        Tab - 2
    </div>
    <div class="tab-item">
      <span class="icon icon-cancel icon-close-tab"></span>
        Tab - 3
    </div>
    <div class="tab-item tab-item-fixed">
      <span class="icon icon-plus"></span>
    </div>
  </div>
  <div>
    <!-- Content goes here -->
  </div>
</div>
```

Navs

Navs acts as a sidebar for your application. You can think of this as a left side bar in the Mac OS finder window or folder explorer inside the Windows platform. It can be created using plain HTML with the following syntax:

```html
<nav class="nav-group">
  <h5 class="nav-group-title">Favorites</h5>
```

```html
<a class="nav-group-item active">
  <span class="icon icon-home"></span> connors
</a>
<span class="nav-group-item">
 <span class="icon icon-light-up"></span> Photon
</span>
<span class="nav-group-item">
  <span class="icon icon-download"></span> Downloads
</span>
<span class="nav-group-item">
  <span class="icon icon-folder"></span> Documents
</span>
<span class="nav-group-item">
  <span class="icon icon-print"></span> Applications
</span>
<span class="nav-group-item">
  <span class="icon icon-signal"></span> AirDrop
</span>
<span class="nav-group-item">
  <span class="icon icon-cloud"></span> Desktop
</span>
</nav>
```

Tables

Photon provides `table` class to display tabular data. The HTML structure is as follows:

```html
<table class="table-striped">
  <thead>
    <tr>
      <th>Name</th>
      <th>Kind</th>
      <th>Date Modified</th>
      <th>Author</th>
    </tr>
  </thead>
  <tbody>
    <tr>
      <td>bars.scss</td>
      <td>Document</td>
      <td>Oct 13, 2015</td>
      <td>connors</td>
    </tr>
    <tr>
      <td>base.scss</td>
      <td>Document</td>
```

```
      <td>Oct 13, 2015</td>
      <td>connors</td>
    </tr>
    <tr>
      <td>button-groups.scss</td>
      <td>Document</td>
      <td>Oct 13, 2015</td>
      <td>connors</td>
    </tr>
  </tbody>
</table>
```

It's a simple UI framework specifically for Electron or desktop applications. Once you have plugged most of the component into the web page, you can get a user interface, which is very similar to the Mac native user interface design, as follows:

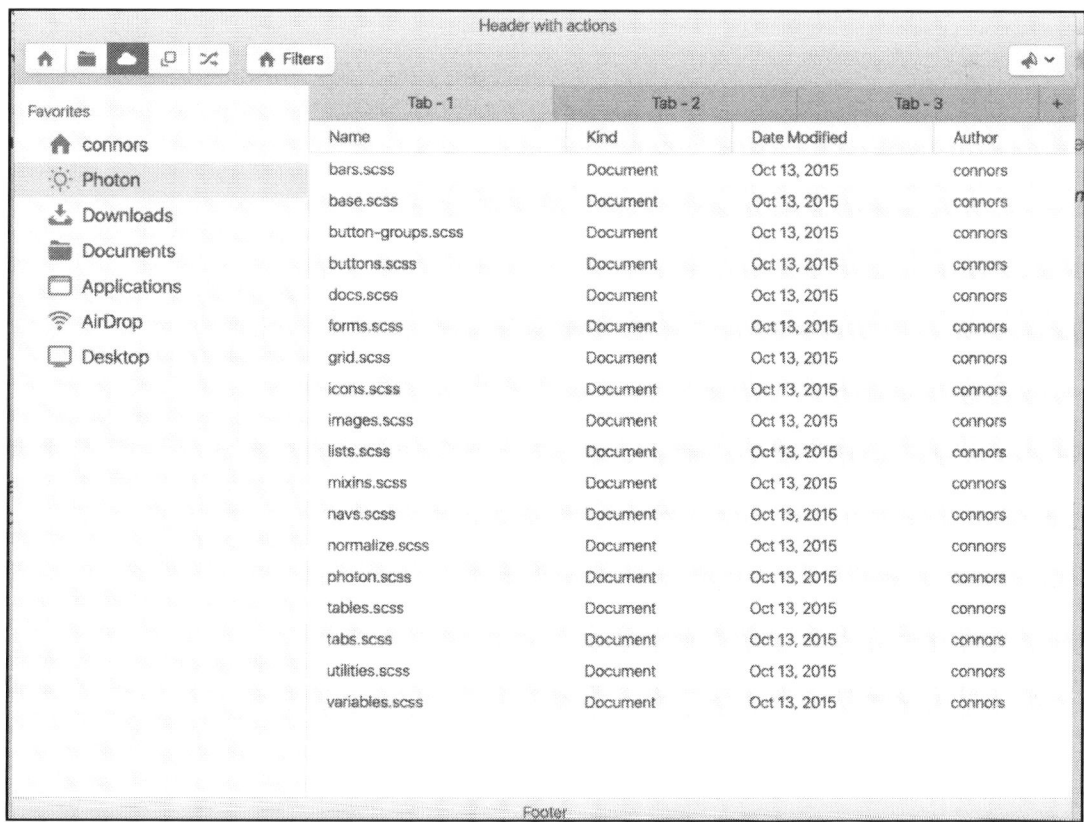

Building a user interface with React desktop

There are not many user interface libraries available specifically for Electron. Most of us may not want to use these libraries as we have the flexibility and power of CSS available in Electron, and we are free to create any type of user interface with it. In this section, let's discuss one more library available for building a user interface. React desktop is a UI component library available for Mac OS and Windows 10. But this is not a general solution. You need to use React to use this library. So let's create a simple application with React and explore how we can integrate a user interface with the React desktop.

The React desktop provides two sets of UI packages, one for Mac and another for Windows 10. Creating an Electron application with React is the same as what we have discussed in previous chapters. You can start with the hello world application that we created in the first chapter to get started with this example. Initialize the application and install the node dependencies by entering the following command into your terminal or command line prompt:

```
npm install --save-dev babel babel-core babel-loader babel-preset-env babel-preset-react css-loader extract-text-webpack-plugin file-loader html-webpack-plugin raw-loader style-loader webpack webpack-dev-server
```

You can also use the yarn for adding the dependencies. Use the following command if you are using the yarn:

```
yarn add --dev babel babel-core babel-loader babel-preset-env babel-preset-react css-loader extract-text-webpack-plugin file-loader html-webpack-plugin raw-loader style-loader webpack webpack-dev-server
```

These are the development dependencies. Next, install the application dependencies with the following command:

```
npm install --save electron react react-desktop react-dom webpack-target-electron-renderer
```

Use the similar step that we did for development dependencies if you want to use the yarn as your package management tool.

You are already familiar with most of these dependencies. All the development dependencies are for webpack and its loaders. Instead of TypeScript we will be using ES2015/2016 and Babel is used to transpile the ES6 to ES5. If you are new to Babel; it's a transpiler for writing next generation JavaScript. With Babel, you can use the latest ECMA Script language features. Babel will transpile your code into the ES5 before running your application. Electron supports most of the ES2015 features, but we still need to use Babel especially when using it with React. This is because we need to write JSX with React, which does not have support natively in any of the browsers. Babel can transpile React's JSX code into the normal JavaScript calls.

Like we did in the previous chapter, let's configure the webpack to load and bundle the JavaScript modules inside the application. Create a webpack configuration file with the following content. Create a new file called `webpack.config.js` in your project directory:

```js
const path = require('path');
const webpack = require('webpack');
const HtmlWebpackPlugin = require('html-webpack-plugin');

module.exports = {
  // The base directory for resolving entry points
  context: __dirname,

  // Source map configuration
  devtool: 'inline-source-map',
  entry: {
    app: path.resolve(__dirname, './src/app.js')
  },
  output: {
    path: path.resolve(__dirname, './build'),
    publicPath: './',
    filename: '[name].js',
    sourceMapFilename: '[name].js.map',
    chunkFilename: '[id].chunk.js'
  },

  resolve: {
    extensions: ['.js', '.jsx', '.css', '.html'],
    modules: ['./src', 'node_modules']
  },
  devServer: {
    contentBase: './',
    publicPath: '/',
    inline: true,
    lazy: false,
    hot: true,
    historyApiFallback: {
```

```
        verbose: true,
        disableDotRule: false,
      }
    },
    module: {
      rules: [{
        test: /\.jsx?$/,
        loader: 'babel-loader',
        exclude: [/node_modules/],
        options: {
          babelrc: false,
          presets: [ 'env', 'react']
        }
      },
      {
        test: /\.html$/, loader: 'raw-loader'
      },
      {
        test: /\.(png|jpe?g|gif|svg|woff|woff2|ttf|eot|ico)$/,
        loader: 'file-loader?name=dist/[name]-[hash].[ext]'
      },
      {
        test: /\.css$/,
        loader: ['style-loader', 'css-loader']
      }
      ]},

    node: {
      global: true,
      progress: false,
      crypto: 'empty',
      module: false,
      clearImmediate: false,
      setImmediate: false,
      __dirname: false,
      __filename: false
    },
    plugins: [
      new HtmlWebpackPlugin({ template: './src/index.html' }),
      new webpack.IgnorePlugin(new RegExp("^(fs|ipc)$"))
    ]
};
```

This is a minimal configuration to run React if you are using ES6 and JSX. This means that you can still use the React event without ES6 and JSX. In that case, you don't have to use all these tools and configurations and you can simply pull the scripts into the web page using script tags. We now have a basic webpack configuration file. Let's update the `main.js` file which runs the main process with the following code. The code is same as the previous chapter code, the only difference is that we have integrated the webpack build process into the main process in development mode:

```
const { app, BrowserWindow } = require('electron');

let win = null;

// index.html flle path
let appUrl = `file://${__dirname}/build/index.html`;

// Configure Webpack Dev Server
if (process.env.NODE_ENV == 'development') {
  console.log('Bundling webpack...');
  const webpack = require('webpack');
  const webpackDevServer = require('webpack-dev-server');
  let config = require('./webpack.config.js');
  config.entry.app = [
    "webpack-dev-server/client? http://localhost:8080/",
    "webpack/hot/dev-server",
    "./src/app.js"
  ];
  config.output.publicPath = '/';
  config.plugins.push(new webpack.HotModuleReplacementPlugin());
  const compiler = webpack(config);
  const devServer = new webpackDevServer(compiler, { hot: true });
  devServer.listen(8080);

  // Change the application file path to the dev server url
  appUrl = 'http://localhost:8080/';
}

/**
 * Create Electron Browser Window instance.
 * @return {BrowserWindow} win
 */
function createElectronShell() {
  // Initializes the new browser window
  win = new BrowserWindow({ width: 800, height: 600 });

  // Load the html file into the browser window
  win.loadURL(appUrl);
```

Crafting User Interface

```
    // Release the instance variable when the window is closed
    win.on('closed', () => {
      win = null;
    });
  }

  app.on('ready', createElectronShell);

  app.on('window-all-closed', () => {
    if (process.platform !== 'darwin') app.quit();
  });

  app.on('activate', () => {
    if (win == null) createElectronShell();
  });
```

Let's create our entry file, called `app.js`, as follows:

```
import './style.css';
import React, { Component } from 'react';
import ReactDOM from 'react-dom';

export default class AppComponent extends Component {
  constructor() {
    super();
  }

  render() {
    return (
      <div style={{ padding: 10 }}>
        <h1>Hello Electron From React</h1>
      </div>
    );
  }
}

ReactDOM.render(<AppComponent />, document.getElementById('root'));
```

This is fairly simple code that prints Hello Electron into the screen. The last section of the preceding code is an important part, the render method. This method will render the DOM element by creating a virtual DOM. This way of embedding tags inside JavaScript is called JSX.

Now update the `index.html` file with the following content. This will first connect to the webpack development server and it will include the compiled bundle using script tags:

```
<!DOCTYPE html />
<html>
  <head>
    <base href="./">
    <title>Hello Electron</title>
    <meta charset="UTF-8" />
    <meta name="viewport" content="width=device-width, initial-scale=1" />
  </head>
  <body>
    <div id="root">
    </div>
  </body>
</html>
```

The webpack dev server will be available at port 8080 and the Electron shell can load the page from this development server URL. It also provides the hot module reload functionality by watching your source code filesystem and injecting the module to runtime whenever a source file is changed.

Instead of running the application manually, let's automate it by adding some script to the `package.json` files:

```
"scripts": {
  "start":   "electron .",
  "dev": "NODE_ENV=development electron .",
  "build": "webpack"
}
```

Now you can run the electron with webpack bundling system together with `npm run dev` command. The production mode can be activated just by running the `npm start` command from your terminal.

Most Electron applications will have to work with built-in Electron/node modules, such as filesystem and the IPC module. The problem with webpack is that it cannot compile the native node or Electron modules as it is meant to be executed in a browser environment. But in the case of Electron, we have both browser environments and node environments available in the web page. So we need to tell webpack to ignore those modules exposed by Node.js and Electron when compiling the bundle. For this purpose, webpack offers a plugin called the ignore plugin, which can be used to exclude some modules from the bundling process.

Add the following line to your webpack configuration file's plugin section:

```
plugins: [
  new webpack.IgnorePlugin(new RegExp("^(fs|ipc)$"))
]
```

This tells webpack to exclude the fs and IPC modules from the bundling process so that the webpack will never search for these module dependencies.

React desktop

Like Photon, React desktop provides native-like user interface widgets to be used in Electron and the nw.js application. But here it provides a more comprehensive set of widgets. The same set of component sets is available for both Mac and Windows as separate packages. The only advantage of using these kinds of a library is that they provide native looks like widgets and CSS components. As the Electron renders your application into a web page, you can use any of the frameworks that you are using for developing your web applications. In this section, let's discuss these widgets and use it with Electron and React for building a desktop application.

Install the library using npm as follows:

npm install react-desktop --save

Let's create some basic user interface with the react-desktop library. Here we are not going to cover all the components. We will be creating a small UI piece of code to get the details of how this kind of frameworks works. Let's update our app.js with following code:

```
'use strict';
import ReactDOM from 'react-dom';
import React, { Component } from 'react';
import { View, TitleBar } from 'react-desktop/macOs';

import './style.css';

export default class AppComponent extends Component {
  constructor() {
    super();
    this.state = { isFullscreen: false };
  }
  render() {
    return (
      <div>
```

```
            <TitleBar
              controls
              title="Electron - React Desktop"
              isFullscreen={this.state.isFullscreen}
              onCloseClick={() => console.log('Close window')}
              onMinimizeClick={() => console.log('Minimize window')}
              onMaximizeClick={() => console.log('Mazimize window')}
              onResizeClick={() => this.setState({ isFullscreen:
!this.state.isFullscreen })}
            />
            <div style={{padding: 10}}>
            </div>
          </div>
      );
    }
}
ReactDOM.render(<AppComponent />, document.getElementById('root'));
```

It's just a basic React component. It renders the Titlebar component into the webpage. You can see various events related to the Titlebar component for close, minimize, and maximize. You need to manually implement those methods and attach the proper behavior to the Electron window shell. Let's look at some of the components provided by the React desktop in detail.

Buttons

A simple button can be easily created using React desktop as follows:

```
import React, { Component } from 'react';
import { Button } from 'react-desktop/macOs';

export default class extends Component {
  render() {
    return (
      <Button color="blue" onClick={() => console.log('Clicked!')}>
        Press me!
      </Button>
    );
  }
}
```

You need to change the import section when targeting for windows to get the native windows look and feel:

```
import { Button } from 'react-desktop/windows';
```

Windows

Modal dialog boxes are essential when working on web applications. When working with Electron, Electron desktop provides native-like window widgets:

```
import React, { Component } from 'react';
import { Window, TitleBar, Text } from 'react-desktop/macOs';

export default class extends Component {
  render() {
    return (
      <Window
        chrome
        height="300px"
        width="300px"
        padding="10px">
        <TitleBar  controls/>
        <Text>Hello World</Text>
      </Window>
    );
  }
}
```

The preceding code itself explains everything about the components and its properties. This example uses the Mac OS version of the Window component and it provides an OSX native look and feel as follows:

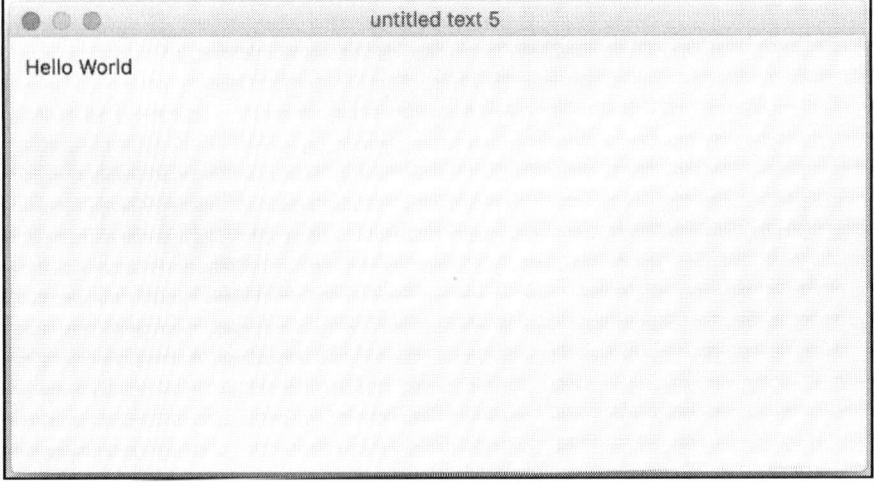

If you want to use the Windows version of this component or any other React desktop component, then you need to use the Windows package available inside the `react-desktop` library. You just need to change the import section as follows:

```
import { Window, TitleBar, Text } from 'react-desktop/windows';
```

When working on a real-world project, it's always better to import the packages based on the current platform. The same code written previously will look as follows on a Windows machine:

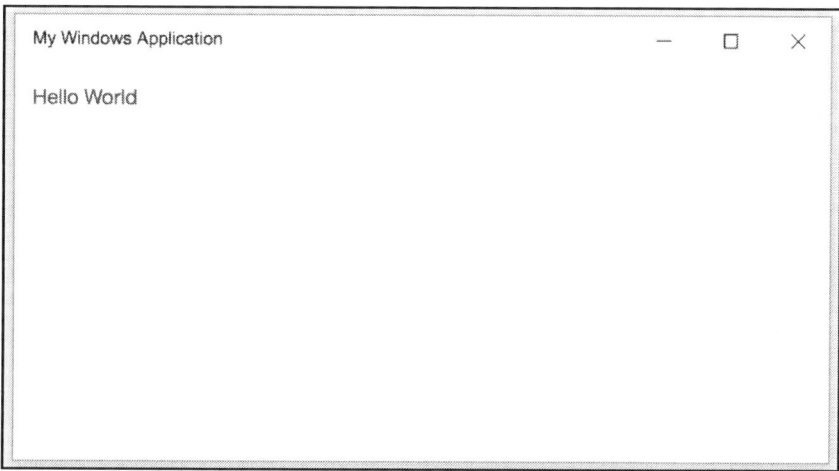

Not all the components are available on both platforms. You need to carefully craft the user interface based on the target platform. For example, for OSX there is a component called segmented control available that provides a tab-like navigation control. But this is not available on Windows, instead you need to use NavPane or any other matching control to achieve the same functionality.

Segmented Control

This provides a tab-like interface, which is most common in OSX settings pages. The `SegmentedControl` component expects it's child views as `SegmentedControlItem` components. See thee following example:

```
import React, { Component } from 'react';
import { SegmentedControl, SegmentedControlItem, Text } from 'react-desktop/macOs';

import ListView from './ListView';
```

```
import NavPane from './NavPane';
import Window from './Window'

export default class extends Component {
  constructor() {
    super();
    this.state = { selected: 1 }
  }
  render() {
    return (
      <SegmentedControl box>
        {this.renderItems()}
      </SegmentedControl>
    );
  }

  renderItems() {
    return [
      <SegmentedControlItem
        key={0}
        title="Window"
        selected={this.state.selected === 1}
        onSelect={() => this.setState({ selected: 1 })}>
        <Window />
      </SegmentedControlItem>,
      <SegmentedControlItem
        key={1}
        title="Nav Pane"
        selected={this.state.selected === 2}
        onSelect={() => this.setState({ selected: 2 })}>
        <NavPane color='#cc7f29' theme='light' />
      </SegmentedControlItem>,
      <SegmentedControlItem
        key={2}
        title="List View"
        selected={this.state.selected === 3}
        onSelect={() => this.setState({ selected: 3 })}>
        <ListView />
      </SegmentedControlItem>
    ];
  }
}
```

Here is how the output should look:

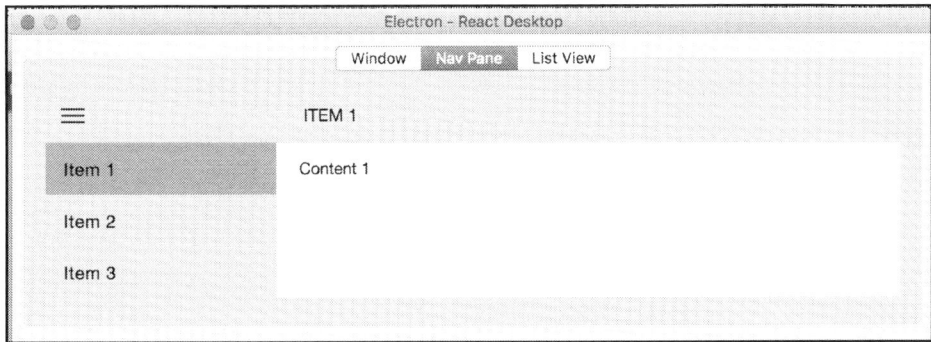

NavPane

The NavPane component is almost the same as the preceding component, but it targets the window platform. This also provides the same behavior of Segmented Control with the navigation bar on the side. Create a react component called NavPane.js inside src directory with following content:

```
import React, { Component } from 'react';
import { NavPane, NavPaneItem, Text } from 'react-desktop/windows';

export default class extends Component {
  constructor() {
    super();
    this.state = {
      selected: 'Item 1'
    };
  }
  render() {
    return (
      <NavPane openLength={200} push
        color={this.props.color}
        theme={this.props.theme}>
        {this.renderItem('Item 1', 'Content 1')}
        {this.renderItem('Item 2', 'Content 2')}
        {this.renderItem('Item 3', 'Content 3')}
      </NavPane>
    );
  }

  renderItem(title, content) {
```

Crafting User Interface

```
    return (
      <NavPaneItem
        title={title}
        theme="light"
        background="#ffffff"
        selected={this.state.selected === title}
        onSelect={() => this.setState({ selected: title })}
        padding="10px 20px"
        push>
        <Text>{content}</Text>
      </NavPaneItem>
    );
  }
}
```

This is how it should look:

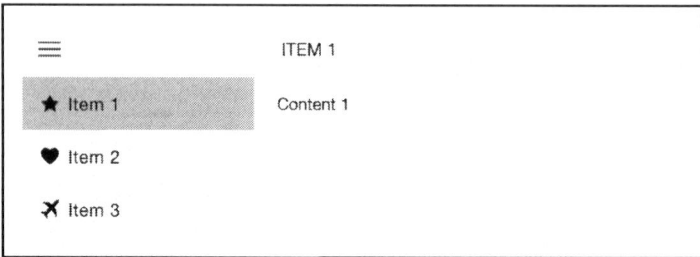

The list view

The most complex user interface pieces are the data table and list view. React desktop provides a list view component with a comprehensive set of features and properties. This is a highly customizable component. Creating the list view can be done as follows:

```
import React, { Component } from 'react';
import {
  ListView,
  ListViewHeader,
  ListViewFooter,ListViewSection,
  ListViewSectionHeader,
  ListViewRow, ListViewSeparator,
  Text
} from 'react-desktop/macOs';

export default class extends Component {
  constructor() {
    super();
```

Chapter 5

```
    this.state = { selected: null };
  }

  render() {
    return (
      <ListView background="#f1f2f4" width="240" height="200">
        <ListViewHeader>
          <Text size="11" color="#696969">Order by name</Text>
        </ListViewHeader>
        <ListViewSection header={this.renderSectionHeader('My Section')}>
          {this.renderItem('Item 1', 'This is the first item.')}
          {this.renderItem('Item 2', 'This is the second item.')}
          {this.renderItem('Item 3', 'This is the third item.')}
        </ListViewSection>
        <ListViewSeparator/>
        <ListViewSection header={this.renderSectionHeader('My Section 2')}>
          {this.renderItem('Item 4', 'This is the fourth item.')}
          {this.renderItem('Item 5', 'This is the fifth item.')}
          {this.renderItem('Item 6', 'This is the sixth item.')}
        </ListViewSection>
        <ListViewFooter>
          <Text size="11" color="#696969">Status</Text>
        </ListViewFooter>
      </ListView>
    );
  }

  renderSectionHeader(title) {
    return (
      <ListViewSectionHeader>
        {title}
      </ListViewSectionHeader>
    );
  }

  renderItem(title, info) {
    return (
      <ListViewRow
        onClick={() => this.setState({ selected: title })}
        background={this.state.selected === title ? '#d8dade' : null}>
        <Text color="#414141" size="13">{info}</Text>
      </ListViewRow>
    );
  }
}
```

This code displays a simple static list. The header and footer can be customized using `ListViewHeader` and `ListViewFooter` components. `ListViewSection` defines a section inside the list view data. You can think of it as a grouping inside the data. The `ListViewRow` component can be used to render each row's content. The preceding example just displays a simple text inside the list row.

More details about React desktop and its components are available in the official documentation (http://reactdesktop.js.org/docs/). It provides only a basic set of components. For a complex user interface requirement, you always need to consider using any of the frameworks available for web user interface development.

Awesome Electron

Awesome Electron is a curated list of awesome Electron development resources that are available on GitHub. Nowadays, the community is maintaining this awesome list for most technologies. Referring to this list will give you a more detailed picture about Electron. You can get details about the projects created on Electron, both open source, and closed source, and there are also a lot of useful resources listed in this list.
Visit: https://github.com/sindresorhus/awesome-electron, and check out the details.

Summary

What we have discussed in this chapter is crafting user interfaces using some of the available libraries. But as always, these frameworks are not necessary to build user interfaces. CSS is much more powerful for building user interfaces to any extent. Expertise in CSS, with a little more web development experience, can help you create an amazing native user interface for Electron or any other desktop application. You can even continue working on Bootstrap, angular/react--material, or any other framework along with these frameworks.

In the next chapter, we will see how Node.js can be used inside our Electron application. We will be looking at the following topics in the next chapter:

- Using Node.js modules with Electron
- Using relational databases directly from Electron using Electron
- Using ORM frameworks from Electron
- Using a brand new package management tool called `yarn` instead of `npm`

6
Using Node.js with Electron

Node.js is an open source JavaScript runtime environment, which also provides the base line for Electron and its runtime. Both technologies are built on top of Google's V8 JavaScript engine and share a lot of common functionalities. Electron leverages us to use the Node.js inside the renderer process or web page directly without any extra effort. So, with Electron, you have the full power of Node.js and its runtime, which gives you enough flexibility to create powerful desktop applications with full access to the native desktop environment. In this chapter, we will be covering how we can use the Node.js runtime and npm modules inside our Electron application. You can use third-party Node.js modules directly from npm inside Electron. It's very straightforward to use these modules inside Electron. You can start using them directly without any extra configuration. So, theoretically, we have nothing to explain about using the Node.js inside the Electron application. But let's check how this works practically in real-world applications. We will be looking at the following things in this chapter. Most of this chapter covers practical examples of using Node.js and Electron together to create wonderful desktop applications.

- Managing your data stores using MySQL and Node.js inside your Electron application
- Accessing hardware from your Electron application
- Using Native Node.js Modules inside Electron applications
- Using TypeScript and ES 2015/2016 to write an Electron application

As I said, the real power of Electron comes when you use Node.js in your web pages. So, let's explore the possibilities of Electron together with Node.js inside your application.

Managing data stores

Node.js provides a number of third-party libraries to retrieve data from the database. These libraries provide the same power and flexibility that other languages provide to access the database. With Node.js, you are able to work with most of the available SQL and NoSQL databases. This section describes how we can access data from relational databases directly from the Electron application. Here, we use MySQL database as the backend for our application.

For demonstration purposes, let's create a small database with a single table. Create a MySQL database called `customer_manager` to get started with our sample. You can use any database of your choice, but you need to use the corresponding Node.js bindings to access the data from the database. Create the database with the following command or use any MySQL GUI tools like MySQL workbench to create the database:

```
CREATE DATABASE customer_manager;
```

Add a table called `customers` in the newly-created database. Use the following sample query to create the table:

```
USE customer_manager;
CREATE TABLE customers (
  id INT NOT NULL AUTO_INCREMENT PRIMARY KEY,
  customer_name VARCHAR(50) NOT NULL,
  customer_address VARCHAR(128),
  customer_email VARCHAR(30),
  customer_telephone VARCHAR(30),
  customer_mobile VARCHAR(30),
  customer_date_of_birth DATE,
  remarks VARCHAR(300)
);
```

As you can see, this is a very basic table, which stores basic information about customers. We don't need to get into the details of database programming in this book, which is not in its scope. But let's cover some basic database operations with Angular 2 and Electron on top of the sample application that we created in the second chapter.

Open the `Chapter06/Example01` from the code bundle. You can find an Angular application similar to the code that we had created in the previous chapters.

Using the Node MySQL driver

There is a popular MySQL driver available for Node.js which is a pure JavaScript implementation. If you want to use some other database, then use a suitable library for that database. Using this driver is very simple and straightforward. To query a database object, you simply create a connection to the database configuration and start hitting the query. A simple Node.js example to query the database is as follows:

```
const mysql = require('mysql');

const connection = mysql.createConnection({
  host     : 'localhost',
  user     : 'root',
  password : 'password',
  database : 'customer_manager' //your database name here
});

// Connect to the data base
connection.connect();

connection.query('SELECT * FROM customers, function(err, rows) {
  if (err) throw err;
  console.log(rows.length);
});

connection.end();
```

Creating the database connection is simple and can be done using the `createConnection` method with your database configuration as parameters. Once the connection object is ready, then you need to connect to the database using the `connect` method. Then you can start querying the database object using the `query` method, which will provide the result in the callback function. `connection.end()` will close the connection. But the recommended way to connect to the database is as follows:

```
const connection = mysql.createConnection({
 // Your database config here
});
connection.connect(function(error) {
  if(error) {
    console.log(error);
    return;
```

Using Node.js with Electron

```
  }
  connection.query('SELECT * FROM Customers', function(err, rows) {
    if(err) {
      console.log(error);
      return;
    }
    console.log(rows.length + ' record found');
  });
});
```

A direct call to the `connection.query` will also establish the connection in an implicit way, and that can also work in our case.

Installing dependencies

Let's return to our angular application. Install `mysql` library from `npm` or `yarn` as follows:

```
npm install mysql --save
# -- OR --
yarn add mysql
```

As we are working with Angular 2 and TypeScript, we need to type definition files so that the TypeScript compiler won't complain about a MySQL module definition error. Install the Typing as follows:

```
npm install @types/mysql --save-dev
# -- OR --
yarn add --dev @types/mysql
```

Creating a database service

Create a new Angular service inside the `src` folder and name it `app.service.ts`. This service will do all operations and will serve the data to the UI component directly from the database. Here, webpages can directly access the database using this service. Add the following content into the service:

```
import { Injectable } from '@angular/core';
import * as mysql from 'mysql';

const connection = mysql.createConnection({
  host: 'localhost',
  user: 'root',
  password: 'password', // Your database password
```

```
    database: 'customer_manager'
});

@Injectable()
export class AppService {
}
```

Use your database username and password to create the MySQL connection object. Update the preceding Angular service template with real database access scripts inside. Add the connection object into the service inside the constructor as follows:

```
import { Injectable } from '@angular/core';
import * as mysql from 'mysql';

const connection = mysql.createConnection({
  host: 'localhost',
  user: 'root',
  password: 'password', // Your database password
  database: 'customer_manager'
});

@Injectable()
export class CustomerService {
  connection: any;
  constructor() {
    this.connection = connection
  }
}
```

This creates a connection to the database using MySQL module. Now let's add the functionality to this service. Add a new method called `getCustomers` to get a list of all customers:

```
getCustomers(): Promise<any> {
  const QUERY = `SELECT * FROM  customers`;
  return new Promise((resolve, reject) => {
    connection.query(QUERY, (error:any, data:any) => {
      if (error) {
        reject(error);
        return;
      }
      resolve(data);
    });
  });
}
```

Using Node.js with Electron

This is just a plain select query and there is nothing complicated in this code. This queries the data from the database and returns into the promise as a resolver callback. Next, add customer filter queries as follows to the `AppService.ts` file inside the class:

```
getCustomerById(id: any): Promise<any> {
  const QUERY = `SELECT * FROM customers WHERE id=?`;
  return new Promise((resolve, reject) => {
    connection.query(QUERY, [id], (error: any, data: any) => {
      if (error) {
        reject(error);
        return;
      }
      resolve(rows);
    });
  });
}

public getCustomerByName(name: string): Promise<any> {
  const QUERY = `SELECT * FROM customers WHERE name LIKE '${name}%'`;
  return new Promise((resolve, reject) => {
    connection.query(QUERY, [name], (error: any, data: any) => {
      if (error) {
        reject(error);
        return;
      }
      resolve(data);
    });
  });
}
```

This query gives customers by name and customer id. If you have previous experience in database programming, then you know this is a very basic thing. Add the `createCustomer` method into the service so that user can add the customer into the database:

```
createCustomer(customer: any): Promise<any> {
  const QUERY = "INSERT INTO customers SET ?";
  return new Promise((resolve, reject) => {
    connection.query(QUERY, customer, (error: any, data: any) => {
      if (error) {
        reject(error);
        return;
      }
      resolve(data.insertId);
    });
  });
}
```

Finally, add the code for the update and delete the customer method to the `AppService` class:

```
    deleteCustomer(id: number): Promise<any> {
      const QUERY = "DELETE FROM customers WHERE id = ?";
      return new Promise((resolve, reject) => {
        connection.query(QUERY, [id], (error: any, data: any) => {
          if (error) {
            reject(error);
            return;
          }
          resolve(data.affectedRows);
        });
      });
    }

    updateCustomer(customer: any): Promise<any> {
      const QUERY = "UPDATE customers SET name = ? WHERE id = ?";
      return new Promise((resolve, reject) => {
        connection.query(QUERY, [customer.name, customer.customer_id], (error: any, res: any) => {
          if (error) {
            reject(error);
            return;
          }
          resolve(res);
        });
      });
    }
```

The service provides simple **CRUD** operation functionality with customer data. Each method returns a JavaScript promise, with MySQL connection query results resolved in its body. That's all for accessing the database from a Node.js/Electron application. Now, let's create a simple user interface to display this data.

Let's add a popular user interface library, and bootstrap into the project to build our user interface. You can use npm or the direct download method to get the library. Download the library and copy the content into the `src` folder. Last, add the style sheet reference into the `index.html` file. There are couple of Angular 2 implementations of Twitter Bootstrap available. You can also use those for your real-world applications. In our case, just grab the CSS file in the source using a link tag.

Using Node.js with Electron

Update the `app.component.html` template file with the following content. Basically, it's a two-column layout with a customer list on the left side and an editor view in the right-side panel:

```
<div class="app-container">
  <header class="app-header">
    <section class="quicklaunch-bar">
      <div class="app-logo">
        <span class="app-logo__title">Customer Manager</span>
      </div>
    </section>
  </header>
  <div class="app-body">
    <div class="app-list">
      <ul>
        <li [ngClass]="{ 'active': customer.id === _customer.id }"
*ngFor="let _customer of customers;let idx = index">
          <a (click)="setCustomer(_customer, idx)">
            {{_customer.customer_name}}
          </a>
        </li>
      </ul>
    </div>
    <div>
      <div class="app-form">
        <div class="form-group">
          <label>Customer Name</label>
          <input type="text" style="width: 300px"
class="input"[(ngModel)]="customer.customer_name" />
        </div>
        <div class="form-group">
          <label>Email</label>
          <input type="text" class="input" style="width: 300px"
[(ngModel)]="customer.customer_email" />
        </div>
        <div class="form-group">
          <label>Address</label>
          <input type="text" class="input" style="width: 300px"
[(ngModel)]="customer.customer_address" />
        </div>
        <div class="form-group">
          <label>Phone</label>
          <input type="text" class="input" style="width: 300px"
[(ngModel)]="customer.customer_mobile" />
        </div>
        <div class="cta-wrapper">
          <button class="btn btn-default"
```

```
            (click)="addNewCustomer()">
                  Add
              </button>
              <button class="btn btn-primary" (click)="saveCustomer()">
                  Save
              </button>
              <button class="btn btn-primary" (click)="cancel()">
                  Cancel
              </button>
              <button class="btn btn-primary" (click)="deleteCustomer()">
                  Delete
              </button>
          </div>
       </div>
    </div>
  </div>
</div>
```

Open the Angular component definition file, and then inject the customer service into the component. We are already familiar with dependency injection in Angular 2. Update the `app.component.ts` file as the following:

```
import { Component } from '@angular/core';
import { AppService } from './app.service';

import './style.css'

@Component({
  selector: 'electron-app',
  templateUrl: './app.component.html'
})
class AppComponent implements OnInit {
  constructor(private service: AppService) {
  }
}
```

We have just injected the service into the component. Now retrieve the data into the component from the database using the customer service. Update the component with the following code:

```
class AppComponent {
  public customers: Array<any> = [];

  constructor(private _customerService: CustomerService) {
  }

  ngOnInit() {
```

```
      // Load data from mysql database
      this.service.getCustomers().then(data => this.customers = data; });
    }
}
```

That's all for listing customer data using MySQL and Electron. We don't have any server implementation, you can directly connect to the database from the Node.js and Electron application. Let's add more functionalities to the application. When users select customer data, it should be copied to the form displayed on the right side of the application. Add click listener to each row of customers, and when selecting the row data, set the value of the current customer to the selected data so that the form will be affected by the corresponding values:

```
class AppComponent {
  public customers: Array<any> = [];
  public customer: any = {};
  public currentSelectedIndex: number = -1;
  constructor(private service: AppService) {
  }
  ngOnInit() {
    //...
  }
  setCustomer(customer: any, idx: number) {
    this.customer = customer;
    this.currentSelectedIndex = idx;
  }
}
```

Now, whenever you select a customer, the form will be updated with the selected customer information. Add the update functionality to the component on a click of the save button. The following code checks the operation mode based on the customer id. If the customer id is null or empty, then it will execute the insert function and if there is a value present, then the operation will be an update on the database. Update the `AppComponent` as follows to add the update and insert the functionality:

```
import { Component } from '@angular/core';
import { CustomerService } from './customer.service';

@Component({
  //...
})
class AppComponent {
  public customers: Array<any> = [];
  public customer: any = {};
  //....
  setCustomer(customer: any, idx: number) {
```

```
    }

    saveCustomer() {
      if (!this.customer.id) {
        this.service.createCustomer(this.customer).then(data => {
          this.customer.id = data;
          this.customers.push(this.customer);
          this.customer = {};
        });
      } else {
        this.service.updateCustomer(this.customer);
      }
    }

    addNewCustomer() {
      this.customer = {};
      this.currentSelectedIndex = -1;
    }
  }
```

I am leaving the validation and other functionalities for you. We just need to demonstrate the database operation with Electron. The rest of the things are the same as your normal web applications. Add the function to delete the record into the component:

```
class AppComponent {
  //.....
  deleteComponent() {
    if (this.currentSelectedIndex !== -1) {
      this.service.deleteCustomer(this.customer.id)
          .then(affectedRows => {
        if (affectedRows > 0) {
          this.customers.splice(this.currentSelectedIndex, 1);
        }
      });
    }
  }
}
```

The application is ready for execution now. Run the application with the `yarn start` and you should get the following screen as output:

Accessing hardware

We have checked how we can connect to the database directly from Electron without using any web server or any other type of server implementation. But the database is not the only native part that we need to access when developing a desktop application. Usually, you will have to access the hardware and sometimes you may need to do some computations that need more memory and resources. In this section, let's check how we can access the hardware and operating system components from an Electron application.

With Node.js, we can write native add-ons/libraries, which are dynamically linked, shared objects written in C or C++, and these can be loaded into the Node.js runtime using the standard require function. So, basically, you can write some C or C++ code that can be used inside your Node.js application. But there are some prerequisites to using the native modules inside Node.js.

As this code is written in C or C++, we need to compile and link the compiled object in order to use it inside the Node.js application. So, when using these types of npm modules that contain native C or C++ code, we need to follow some additional steps to use these libraries inside our Electron or node applications. Let's check how these types of libraries can be used inside our Electron application. In the first part of this section, we will use an existing library available in npm and will check how we can use native third-party libraries. We use a famous printer module node-printer, which provides access to native printers and their functionalities. In the second part, we will create a small hello world library using C++ and link it into the Electron shell using the infrastructure provided by Node.js.

Developing a native module is a little bit more complex, as you need to have knowledge of multiple domains and languages to achieve it. Also, you need to have a C/C++ compiler and Python installed on your system.

Make sure you have Python 2.x installed on your system. On a Windows machine, you also need to have Visual Studio 2013 installed on the system. The express version of Visual Studio is enough for our purpose. Since Electron uses a different version of V8 engine, the normal Node.js native module build workflow will not fit for Electron. There are multiple ways to build a native module with Electron. Here, let's try the simplest way. Visit Electron docs for more information about building a native Node.js module against Electron.

Whenever you install a native module, you need to rebuild that module against Electron. We have npm module available, which provides an executable to rebuild the Node.js module against the version of Node.js module that your Electron application uses.

Install the package:

```
npm install --save-dev electron-rebuild
# -- OR --
yarn add --dev electron-rebuild
```

Then whenever you install a new npm package, run `electron-rebuild`:

```
./node_modules/.bin/electron-rebuild
# -- On Windows use --
.\node_modules\.bin\electron-rebuild.cmd
```

The printer module is a native binding for printers on POSIX and Windows from Node.js runtime. Install the node-printer module from npm:

```
npm install printer --msvs_version=2013
# -- OR --
yarn add printer --msvs_version=2013
```

Once you install any npm module run the `electron-rebuild` command to build the module against your electron binaries.

You can also manually rebuild the native modules using `node-gyp` utility instead of using `electron-rebuild`. Install `node-gyp` library, which is a cross-platform command-line tool written in Node.js for compiling native add-on modules for Node.js. It takes away the pain of dealing with the various differences in the build platform. There are some prerequisites to run `node-gyp` with your native node modules. You can find a list of these at (https://github.com/nodejs/node-gyp) for various platforms. Install `node-gyp`:

```
npm install -g node-gyp
# -- OR --
yarn add global node-gyp
```

You can rebuild the printer module using `node-gyp` using the following command. The target argument specifies the version of your electron which is installed locally in your project:

```
node-gyp rebuild --target=1.7.6 --arch=x64 --dist-url=https://atom.io/download/atom-shell
```

Now it's ready to use inside your Electron application. Import the printer module using the standard require function and you can get all the available connected printers using the `getPrinters()` method in your main process or renderer process:

```
const printer = require('printer');
// List down all the printers installed on your system
printer.getPrinters();
```

Creating a native add-on

There are some situations where you want to access the native operating system component, which is not exposed by Electron or any other third-party Node.js modules. In this case, you will be forced to write the native add-ons that can access and manipulate the native operating system components at any level. So, let's check how we can write a simple native add-on using C++ and use it inside the Electron shell or web pages that you rendered inside the Electron shell. The following tools are needed to build our native add-on:

- `node-gyp`: A cross-platform tool for compiling native add-on modules
- `nan`: A tool for making add-on development easier across Node versions

Install the tools with the following command:

```
npm install --save node-gyp nan
#--OR--
yarn add node-gyp nan
```

You also need to install the node-gyp to your global npm cache with the following command from your terminal:

```
yarn add global node-gyp
```

Open the `Example03` folder and your `package.json` file should be updated with `gypfile: true` entry as follows:

```
{
   name: 'example03',
   gypfile: true, // add this line
   dependencies: {..},
}
```

Create a new file called `binding.gyp` inside the root of the project and add the following content into it:

```
{
  "targets": [
    {
      "target_name": "sum",
      "sources": [ "sum.cc"]
    }
  ]
}
```

This is a very basic example that calculates the sum of two numbers. It has nothing to do with your real-life scenarios. But I just want to provide you with an example of creating and using native add-ons inside the Electron application. Refer to V8 implementation and API docs for more information about the native add-n API:

```
#include <node.h>

namespace electron {
    using v8::Exception;
    using v8::FunctionCallbackInfo;
    using v8::Isolate;
    using v8::Local;
    using v8::Number;
    using v8::Object;
    using v8::String;
```

```
        using v8::Value;

        void Multiply(const FunctionCallbackInfo<Value>& args) {
            Isolate* isolate = args.GetIsolate();

            if(args.Length() < 2) {
    isolate->ThrowException(Exception::TypeError(String::NewFromUtf8(isolate,
    "Wrong number of arguments")));
                return;
            }

            double value = args[0]->NumberValue() * args[1]->NumberValue();
            Local<Number> num = Number::New(isolate, value);

            args.GetReturnValue().Set(num);
        }

        void Add(const FunctionCallbackInfo<Value>& args) {
            Isolate* isolate = args.GetIsolate();

            if(args.Length() < 2) {
    isolate->ThrowException(Exception::TypeError(String::NewFromUtf8(isolate,
    "Wrong number of arguments")));
                return;
            }

            double value = args[0]->NumberValue() + args[1]->NumberValue();
            Local<Number> num = Number::New(isolate, value);

            args.GetReturnValue().Set(num);
        }

        void Init(Local<Object> exports) {
            NODE_SET_METHOD(exports, "multiply", Multiply);
            NODE_SET_METHOD(exports, "sum", Add);
        }

        NODE_MODULE(addon, Init);
}
```

Once the source is ready, configure the add-on using `node-gyp` with the following command:

```
node-gyp configure build
```

The filename extension of the compiled add-on binary is .node, and the Node.js standard require function is written to look for files with the .node file extension and initialize those as dynamically linked libraries. You can access the methods written in the preceding code easily using the standard require function as follows:

```
var addonProto = require('./build/Release/sum');
var sum = addonProto.sum(1,2);
console.log(sum);
```

Because of your Electron's Node.js version difference, you need to rebuild the native add-on against your Electron shell, which we already covered in this chapter.

Using TypeScript and ES2015 with Electron

We have already used TypeScript throughout this book for building the user interface. Also, in Chapter 5, *Crafting User Interface*, we checked how we can use ES2015 and React to build our user interface. Most of the ES2015 language features are already supported by the latest version of Node.js. As Electron is constantly aligning with the latest Node.js version, we can use most of the ES2015 features without using any additional tools. But, the ES specification is continuously updating and new features are being added each year. So, in order to use the latest ES features, we need to use a transpiler like Babel along with Electron. The transpiler will compile our code into ES2015 or ES5. With TypeScript, you can also use the latest ES features in addition to the TypeScript language features. Like in the browser, TypeScript is not supported by the Electron shell natively. You will have to compile the TypeScript code into JavaScript using TypeScript compiler to run the application. Let's look at how we can use TypeScript and ES2015/2016 to build the Electron application, including the main process.

TypeScript is a typed language, and you need to have type definitions available in your project for all the JavaScript code you are using in the project. These definition files can be downloaded using npm. If you can't find type definition for a specific library, then you need to manually create a minimal type definition file so that the TypeScript compiler won't complain about unknown modules and libraries.

Again, let's use the hello world scenario and build a small application using TypeScript. We will also check how we can use ES2015 and Flow.js to build the same application in the coming section. Install the TypeScript and Electron dependencies to initialize the project, as we did in the previous chapters. Next, add a new file called `tsconfig.json` to the project root. Put it in the same place as your `package.json` file. The presence of the `tsconfig.json` file in the directory indicates that the directory is the root of the TypeScript project. This configuration file provides compiler options for the TypeScript compiler required to compile the project. Add the following content into the `tsconfig.json`:

```
{
  "compilerOptions": {
   "target": "ES5",
    "module": "commonjs",
    "moduleResolution": "node",
    "sourceMap": true,
    "emitDecoratorMetadata": true,
    "experimentalDecorators": true,
    "removeComments": false,
    "noImplicitAny": false,
    "jsx": "react"
  },
  "exclude": [
   "node_modules"
  ]
}
```

Details about all available compiler options are available at: https://www.typescriptlang.org/docs/handbook/tsconfig-json.html.

Copy the `main.js` file that we created in the previous chapter. Basically, TypeScript is a super set of JavaScript. So, the code written in JavaScript is a valid TypeScript code. Rename the `main.js` file as `main.ts` file. And update the content as follows:

```
import { app, BrowserWindow } from 'electron';

let win: any;

// index.html flle path
const appUrl: String = `file://${__dirname}/index.html`;

function createElectronShell() {
  // Initializes the new browser window
  win = new BrowserWindow({ width: 800, height: 600 });
```

```
  // Load the html file into the browser window
  win.loadURL(appUrl);

  // Release the instance variable when the window is closed
  win.on('closed', () => {
    win = null;
  });
}

app.on('ready', createElectronShell);
app.on('window-all-closed', () => {
  if (process.platform !== 'darwin') app.quit();
});
app.on('activate', () => {
  if (win == null) createElectronShell();
});
```

The Typescript definition for Node.js and Electron should be installed before compiling the TypeScript code into JavaScript. This can be installed using npm as follows:

```
npm install –save-dev @types/node @types/electron
```

Once the type definition files are installed, the code can be then compiled into JavaScript using the tsc command inside your current working directory. If you have not installed the typescript globally, the tsc command won't be available in your path. Compiled JavaScript will be generated inside the same directory with the same file name. After compiling the application, you can use the same Electron command to run the application inside the workspace directory. You can use the following command to run the both compiler and electron together. You can either use tsc command if you have the typescript available in the global path. Here we are using local typescript binaries:

```
"./node_modules/.bin/tsc" && electron main.js
```

Summary

In this chapter, we checked how we can use Node.js libraries inside the Electron shell. Connecting to a data store is very easy from the Electron shell, and it can be achieved without having any additional server implementations. You can use any type of database and dialect with Electron. If you have a custom requirement that needs to access the native operating system, then you can use the Node.js native add-on, which is also supported by Electron. Last, we checked how we can write our application using TypeScript. The static type checker will give you a much easier development workflow by highlighting syntax errors on development time inside your editor.

In the next chapter, we will dive deeply into the Electron API. It provides support for various operating system APIs. We will look into the details of these APIs in the next two chapters.

7
Deep Dive into Electron API - 1

Electron provides a rich set of APIs that leverage us to create a powerful desktop application, which gives us full control over native operating system APIs. We had discussed various aspects of the Electron application development, but we did not get into the details of the Electron APIs. In this chapter and the next chapter, we will be discussing the Electron API in detail. Most of the APIs discussed here should be working well with all major operating systems. Some of the features/APIs are designed specifically for certain platforms; this will be discussed accordingly. We will be checking the following points in detail in this chapter:

- Inter-process communication with ipcRenderer & ipcMain modules
- Protocol management and defining custom protocols
- Managing and accessing the system preferences
- Networking API
- Monitoring power state and managing the power
- Various other minor Electron APIs

The features that we will discuss here are readily available in Electron shell without using any third-party npm modules. In addition to the above points, we will also discuss some other internal APIs corresponding to node modules that can be used as a replacement of built-in modules in detail in this chapter.

Inter-process communication with IPC module

In one of the previous chapters, we went through some of the examples about the IPC module. In a multi-process architecture model, such as Electron and chromium, it's essential to communicate between the each of the processes. Electron's IPC module facilitates this communication between the main process and renderer process in a simple yet powerful way; depending on your context, you need to choose between them. For example, in order to communicate from the main process to renderer process, you should use the IPCRenderer module. The IPCMain module should be used if you want to send messages or communicate from the main process to renderer process.

Basically, an IPCMain and IPCRenderer module is an event emitter, which emits the event that can be subscribed in other processes. These modules provide some methods that you can use to send synchronous and asynchronous messages between different processes, in our case, it's main process and renderer process. You will have to use these modules heavily when you working with Electron because Electron's standard user interface components and some other modules are only available in the main process. So, you will have to send the message to the main process in order to execute these modules.

IPCRenderer

This module sends the message to the main process from the renderer process. You can also receive the reply from the main process using this module. Here is an example of sending and receiving the messages between the main process and renderer process:

```
const { ipcRenderer } = require('electron');

// Get the config version Synchronous
let version =  ipcRenderer.sendSync('app-config-get-sync', 'version');
console.log('Application configuration version is ' + version);

// Listen for main process to send app-config-get-async
// event with version in argument field
ipcRenderer.on('app-config-read', (event, args) => {
    console.log('configuration version : ' + args);
});

// Send asynchronous message to main process
ipcRenderer.send('app-config-get-async', 'version');
```

For both processes, this is the way to send and receive the messages. Like in this example, you can send the asynchronous message using the `ipcRenderer.send` method. Custom event name and event data should be passed as the parameter. You can use any string as the event name. However, the same string should be used to subscribe the event in another process. These messages can be subscribed in other process using the method in a similar way that we do when manipulating the DOM events. When subscribing the event, the callback function will have two arguments in it, the event metadata and the data passed from the other process as a response to this message.

As I said earlier, you will have to use this module a number of times when developing an Electron application. There is number of APIs in the Electron that is only available in the main process, and to start executing these APIs, you need to send the message to those process using this module. For example, `MenuBar`, `MenuItem`, and `BrowserWindow` are some the examples that are only available in the main process. Basically, most of the native user interface components, such as `Menu`, are only available in the main process. To use these APIs inside the renderer process, you need to send the messages to the main process to invoke the APIs for renderer process. These APIs will continue to run as a part of the main process and not as part of renderer process. For example, let's take a look at a classic example of the settings page. Imagine a common scenario that always happens in the application development. When the user does some action, such as clicking on a link, we need to open a settings window. The problem here is that you need to use the `BrowserWindow` class to open a new window. However, as this class is available only on the main process, you cannot directly instantiate this class. You need to do something like the following to make it work:

```
//In your main process
const { BrowserWindow, ipcMain } = require('electron');

let settingsWindow = null;
ipcMain.on('app-settings', (event, args) => {
  settingsWindow = new BrowserWindow({ width: 450, height: 400 });
  settingsWindow.on('close', () => {
    settingsWindow = null
  });
  settingsWindow.loadURL(`file://${__dirname}/settings.html`);
});
```

This should be added into your `main.js` file, which means your main process. This simply listens for a message or event called `app-settings` and creates a `BrowserWindow` with settings page loaded into it. In your web page, you need to send the message to the main process to show this settings page, as follows. Place this code as part of your click event:

```
// In your renderer process
const { ipcRenderer } = require('electron');

let settingsBtn = document.querySelector('#settings-btn');
settingsBtn.addEventListener('click', () => {
    ipcRenderer.send('app-settings')
});
```

IPCMain

You can send a message to the renderer process. Both of these modules are lower-level APIs available inside the Electron. Let's take a look at one more example where you can send the IPC response back to the other process with some execution results. Here, the following example reads a configuration data from a file called the `config.json` file. However, the code to read the configuration file is only available in the main process, and renderer process requests the main process to get the configuration version.

Add the following code into your main process (`main.js`):

```
const fs = require('fs');
const { ipcMain } = require('electron');

// Handles the message asynchronously
ipcMain.on('app-config-get-async', (event, args) => {
    readConfigurationAsync((config) => {
        let response = null;
        if(args != null)
            response = config[args];
        event.sender.send('app-config-read', response);
    });
});

// Synchronous Message Handler
ipcMain.on('app-config-get-sync',(event,args) => {
    let config = readConfigurationSync();
    let response = null;
    if(args != null)
        response = config[args];
    event.returnValue = response;
});
```

```
function readConfigurationSync() {
    let config = fs.readFileSync('config.json');
    return JSON.parse(config);
}

function readConfigurationAsync(callback) {
    fs.readFile('./config.json', (error, content) => {
        if(error)
            throw Error('Could not read file');
        if(callback)
            callback(JSON.parse(content));
    });
}
```

For the renderer process section code, refer to the example section inside the `ipcRenderer` section. This demonstrates two modes of messaging, synchronous and asynchronous. As always, you need to pass the callback to get the asynchronous response from the IPC. The `Send` and `sendSync` methods can be used to send the message from one process to another. `Send` will be asynchronous.

IPC is important. However, think about a large-scale application where you will have a lot of tasks related to the main process. Alternatively, you may have to access the native user interface multiple times. Then, we have to send different messages to handle different use cases. This will end up in a number of messages and event subscription in your application, which is not a best practice and hard to maintain.

Electron.js has another module called `remote`; this will give you access to the modules available only inside the main process from the renderer process. It provides a simpler way to do the inter-process communication between the main process and the renderer process, that is, our web page. With this module, our settings page example can be rewritten, as follows:

```
// In your renderer process
const { BrowserWindow } = require('electron').remote;

let settingsWindow = null;
let settingsBtn = document.querySelector('#settings-btn');

settingsBtn.addEventListener('click', () => {
    settingsWindow = new BrowserWindow({ width: 450, height: 400 });
    settingsWindow.on('close', () => { settingsWindow = null });
    settingsWindow.loadURL(`file://${__dirname}/app/settings.html`);
});
```

Here, we did not use the IPC module explicitly, although it's happening in the background. This does not mean that the remote module can replace the `ipcMain` and `ipcRenderer` modules. Behind the scene, the remote module uses these modules, and there will be some use cases where you need to use the IPC module explicitly in your application.

The object returned by the remote object represents an object inside the main module. This object will contain all the exported objects and function from the main module. This means that you can export any custom functions, variables, and objects from your main module that can be accessed from the renderer process using the remote object. However, you need to keep in mind that when you instantiate an object or call a function using the remote module, you are actually invoking an inter-module communication between the main and renderer processes. In our previous example, `settingsWindow` and `BrowserWindow` are remote objects; the new `BrowserWindow()` actually did not create an object inside the renderer process, instead, it created an object inside the main process and corresponding remote object to renderer process.

Our configuration reader example can be also written using the remote module, as follows:

```
//in your main process
export function getConfig() {
    return readConfigurationSync();
}

// in your  renderer process
const { getConfig } = require('electron').remote;
const config = getConfig();
```

All the exported modules from the main process and built-in modules inside the main process are added as getters into the remote module. So, if you are exporting a method from the main module, you can access it through the remote module from the renderer process like above. In a similar way, accessing built-in modules using remote can be done, as shown in the following code; but, be careful to see that these will run inside the main process and not inside the renderer process:

```
const { BrowserWindow, dialog, app } = require('electron').remote;
```

Passing callbacks to the main process

When you are exposing a method to renderer process through the remote object, you can use callbacks in your functions to accept some values from the renderer process. In that way, a two-way communication between the processes is possible using the remote module. The exported method can accept the callback from the renderer process so that you can send processed result back to the main process. However, I recommend that you avoid using callbacks when working with remote module. There are the couple of reasons to avoid the callbacks. Before checking this reason, let's check how this will work in Electron:

```
// In main process
const fs = require('fs');

export function readConfigurationAsync(callback) {
    fs.readFile('./config.json', (content) => {
        if(!content)
            throw Error('Could not read file');
        if(callback)
            callback(JSON.parse(content));
    });
}

// In renderer process
const { readConfigurationAsync } = require('electron').remote;
const config = readConfigurationAsync(cfg => {
    console.log(`Configuration version is - ${cfg.version}`)
});
```

This is the same example that we discussed before, but changed to callbacks. You should be careful when using this; better avoid this always for the following reasons:

- It's very easy to get a deadlock with the callback on remote module inside the renderer process.
- Callbacks passed to the main process will persist until the main process garbage collect them. Because of this, memory leaks can happen very easily.

If you are using it, always ensure that you clean up any references that you have passed through the callback to the main process upon completing the task.

Sharing variables between modules

With the remote module, you can also share a variable between the processes. Any Node.js global can be accessed from the renderer process via remote. The `remote.getGlobal` method provides the value of the variable that you declared inside the main process using global keyword:

```
//in main
const { BrowserWindow } = require('electron')
const win = new BrowserWindow({ width: 700, height: 700 })
global.strVal = "This is string";
global.windowSize = win.getSize();

//in renderer
const { getGlobal } = require('electron').remote;
remote.getGlobal('strVal');
const size = remote.getGlobal('windowSize');

console.log('window size is ' + size);
```

This works the same way as the Node.js global objects. Global objects in Node.js is accessible across all modules in an application. In a similar way, you can access the global objects defined in the application from any other process using the `remote.getGlobal` method inside an Electron application.

Defining custom protocols

A protocol is an important part of a network system. Most of the operations inside a web application are based on the HTTP/HTTPS protocol. When developing with Electron, you can define your own custom protocol. This means that Electron has a built-in protocol module, which provides an easy way to implement custom protocols other than standard protocols. For better clarity, think about Google Chrome browser, which provides custom protocols for accessing its internal pages. For example, to access the settings page from a Chrome browser tab, you just need to navigate to the `chrome://settings` URL. Google Chrome also provides several other URLs with custom Chrome protocol to access its internal pages. This way we can create the custom schema or protocol for our application. So, what is the benefit for this custom protocol? We have several benefits for this. You can assign the application in the operating system to open the links with a specific type of protocol, for example, mail to opening in a mail client. These links can be executed from any web pages, and the application can be opened as a response to this action. Here is an example of the implementation of a built-in file protocol, which is used to access the local filesystem:

```
const { app, BrowserWindow, protocol } = require('electron');
const path = require('path');

let appShell;
let appUrl = 'file://' + __dirname + '/index.html';

protocol.registerStandardSchemes('app');

function createElectronShell() {
    appShell = new BrowserWindow({ width: 800, height: 600 });
    appShell.loadURL(appUrl);

    appShell.on('closed', () => { appShell = null; });
    appShell.webContents.openDevTools();

    protocol.registerFileProtocol('app', (request, callback) => {
        const requestedUrl = request.url.replace('app://', '');
        callback({ path: path.normalize(`${__dirname}/${requestedUrl}`)});

        // Open the file with file api
        appShell.loadURL('file://' + __dirname + requestedUrl);
    });
}

app.on('ready', createElectronShell);

// In your html file
<a href="app://project.txt">Access the file using app protocol</a>
```

This example is a basic example for registering a custom protocol. As shown here, you should only register the custom protocols after the app module emits the ready event. Here, we registered a file protocol, and when a user accesses this protocol, the corresponding file will be loaded into the `BrowserWindow` object.

Protocol modules give us the ability to register different types of protocol schemes. The file protocol, buffer, string, and HTTP are some of the different types of protocol implementation provided by the protocol module. It also provides the options to intercept the protocol, which is already registered with the application. Let's look at how we can implement a settings page that will open using custom protocols similar to the Chrome settings page:

```
const { app, BrowserWindow, protocol } = require('electron');
const path = require('path');

let appShell;
let settingsWindow = null;
```

Deep Dive into Electron API - 1

```
let appUrl = 'file://' + __dirname + '/index.html';

protocol.registerStandardSchemes('app');

function createElectronShell() {
    appShell = new BrowserWindow({ width: 800, height: 600 });
    appShell.loadURL(appUrl);
    appShell.on('closed', () => { appShell = null; });
    appShell.webContents.openDevTools();

    protocol.registerFileProtocol('app', (request, callback) => {
        const requestedUrl = request.url.replace('app://', '');
        if(requestedUrl == 'settings') {
            settingsWindow = new BrowserWindow({ width: 500, height: 500 });
            settingsWindow.on('closed', () => { settingsWindow = null; });
            settingsWindow.loadURL('file://' + __dirname + '/settings.html');
        }
    });
}
app.on('ready', createElectronShell);

// In your html file
<a href="app://settings">Open Settings</a>
```

Intercepting a registered protocol can be done using the `interceptProtocol` methods. For example, if you want to intercept a file request using file protocol and add some custom logic so that the application will do the action before accessing the file, this can be done as follows:

```
protocol.interceptFileProtocol('app', (request, callback) => {
  const requestedUrl = request.url.replace('app://', '');
  if(requestedUrl == 'settings') {
     callback(null);
  }
}, function(error) {
    if(error)
      throw new Error('Error in accessing the file');
   //request is completed
});
```

[160]

Sessions and cookies

Sessions and cookies are important when your application is connected to a remote host. In a web page, by default, you can get the cookie associated with the domain that your web page is loaded from using `cookie` object. In Electron, the `cookies` class provides the access to the `cookie` object for each domain. An instance of this `cookies` class can be accessed by using cookies property of the `Session` class. For example, all the cookies stored in the Electron shell can be queried as follows from your main process:

```
const { session, app, BrowserWindow } = require('electron');

let appShell;
let appUrl = 'file://' + __dirname + '/index.html';

function createElectronShell() {
    appShell = new BrowserWindow({ width: 800, height: 600 });
    appShell.loadURL(appUrl);

    getAllCookies();
}

function getAllCookies() {
    session.defaultSession.cookies.get({}, (error, cookies) => {
       // Cookies can be accessed here using cookies variable
    });
}

app.on('ready', createElectronShell);
```

In this example, the `cookies.get` method will retrieve the cookies stored in the Electron shell. However, we did not pass any cookie name or URL, so that the Electron will list out all the cookies available inside the shell. You can pass the domain and cookie name to get the filtered cookies specific to the passed domain or cookie name. The following example queries all the cookies stored against a specific domain or URL:

```
const { session,BrowserWindow, app } = require('electron'); app.on('ready',
() => {
    let domainFilter = {
        url: 'http://www.google.com'
    };
    session.defaultSession.cookies.get(domainFilter, (error, cookies) => {
        if(error)
            throw new Error('Could not read cookie');

        console.log(cookies);
```

Deep Dive into Electron API - 1

```
    });
});
```

This code gives you all the cookies that are set against the google.com URL. If you pass a name with a URL, you can get the specific cookie assigned to that URL with the name passed:

```
let domainFilter = {
    url: 'http://www.google.com',
    name: 'auth_user'
};
```

This will give the cookie stored with name auth_user against the google.com URL. The same signature can be used to set cookie back to the shell. This will overwrite the cookie if the name already exists:

```
const cookie = {
    url: 'http://www.google.com',
    name: 'auth_name',
    value: 'username'
};
session.defaultSession.cookies.set(cookie, (error) => {});
```

The cookie class provides changed event that can be used to watch the value changes in a cookie. Electron emits this event whenever a cookie is added, deleted, or a value is changed:

```
session.defaultSession.cookies.addEventListener('changed', (
    event, cookie, cause, removed
) => {
if(removed) console.log('Cookie ' + cookie.name + ' is removed');
else console.log('Changed action : ' + cause);
});
```

The removed flag will be true when you remove a cookie from the shell. You can get the type of action you made on a cookie through the cause variable. This returns a string and can be one of the following values:

- explicit
- overwrite
- expired
- evicted
- expired-overwrite

Session

The session module can be used to create or access the browser session present inside each renderer process or the rendered page. The events and methods provided by the session object are very useful: proxy the requests, intercepting the content download and emulating the network usage, and so on. Let's look into the details of the session API.

Session API is a getter property available under web content API. This means that you can access the session of the current page using session property of web content API. We will discuss web content API later in this book. Here is the basic example of getting the current session of a web page inside Electron shell:

```
const { session, app, BrowserWindow } = require('electron');

let appShell;
const appUrl = `file://${__dirname}/index.html`;

function createElectronShell() {
    appShell = new BrowserWindow({ width: 800, height: 600 });
    appShell.loadURL(appUrl);
    // Get default session object
    const ses = appShell.webContents.session;
    console.log(ses.getUserAgent());
}
app.on('ready', createElectronShell);
```

Here, we got a session object already defined with the current window object. To instantiate or create a new session object from scratch, the `session.fromPartition` method can be used. You can use the following code to instantiate the session:

```
const { session } = require('electron');
const _session = session.fromPartition('persist:name');

// Get the user agent from the session object
console.log(_session.getUserAgent());
```

This code will return a session object from the partition if it exists, else it will create a new session object from scratch and return it to the _session variable. Here, partition means from where it should get the session object reference. You need to take care of the following points when working with partitions:

- If the value of the partition starts with partition, the page will use a persistent session available to all pages in the app with the same partition. For example, `session.fromPartition('persist:name')` will check all the pages inside the app for the session with a `'persist'` value equal to its name.

- If there is no persist: prefix, the page will use an in-memory session. If the partition is empty, then default session of the app will be returned.

To create a session with options, you have to ensure that the session with the partition has never been used before. There is no way to change the options of an existing session object.

The session can accept an optional second argument, which can be used to enable or disable cache. However, to use this optional argument, you need to ensure that the session with the same persist name has never been used before. Once you initialize a session with options, you cannot change it.

Intercepting content download

Session object provides an event call `will-download`, which will be emitted when the Electron is about to download a content or an item in a web page. This event is very helpful to monitor the content is being downloaded by the Electron. We can also enable filtering on the downloaded file using this event. `event.preventDefault()` can be used to block a file from being downloaded:

```
const { session } = require('electron');

let count = 0;
session.defaultSession.on('will-download', (event, item, webContents) => {
  // File is blocked
  event.preventDefault();
  count = count + 1;
  if(count < 3) {
    console.log('Downloading file from : ' + item.getURL() + ' is blocked');
  }
  else {
    downloadFileUsingRequestJs(item.getURL());
  }
});

function downloadFileUsingRequestJs(url) {
  require('request')(url, (data) => {
   let filename = url.substr(url.lastIndexOf('/') + 1) ;
    require('fs').writeFileSync('/user/' + filename, data)
  });
}
```

This example prevents the content from being downloaded for three times. Each time it increases the count after preventing the file download. When the count value gets more than three, the file will be downloaded. However, instead of using Electron's native file download methods, we use custom Node.js modules to download the file. Here, we use `request.js` to request the file and on the response from the server node's native filesystem is used to write the content into the disc.

Emulating network using session API

Devtools are an essential part of web development. Nowadays, dev tools provide complex features that help us develop a better application. With Chrome Developer Tools, the network tab provides you network emulation feature. Dev tools can emulate various network conditions so that you can check how the application will behave in different network conditions. For a normal Ajax request from your renderer process still, you can use this dev tool feature from Chrome dev tools. As Electron ships with the latest chromium features, you can use any dev tools features right inside your web page from Electron.

From the main process, you can emulate the network condition using session module. This allows you to mock the application into a specific network condition. For example, to emulate a GPRS connection with 50 KBPS throughput and 500 ms latency, the following code snippet can be used:

```
var appShell = new BrowserWindow({ ... });
//...
appShell.webContents.session.enableNetworkEmulation({
    latency: 500,
    downloadThroughput: 6400,
    uploadThroughput: 6400
});
```

The values are same as the Chrome dev tools options. To emulate the offline mode, set `offline` to true inside the option:

```
appShell.webContents.session.enableNetworkEmulation({ offline: true });
```

Disabling any emulation already active for the session can be done as follows:

```
appShell.webContents.session.disableNetworkEmulation()
```

Intercepting permission requests

If your application is requesting some remote resource and that resource asks for some local permissions, such as accessing your geographical location, the shell will prompt you to allow or deny the permission. This is built into the chromium; the confirmation message is automatic. You can customize this permission request and do some action programmatically. The session API provides access to this permission dialog where you can customize the default behavior:

```
const { session, BrowserWindow } = require('electron');

let appShell = new BrowserWindow({ ... });
let session = session.fromPartition('partition:name');
if(!session)
   session = appShell.webContents.session;


session.setPermissionRequestHandler((webContents, permission, callback) =>
{

   if (webContents.getURL() === 'maps.google.com' && permission === 'geolocation') {
      return callback(false);
   }

   if (webContents.getURL() === 'youtube.com' && permission === 'fullscreen') {
      return callback(false);
   }

   callback(true);

});
```

This gets the session with partition name or uses the default browser window session. The `setPermissionRequestHandler` method checks for two types of permission here. If a geolocation request comes from `maps.google.com`, then deny it. Also, we are denying a fullscreen permission request from `www.youtube.com`. If you pass the callback with `false` as the parameter, then the permission will be denied; use `true` to grant the permission. The permission argument passed in the listener is a string value, which indicates the type of the permission being requested. Possible value for this arguments are, as follows:

- `media`
- `geolocation`

- `notifications`
- `midiSysex`
- `pointerLock`
- `fullscreen`
- `openExternal`

Managing file download

In the preceding section, we had discussed how we can intercept a file download from the remote host. We could completely override the download behavior using the `'will-download'` event and the `DownloadItem` class. Using this event, we can also customize the default file download behavior. The `DownloadItem` class is much powerful and provides various methods to play with the content being downloaded.

When you download a file inside the Electron, a new instance of `DownloadItem` is being created. This class is an event emitter, which also provides some utility function that can be used to control the file. This class is used inside the `'will-download'` event of the session class:

```
// In the main process.
const { session, BrowserWindow, ipcMain } = require('electron')

let appShell = new BrowserWindow();

appShell.webContents.session.on('will-download', (event, item, webContents) => {

  ipcMain.send('download-start', item.getURL());

  let onContentDownloadUpdated = (event, state) => {
    switch (state) {
      case 'interrupted':
        ipcMain.send('interrupted', 'Download is interrupted, restart it again');
        break;
      case 'progressing':
        if (item.isPaused())
          ipcRenderer.send('download-paused', item);
        else
          ipcMain.send('download-progress', item, item.getReceivedBytes());
        break;
    }
```

```
  };

  item.on('updated', onContentDownloadUpdated);

  let onContentDownloaded = (event, state) => {
    if (state === 'completed') {
      ipcMain.send('download-finished');
      console.log('Download successfully')
    } else {
      ipcMain.send('download-failed');
      console.log(`Download failed: ${state}`)
    }
  };
  item.once('done', onContentDownloaded);
});
```

The preceding code simply watches for a `'will-download'` event, and whenever the Electron downloads a file this will notify the user about the state of the file being downloaded accordingly. The second parameter inside the event handler callback is an instance of the DownloadItem class. Basically, this is an event emitter that provides two events--`'updated'` and `'done'`--which is emitted in when the file upload is in progress and when it is finished. You can subscribe the updated event so that you can watch each updates happening on the file. The callback parameter `'state'` will provide you the current state of the downloaded item. Once it's finished downloading, the object will emit done event with state equal to completed. This event will be triggered even if the download operation is canceled or interrupted and can't be resumed. The callback provides you a parameter called state. The value of the state can be `'completed'`, `'canceled'`, or `'interrupted'` depending on the state of the download operation status.

The DownloadItem class provides more helper functions that give more control over the downloading files. The basic pause, resume, or cancel operation on a file can be done using downloadItem.pause(), downloadItem.resume(), and downloadItem.cancel() functions, respectively.

When you download a file by clicking on a link or using any type of redirect, normally the browser will ask you the path to save the file by opening a file dialog. Alternatively, the browser will save the file into the default download location. The Electron also behaves like standard browsers. You can override this file dialog by setting the file path inside the `'will-download'` event handler. This will set the local path for the file to be downloaded. If you did not set this path, then the Electron will prompt for the save dialog so that the user has to save it manually into the disk:

```
// In the main process.
const { session, BrowserWindow, ipcMain } = require('electron')
```

```
let appShell = new BrowserWindow();

win.webContents.session.on('will-download', (event, item, webContents) => {
  item.setSavePath('/user/home/desktop/file.pdf');
  //...
});
```

Native system dialogs

When you download a new file, the Electron shell will automatically ask you to select a location to save the file in your disc. The previous example shows you how to override this behavior by setting a file path for each download in your application. What if, you need to show the save dialog programmatically? Let's check how we can show native dialog API to work with dialog boxes, such as file dialog, custom alerts, and information messages.

Usually, you don't need to access native renderer process from your web pages since you have JavaScript dialog API. We won't have to use that as well, as we have custom JavaScript user interface plugins available for better dialog and windows. However, in the main process, as the context is different, we need to use some native window API as we don't have any user interface present for that process. Luckily the Electron provides a dialog API, which gives access to native dialog user interface component from the main process. Open your main.js or your main process code and use the following code to simply open a file open dialog. Let's take the same previous example of the file download event. In that example, if we call setSavePath, then the Electron will save the file into that location with the specified filename. So, let the user select the location using custom file save dialog option. Even if you did not use setSavePath, the default file save dialog will be opened by default. Here, we will do this manually:

```
const { session, app, BrowserWindow, dialog } = require('electron');

let appShell;
let appUrl = 'file://' + __dirname + '/index.html';

function createElectronShell() {
 appShell = new BrowserWindow({ width: 800, height: 600 });
 appShell.loadURL(appUrl);

 appShell.webContents.session.on('will-download', (event, item,
webContents) => {

   let result = dialog.showSaveDialog({
       properties: [
         'openDirectory'
```

```
            ]
        });

            if (result && result.length > 0)
                item.setSavePath(result[0] + '/file_name.pdf');
            else
                event.preventDefault();

    let onContentDownloadUpdated = (event, state) => {};
    item.on('updated', onContentDownloadUpdated);

    let onContentDownloaded = (event, state) => {};
    item.once('done', onContentDownloaded);
    });
}
app.on('ready', createElectronShell);
```

This shows the same file save dialog box and will return an array of selected file location that we then pass into the `setSavePath` method. If the user cancels the dialog, we use `event.preveDefault` to cancel the download. The same way you can show the `openFileDialog` from your web page. Dialog API has another method named as `showSaveDialog`, which can be used to show the `openFileDialog`:

```
<!DOCTYPE html>
<html>
<head>
    <script type="text/javascript">
        const { dialog } = require('electron').remote;
        window.onload = function () {
            document.getElementById('btn').onclick = function () {
            let result = dialog.showOpenDialog({
                properties: [
                    'openFile',
                    'openDirectory'
                ],
                filters: [
                    { name: 'Text', extensions: ['txt'] }
                ]
            });
            if(result && result.length > 0) {
              let file = result[0];
              console.log(file);
            }
          }
        }
</script>
</head>
```

```
<body>
 <button id="btn">Show Dialog</button>
</body>
</html>
```

This opens an open file dialog that can select a single or multiple files with a .txt extension. The dialog opens in the main process, and this will block your renderer process until you close the file dialog. File dialog can be customized by providing additional configurations:

```
let result = dialog.showOpenDialog({
    title: 'Select a text file',
    defaultPath: '/Users/Profile/Desktop',
    buttonLabel: 'Select Text File',
    properties: [
       'openFile',
       'openDirectory'
    ],
    filters: [
      { name: 'Text', extensions: ['txt'] }
    ]
});
```

Here, title will set the dialog title, and you can customize the button label using buttonLabel options. You can filter the type of the file that should be selected using the filter array inside the parameter. For example, you can restrict the various type of file extensions, as follows:

```
let result = dialog.showOpenDialog({
    title: 'Select a text file',
    defaultPath: '/Users/Profile/Desktop',
    buttonLabel: 'Select Text File',
    properties: [
       'openFile',
       'openDirectory'
    ],
    filters: [
        {name: 'Images', extensions: ['jpg', 'png', 'gif']},
        {name: 'Text Files', extensions: ['txt']},
        {name: 'All Files', extensions: ['*']}
    ]
});
```

When providing the list of extensions, you don't have to use any wild card letters or dot, such as *.txt or .txt. To list all the files, use * as extensions so that all the files under the directory can be selected.

The properties options can be used configure the file selection type inside the file dialog. Properties option accepts an array that accepts the following values:

- openFile
- openDirectory
- multiSelections
- createDirectory
- showHiddenFiles

You can pass single or multiple values from the preceding list. The last parameter for the openFileDialog method is a callback function, which gives you the list of files that are selected using dialog. The callback is optional. If it is passed, the operation will be asynchronous, else this will be synchronous and the function will return the filenames as the return value.

Generic dialog boxes

Dialog module also provides some generic dialog functions that can be used to display information dialogs or error messages to the user. When working with renderer process, mostly you don't need to use these methods as the web view provides normal JavaScript alert and confirm method. Else, you can even use the modal dialog boxes that JavaScript libraries provide, such as the bootstrap modal box. This can be useful to display the crash report and any error messages from the main process.

Here is the example for showing a warning message. In a similar way, you can show error, information, or any other type of message box by just setting the type option:

```
<!DOCTYPE html>
<html>
<head>
<script type="text/javascript">
const { dialog } = require('electron').remote;
window.onload = function () {
document.getElementById('btn').onclick = function () {
  let result = dialog.showMessageBox({
     type: 'warning',
     buttons: ['Ok'],
     title: 'Warning',
```

```
        message: 'Warning!, Battery is low',
        detail: `Lorem Ipsum is simply dummy text of the printing and
typesetting industry. Lorem Ipsum has been the industry's standard dummy
text ever since the 1500s, when an unknown printer took a galley of type
and scrambled it to make a type specimen book. `
      });
  }
}
</script>
</head>
<body>
<button id="btn">Show Dialog</button>
</body>
</html>
```

This will show you a warning message when you click on the button from your web page. You can use this API in your main process also to notify any system events. The following screen shows the output for this code:

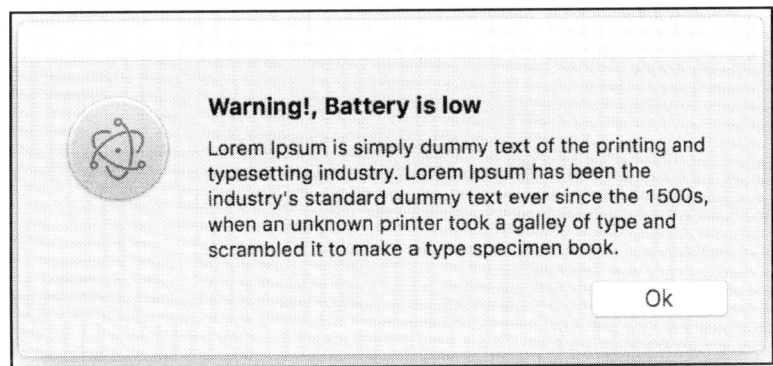

This returns the index of the button clicked from the buttons array. You can pass a callback if you want to make this dialog API call asynchronous. The value of the type can be none, info, error, question, or warning depending upon your requirement.

Working with clipboard

In Electron API, there are some modules that can be accessed from both renderer process and main process. Clipboard is such module that is available in both processes. This module can be used to access the clipboard data, which is present inside the native operating system. It provides a rich set of API to manipulate the clipboard data. Here is a small example that writes the text content of a paragraph element in DOM to the clipboard on the click of a button:

```html
<!DOCTYPE html>
<html>
<head>
<script type="text/javascript">
const { dialog, clipboard } = require('electron').remote;

window.onload = function () {
    document.getElementById('btn').onclick = function () {
        let el = document.getElementById('content');
        clipboard.writeText(el.innerText);
        dialog.showMessageBox({
            type: 'info',
            buttons: ['Ok'],
            message: 'Text copied to the clipboard!',
        });
    };
};
</script>
</head>
<body>
 <p id="content">
 This element content will be copied to clipboard on click of the button
 <button id="btn">Copy</button>
 </p>
</body>
</html>
```

This writes a plain text in the clipboard. In a similar way, you can read text from the clipboard using the `readText` method, as follows:

```
const { clipboard } = require('electron');

// read the clipboard data as plain string
let clipboardData = clipboard.readText();
console.log(clipboardData);
```

You can read/write HTML, RTFText, and image to and from the clipboard data. For example, to read/write HTML data, the preceding example can be written, as follows:

```
<!DOCTYPE html>
<html>
<head>
<script type="text/javascript">
const { dialog, clipboard } = require('electron').remote;

window.onload = function () {
    document.getElementById('btn').onclick = function () {
        let el = document.getElementById('content');
        clipboard.writeHTML(el.innerHTML);
    };
};
</script>
</head>
<body>
 <p id="content">
 This element content will be copied to clipboard on click of the button
 <button id="btn">Copy</button>
 </p>
</body>
</html>
```

However, if you are writing anything other than a text content to clipboard, then you need to use corresponding read method to read that type of data. Here, to read the HTML string copied to the clipboard, we need to use the `readHTML()` method:

```
let copiedData = clipboard.readHTML();
```

Clipboard also supports RTFText:

```
const { clipboard } = require('electron');

// writes into the clipboard
clipboard.writeRTF('Some RTF String');

// This can be read as follows
clipboard.readRTF();
```

To deal with the image in clipboard, you need to create a native image object to write into the clipboard. `readImage` and `writeImage` methods give you the access to the clipboard to work with the image. `readImage` will return the image in the clipboard as native image instance. To write an image from the local filesystem to clipboard, the following can be done:

```
const { nativeImage, clipboard } = require('electron');
let image = nativeImage.createFromPath('/Users/Downloads/Image.png');
clipboard.writeImage(image);

//Images can be read as
let clipboardImage = clipboard.readImage();
```

The entire clipboard content can be cleared using the `clear` method:

```
const { clipboard } = require('electron');
clipboard.clear();
```

Managing display and power sleep mode

In some scenarios, we may need to control the machine or block the machine from entering into sleep mode. For example, if you are developing a media player application, the system should not go to sleep mode when playing a video, or your app should never turn off the power when playing the audio. Electron's `powerSaveBlocker` module gives you the access to the power and display mode. You can use this module to prevent the system from entering the low power mode. As we discussed, a classic example of this scenario is a video player. When the user clicks on the play button, you can ask this module to prevent low power mode, and you can stop monitoring the power state change when the user stops the playback. Here is an example for the `powerSaveBlocker` module:

```
<html>
<head>
</head>
<body>
<script language="javascript">
const { powerSaveBlocker } = require('electron').remote;
document.addEventListener("DOMContentLoaded", init, false);

  function init() {
    var video = document.getElementById("video");
    var _ref = null;
    video.addEventListener("play", () => {
        _ref = powerSaveBlocker.start('prevent-display-sleep');
```

```
    });

    video.addEventListener("stop", () => {     powerSaveBlocker.stop(_ref);
    });
}

</script>
<video id='video' controls preload='none'
 poster="http://media.w3.org/2010/05/sintel/poster.png">
    <source id='mp4'
      src="http://media.w3.org/2010/05/sintel/trailer.mp4"
      type='video/mp4'>
    <p>Your user agent does not  support the HTML5 Video element.    </p>
</video>
</body>
</html>
```

The start method accepts type argument, which can accept two values:

- `prevent-app-suspension`
- `prevent-display-sleep`

`prevent-app-suspension` prevents the application from being suspended. This will keep the system active, but allow the screen to be turned off. This can be used when you download a file or playing an audio. To keep display active, use `prevent-display-sleep` value. This will return an integer value representing the blocker id. This blocker id should be passed to the `stop` method to stop `powerSaveBlocker` from watching the power state change.

Monitoring power changes

To watch different power states in your machine, we use the `powerMonitor` module, which is available in Electron module. It provides events that you can use to watch various power states with your machine. Basically, this module provides four events--`suspend`, `resume`, `on-ac`, and `on-battery`. These events should be attached to the context only after the app emits the ready event. The following is the example to monitor the power state of your machine from the application:

```
const electron = require('electron');
const{app, BrowserWindow, dialog } = electron;

let appShell;
const appUrl = `file://${__dirname}/index.html`;
```

```
function createElectronShell() {
 appShell = new BrowserWindow({ width: 800, height: 600 });
 appShell.loadURL(appUrl);

 electron.powerMonitor.on('suspend', () => {
    dialog.showMessageBox({
      type: 'warning',
      buttons: ['Ok'],
      title: 'Warning',
      message: 'The system is going to sleep'
    })
 })

 electron.powerMonitor.on('on-ac', () => {
    dialog.showMessageBox({
      type: 'info',
      buttons: ['Ok'],
      title: 'Warning',
      message: 'System changes to ac-power'
     });
 });

 electron.powerMonitor.on('on-battery', () => {
     dialog.showMessageBox({
      type: 'warning',
      buttons: ['Ok'],
    message: 'System changes to battery power'
 });

 });

 }
 app.on('ready', createElectronShell);
```

Like the preceding code, you can watch for a different power state of your application. You can watch `suspend, on-ac, on-battery,` and `resume` event using the `powerMonitor` module. You should not attach any event handler to the `powerMonitor` class until your application emits the ready event.

Networking from the main process

There are a number of libraries available in Node.js for creating and managing network requests. When it comes to choosing your browser, you have the standard `XMLHttpRequest` and `fetch` modules available. With Electron, as the Node.js context is available in both the main and the renderer process, you have as many choices as the Node.js has. Any third party or built-in networking module can work with the Electron. Other than all these modules, Electron provides access to the chromium native networking library that can be used inside the main process. There is some advantage of this library over others, as it provides better support for web proxy. The API specifications are same as the Node.js built-in HTTP module. So, you won't feel any differences to use this library in terms of syntax and usage. As I already mentioned, this module provides some key benefits over other libraries, such as the Node.js HTTP module:

- It manages the system proxy configuration and supports proxy PAC configuration files
- Various authentication methods for authentication proxies are supported

The following example shows the Electron net API that may be used:

```
<!DOCTYPE html>
<html>
<head>
 <script type="text/javascript">
 const { net } = require('electron').remote;
 window.onload = function () {
    let isLoading = true;
    let responseText = "";
    const request = net.request('https://www.endpoint.com')
    request.on('response', (response) => {
      if(response.statusCode == 200) {
        console.log(`HEADERS: ${JSON.stringify(response.headers)}`)
        response.on('data', (chunk) => {
          responseText += `${chunk}`
        });
        response.on('end', () => {
          isLoading = false;
          console.log(responseText);
        })
      }
   })
   request.end()
 };
 </script>
</head>
```

```
<body>
 <p id="content">
 </p>
</body>

</html>
```

Here, we use the net module inside the renderer process using the remote module. The net module is available only in the main process. You might not need to use this module in your web pages, as we have `fetch` and `XMLHttpRequest` available in web pages. If you have worked with the Node.js HTTP module before, this syntax should be familiar to you. The syntax is same as HTTP or requestJS libraries.

The net modules basically create a network request using the `ClientRequest` class. Basically, when you pass arguments into the `net.request` method, this creates a `ClientRequest` object with the same parameters. For example, you can create a request using net API, which will be converted as the `ClientRequest` object, as follows:

```
const { net, ClientRequest } = require('electron').remote;

// Creating a request using net.request method
let request = net.request({
  host: 'api.google.com',
  port: 8080,
  protocol: 'https',
  method: 'POST'
});

// The above will be converted into the following
let request = new  ClientRequest({
  host: 'api.google.com',
  port: 8080,
  protocol: 'https',
  method: 'POST'
});
```

`net.request` method actually returns an object of the `ClientRequest` class. This class has utility functions and events to manage each part of a request-response cycle. If your server requires a credential to log in, you need to subscribe the login event to send the authentication credentials to the server. This event will be triggered if the request asks for authentication. You can pass the authentication credentials using this event, as follows:

```
const request = net.request('https://www.endpoint.com')
    request.on('response', (response) => {
       response.on('data', (chunk) => {
          // Process your data chunks
```

```
        });
        response.on('end', () => {
            //response finished
        })
        response.on('login', (info, callback) => {
            callback(username, password);
        })
    })
    request.end()
```

If you pass username and password back in callback, then the authentication will be canceled.

Managing web requests

The session object that we checked before provides some cool features that can be used to intercept, filter, or monitor any requests sending from the application. Session object provides a getter property--webRequest--that can be used to manage all types of network request happening inside your application. Here is a simple example of how we can use the web request API. This piece of code blocks all the request to google.com:

```
const { session } = require('electron')

const filter = {
  urls: [
    '*://*.google.com/*'
  ]
};

session.defaultSession.webRequest.onBeforeRequest(filter, (details, callback) => {
 callback({cancel: true });
})
```

This adds an event listener for the beforeRequest event. This event will be fired before each request is being sent to the remote host. Here, we check the hostname and the protocol and if it matches the request, it will be canceled by passing cancel flag true. You can also redirect the request in the same way by passing redirectURL, as follows:

```
session.defaultSession.webRequest.onBeforeRequest(filter, (details, callback) => {
 callback({cancel: false, redirectURL: 'http://www.bing.com' });
})
```

This API provides a lot of useful features that can help us when dealing with the network requests. All the functions that this method provides accepts two arguments, a `filter` parameter which is optional, and `listener` function. Basically, this module only provides some events that can be hooked into various stages of a network request. In this way, you can have the control on all the requests that your application sends.

Let's take a look at how this can be used for handling the exception. This module is very helpful to provide an application-level exception handling when some error occurs in your particular network request life cycle, such as the server returning 500 error, network resource not being found, and so on:

```
//In your main process
const { session, dialog } = require('electron')

session.defaultSession.webRequest.onErrorOccurred([], (details) => {
    dialog.showMessageBox({
        title: 'Error',
        buttons: ['Ok'],
        message: 'Error on your request',
        detail: 'The requested resource not found or there is some
unexpected server error occurred n ' + details.url
    });
    //details.error will give you the error description
    console.log(details.error);
});
```

Another scenario is if you want to monitor each network request inside the application. This is a common scenario when developing an application that you want to create a log for all the network requests inside the application. `webRequest` API provides `onBeforeRequest`, `onCompleted`, and `onErrorOccured` events, which can be used for this purpose, as follows:

```
//In your main process
const { session, dialog } = require('electron')

session.defaultSession.webRequest.onBeforeRequest([], (details) => {
    log('Requesting ' + details.url);
});

session.defaultSession.webRequest.onCompleted([], (details) => {
    log('Response received successfully from ' + details.url);
});

session.defaultSession.webRequest.onErrorOccurred([], (details) => {
    log('Error on request ' + details.url + ', details: ' + details.error);
});
```

```
function log(msg) {
   Logger.log(msg, new Date())
}
```

Other than just intercepting a request, you can also update the request data such as header before sending the request. This is extremely useful in some situation where the server accepts authentication tokens in the request header so that you don't have to take care of sending the auth header each time for each request. Instead, you can use this event and add the harder using this event, as follows:

```
const { session } = require('electron');

session.defaultSession.webRequest.onBeforeRequest(filter, (details,
callback) => {
  let token = getAuthenticationToken();
  if (token == null) callback({cancel: false, redirectURL: 'login.html' })
  else callback({ cancel: false });
})

session.defaultSession.webRequest.onBeforeSendHeaders(filter, (details,
callback) => {
 let token = getAuthenticationToken();
 details.requestHeaders['Authorization'] = 'Bearer ' + token;
 callback({ cancel: false, requestHeaders: details.requestHeaders })
})

function getAuthenticationToken() {
 return somePersistantStorage.getToken();
}
```

The callbacks inside these listeners will give you event details object, which has the complete information about requests, such as URL, request method, resource types, and so on.

Summary

So far, we have checked various Electron APIs. This gives you more control over your web page than a traditional web page running inside a browser. You can control each and every piece of the application when it is run from the Electron shell. The API is very powerful, and new features are actively added into the Electron on a daily basis. We will continue with API in the next chapter. In the next chapter, we will check how we can use the webContent API and web view. This gives you more access to the rendered web page content. We will also check some of the Electron UI components and UI action components, such as keyboard shortcut and menu in the next chapter.

8
Exploring Electron API - 2

The last chapter was about the details of the Electron API. We have gone through how we can utilize the API to manage both the main and renderer processes. Unlike other hybrid frameworks, the Electron provides deep access to the native shell using its API. We will continue exploring the Electron API in this chapter. Like in the preceding chapter, we will check the API details with some of the real-world usage examples. The following points will be discussed in this chapter:

- Managing the browser window content using web content API
- Embedding the external content using web view
- The extended Node.js process object
- Managing the rendered page
- WebFrames

You won't use most of these techniques in a simple Electron application. However, for a complex and large-sized application, you should be having full control over the Electron shell and the rendered web page. Also, you will have to access the operating system components through these APIs.

Managing the web page using webContents

The `webContents` class is one of the most important classes available inside the Electron to work with the rendered web page from the main process. Basically, this class is an event emitter that is responsible for rendering and controlling a typical web page inside the browser window. So, you can use this class to manage your web page behavior and customize the rendering pipeline in your Electron shell or browser window. Reference to this API can be retrieved using getter property inside the `BrowserWindow` class, as follows:

```
// In your main process
const { BrowserWindow } = require('electron');
var appShell = new electron.BrowserWindow({
    width: 600,
    height: 400
});

win.loadURL(`file://${__dirname}/index.html`)
win.on('closed', () => appShell = null);

// access the webContent object
var content = appShell.webContents;
```

This class provides a number of events that can be hooked into the various stages in a page-rendering pipeline. You can manage every aspect of page rendering and the page life cycle using this class. This class is only available in the main process, and the events should be handled inside the main process. As you can see in the preceding code snippets, we are getting the reference to the `webContent` API using the `appShell` object in which your page is rendered.

One of the common event you need to deal with is the `did-finished-load` event. This emits when the content is loaded into the browser window. The call will be done right after the web page dispatches the onload event from the JavaScript context. You can use this event as an alternative to the JavaScript window onload event, but inside the main process. For example, `did-finish-load` event can be written as follows:

```
const { BrowserWindow } = require('electron');
var win = new electron.BrowserWindow({
    width: 600,
    height: 400
});

win.loadURL(`file://${__dirname}/index.html`)
win.on('closed', () => appShell = null);

let content = win.webContents;
```

```
contents.addListener('did-start-loading', function (e) {
  console.log('Started loading the web page')
});

contents.addListener('did-finish-load', function (e) {
  console.log('Webpage content loaded');
});

contents.addListener('did-stop-loading', function (e) {
  console.log('Finished/Stopped the page load');
});
```

The preceding code is a simple example that watches various page content load events available inside the Electron `webContents` API. The `did-start-loading` event will be fired right after the Electron request for the content. Once the content is loaded into the browser window from the remote location or a local file successfully, the `did-finish-load` event will be triggered. The last event is the `did-stop-loading`, this will be triggered when the content download stops. This will be triggered even if the action was successful or failure. The `webContents` class also provides a dom ready event, which emits when the frame emits the dom ready event.

Managing the page navigation

You can watch and manage your page navigation once you load the content into the Electron shell. The `webContents` class provides three events to manage the page navigation. Here, navigation means the URL changes like click on the link, change the document's location value, and so on. The `will-navigate`, `did-navigate`, and `did-navigate-in-pages` are the three events provided by the Electron. When you click on a link or the page is about to navigate to the new page, the `will-navigate` event will be triggered first. However, this will not be affected for internal anchor link and page hashes. You can block the navigation using the `event.preventDefault` method inside this event handler. For example, in the preceding chapter, we used the `WebRequest` API to manage all the requests passing through the application. However, that was like a global filter, and whatever requests the application sends will be passed through the `WebRequest` API's registered event listeners. Here, with these three events, we can only manage the page navigations. Also, the `WebRequest` API will be attached to all the browser windows opened in the application, and this will be attached to a specific window and its web view:

```
const { BrowserWindow, app } = require('electron');
let appShell;
const onClosed = () => {};
```

```
function createMainWindow() {
  const win = new electron.BrowserWindow({
    width: 600,
    height: 400
  });
  win.loadURL(`file://${__dirname}/index.html`);
  win.on('closed', onClosed);

  const contents = win.webContents;

  // If the url contains the word google.com then block the navigation
  contents.addListener('will-navigate', function (e, url) {
    if (url.indexOf('google.com') != -1) {
      console.log('Navigation to google.com is blocked');
      e.preventDefault();
    }
  });

  // Navigating to the page is finished
  contents.addListener('did-navigate-in-page', function (e) {
    console.log('Finished navigation')
  });

  return win;
}

app.on('ready', () => {appShell = createMainWindow()});
```

This example adds two event handlers to the window to listen to the navigation from the page. The `will-navigate` event will be triggered first when the user clicks on a link or change the value of `window.location`. Here, we check whether the URL contains `google.com`, then block the navigation. Once the page is navigated successfully, the `did-navigate-in-page` event will be triggered. You can use these events to filter your application's navigation to external domains.

Authenticating the web view requests

Another useful event provided by the `webContents` API is the `login` event, which will be emitted when the remote host asks for authentication credentials. You can subscribe this event to send the authentication credentials. The usage of the event is same in multiple Electron modules. Multiple Electron modules emit this event, and the syntax is same for all of these modules:

```
const { BrowserWindow, app } = require('electron');
```

```
let appShell;

function createMainWindow() {
  // Initialize the BrowserWindow here

  const contents = win.webContents;

  contents.addListener('login', function (e, request, authInfo, callback) {
    callback('username', 'password');
  });

  return win;
}
app.on('ready', () => {appShell = createMainWindow()});

app.on('login', (e, request, authInfo, callback) => {
   callback('username', 'password');
});
```

The same `login` event can be triggered either using the `webContent` API as we did inside the `createMainWindow` function or can be done using the `app` module. The behavior is same for both of these methods. You should pass the username and password to authenticate the request.

Capturing the page snapshot

The `webContents` API's `capturePage` can be used to capture the rendered page or an area of the page. The method accepts an optional rectangle as a parameter that can be used to specify the area of the page. The output can be retrieved as the parameter to the callback function. If the rectangle parameter is not passed, the entire page will be captured; here is an example:

```
const fs = require('fs');
const { BrowserWindow } = require('electron');

const win = new BrowserWindow({ width: 600, height: 400 });
const contents = win.webContents;

// captures whole visible page
contents.capturePage(saveImage);

// captures specific area on screen
contents.capturePage({ x: 10, y: 10, height: 400, width: 500 }, saveImage);

// save the captured image to disk
```

```
function saveImage(img) {
  fs.writeFile('capture.png',img.toPng(), function (err) {
    if (err) throw err;
    console.log('Screenshot captured!');
  });
}
```

The output is an instance of the NativeImage class, which provides a lot of useful methods to manipulate the images from inside the Electron application. You can find more about this class at https://github.com/electron/electron/blob/master/docs/api/native-image.md.

Emulating device viewport inside the web view

In the preceding chapter, we discussed emulating various network states using the Electron API from within the application itself. Here, the webContents API provides some way to emulate the different device viewport inside the web view. This emulation works almost same as the Chrome Developer Tool's device toolbar. However, note that this is not as perfect as the device toolbar available inside the developer tools. Use the developer tool to emulate the device viewport. Use the enableDeviceEmulation method to start the emulation for different screen viewports; here is an example:

```
const { app, BrowserWindow } = require('electron');
let appShell;
const appUrl = 'http://www.google.com';

function createElectronShell() {
  appShell = new BrowserWindow({ width: 800, height: 600 });
  appShell.loadURL(appUrl);
  appShell.webContents.enableDeviceEmulation({
    screenPosition: 'mobile',
    screenSize: {
      width: 320,
      height: 500
    },
    scale: 1,
    fitToView: true,
    viewSize: {
      width: 320,
      height: 500
    }
  });
}
app.on('ready', createElectronShell);
```

You might note that if the viewport size is reduced and the outputs are within the specified width and height, then the page will be displayed in the center of the window. The value of `screenPosition` can be either mobile or desktop. Next, you need to specify the height and width of the screen. To stop the emulation mode, you can use `disableDeviceEmulation`, which will return the page to its original state:

```
appShell.webContents.disableDeviceEmulation();
```

Printing and saving the web pages

Usually, browsers provide *Command + S/Control + S* key shortcuts to save the content of the web page into the disk. By default, the Electron does not provide this functionality inside the shell. You need to implement this manually if you really need this in your application. You can use `webContent` API to save or print your web content. Let's take a look at how we can add the default page save behavior into the page that the browsers provide for our application:

```
const { globalShortcut, app, BrowserWindow, dialog } = require('electron');

let appShell;
const appUrl = 'http://www.google.com';
let shortcut;

function createElectronShell() {
    appShell = new BrowserWindow({ width: 800, height: 600 });
    appShell.loadURL(appUrl);

    // Registers the keyboard shortcuts to the save the page
    shortcut = globalShortcut.register('CommandOrControl+S', () => {
        let path = dialog.showSaveDialog({});
        if(path != "") {
            appShell.webContents.savePage(path, 'HTMLComplete',(error) =>
{
            if (!error)
                console.log('Save page successfully')
            });
        }
    });

    if (!shortcut) {
        console.log('Could not register the shortcut')
    }
}
app.on('ready', createElectronShell);
```

```
app.on('will-quit', () => {
  // Unregister all shortcuts.
  globalShortcut.unregisterAll()
})
```

This will show the file dialog on *Command + S* shortcut and will save the current page. The second parameter is `saveType`, and the values can be `HTMLOnly`, `HTMLComplete`, and `MHTML`. Here, we use `globalShortcut` module to register the shortcut. You should be careful when using this module because this shortcut will work even when your application is on background on Mac. All the global shortcuts should be unregistered when the application quits. That can be done in the app module's `will-quit` event. Also, the shortcuts should be registered again on the window focus.

The content of the page can be printed using the `print` and `printToPDF` methods. This is the equivalent of calling the JavaScript `window.print` method. For example, you can print a web page by simply calling the `print` method, as follows:

```
browserWindow.webContents.print({
  silent: true,
  printBackground: true
});
```

The parameter is optional. Here, if you pass the option as silent, the shell will not show a print dialog, and it will take the operating system's default printer to print. By default, the `print` method will not print background color and images from the web page. You can override this behavior by setting `printBackground` to `true` in the options.

The `printToPDF` method prints the page into a PDF document with chromium's preview printing custom settings. The method will return a buffer that contains the PDF data. You can customize the paper settings and printing mode using the argument; refer to the following example:

```
const {
    globalShortcut, app, BrowserWindow, dialog
} = require('electron');
const fs = require('fs');
let appShell;
const appUrl = `file://${__dirname}/index.html`;

function createElectronShell() {
    appShell = new BrowserWindow({ width: 800, height: 600 });
    appShell.loadURL(appUrl);

    //Register the short cut keys
    let shortcut = globalShortcut.register('CommandOrControl+P', () => {
```

```
    const option = dialog.showMessageBox({
      buttons: ["Paper", "Pdf", "Cancel"],
      title: 'Select a type'
    });

    switch (option) {
      case 0:
        appShell.webContents.print({
          silent: true, printBackground: true
        });
        break;
      case 1:
        savePageToPdf();
        break;
    }
  });
  if (!shortcut) {
      console.log('Could not register the shortcut')
  }
}
function savePageToPdf() {
    const path = dialog.showSaveDialog({});
    if (path) {
        appShell.webContents.printToPDF({
            marginType: 0,
            printBackground: false,
            printSelectionOnly: false,
            landscape: false,
            pageSize: 'A4'

        }, (error, data) => {
            if (error) throw error;
            fs.writeFile(path, data, (error) => {
                if (error) throw error
                console.log('Successfully written to pdf!');
            });
        });
    }
}
app.on('ready', createElectronShell);
```

This registers the *Command + P* shortcut with the shell first. Then, the user will be notified to select the print target using the Electron dialog API. The printed PDF is saved into the disk using Node's `fs` module. The page size can be any valid paper size A4, A5, A3, Legal, Letter, or Tabloid.

It can be also a custom object with `width` and `height` specified in micron:

```
appShell.webContents.printToPDF({
    pageSize: { width: 10000, height: 10000 }
});
```

The `webContents` API has a lot more methods to explore. The official documentation and GitHub page can give you the list of each and every method and event that this module provides. Basically, in a browser window, the content of each web page is an instance of this class can be managed using the same.

Embedding guest content using WebView tag

You can use the `WebView` tag to embed the guest or external content into the web page. This acts same as an iframe. However, unlike the iframe, this runs in a separate process. The `WebView` tag provides the same API that the `webContents` class provides. So, you can manage the `WebView` content using the same method that the `webContents` API provides. Here is a simple web browser example that uses the `WebView` tag. This creates a simple custom web browser using the `WebView` tag. Here is what the page HTML looks like:

```
<!DOCTYPE html>
<html>

<head>
  <link rel="stylesheet" href="style.css">
  <link rel="stylesheet" href="fontawesome.css" />
  <script src="app.js"></script>
</head>
 <body>
 <div id="controls">
 <button id="btnBack" disabled="true">
    <i class="fa fa-arrow-left"></i>
 </button>
 <button id="btnForward" disabled="true">
    <i class="fa fa-arrow-right"></i>
 </button>
 <button id="btnHome">
    <i class="fa fa-home"></i>
 </button>
 <button id="btnReload">
    <i class="fa fa-refresh"></i>
 </button>

 <form id="frmLocation">
```

```
<div>
<input id="location" type="text" value="http://www.github.com/">
</div>
<input type="submit" value="Go">
</form>
</div>
<webview src="http://www.google.com/" style="flex: 1"></webview>
</body>

</html>
```

This is a simple HTML with an address bar, created using HTML, and the rest of the screen is filled with a web view. This will load google.com when the window loads. Let's add some functionalities to the button:

```
window.onload = function () {
    let webview = document.querySelector('webview');

    // Go to previous page on back button press
    document.querySelector('#btnBack').onclick = function () {
        webview.goBack();
    };

    //Go forward on button press
    document.querySelector('#btnForward').onclick = function () {
        webview.goForward();
    };

    // navigate to home
    document.querySelector('#btnHome').onclick = function () {
        webview.src = 'http://www.google.com';
    };

    //reload the page
    document.querySelector('#btnReload').onclick = function () {
        webview.reload();
    };

    document.querySelector('#frmLocation').onsubmit = function (e) {
        e.preventDefault();
        webview.src = document.querySelector('#location').value;
    };
}
```

All of these methods come from the `webContents` class. You can also watch various events on `WebView` tag. A page loading cycle can listen as follows:

```
webview.addEventListener('did-start-loading', () => {
    document.body.classList.add('loading');
    isLoading = true;
document.querySelector('#location').value = event.url;
});

webview.addEventListener('did-stop-loading', () => {
    isLoading = false;
});

webview.addEventListener('did-fail-load', () => {
    console.log('Request failed');
});

webview.addEventListener('did-finish-load', () => {
    document.body.classList.remove('loading');
});
```

These are the same event hooks that we discussed in the `webContents` API section. As `WebView` runs in a different process, the communication is always asynchronous. Then, you should use IPC messaging to communicate to and from the `WebView`.

Extended Node.js process

In a Node.js environment, the process object gives control over the process on which the Node.js is running. This is available as a global object inside the Node.js context. Electron provides an extended version of this process object with more functionalities. For a detailed information about the Node.js process, visit https://nodejs.org/api/process.html. Other than Node's process object API properties and events, the Electron process object gives an extra event that can be used to do some initialization purpose after the Electron process has been initialized. The load event provided by this process object is useful to run some initialization blocks right after the Electron process is initialized. Mostly, this is very useful when you turn off the Node.js context in the Electron for your renderer process. Then, you can initialize some of the global Node.js variables inside this event, as the node context is not available inside the renderer process:

```
function someFunction () {
    //implementation
}
const someVariable = 'SomeValue';
```

```
// Add this variable and function to global context, so that this available
in all the application
process.once('loaded', () => {
  global.someFuntion = someFunction;
  global.someVariable = someVariable;
});
```

The process object is accessible from both the main process and the renderer process. The object provides a type property, and its value can be `browser`, that is, main process or `renderer` when accessing from the renderer process.

You can use the process object to crash or hang the main process programmatically. The following methods can be used to hang or crash the process:

```
// Crash the main process
process.crash();

// Hang the main process
process.hang();
```

The object also gives the system memory information and process memory usage information using the following methods:

```
// Gives the memory usage statistics of the current process
const info = process.getProcessMemoryInfo();
```

This will give you the following output:

```
{
  workingSetSize: 44544,
  peakWorkingSetSize: 0,
  privateBytes: 19008,
  sharedBytes: 51340
}
```

All the numbers are in kilobytes. The system memory information can be retrieved, as follows:

```
const info = process.getSystemMemoryInfo();
```

The output gives you an object with total memory size and available free space. It also gives total swap memory size and available free swap memory size when executing in Windows or Linux.

Customizing the browser window

The `BrowserWindow` class is used to create and manage the browser windows. We have used this class throughout this book. It provides a lot of features more than just creating a window. The window can be customized as per your requirement using this class. This class provides a rich set of methods and events; let's look at some of them here in this section.

We have just set the width and height inside the browser. However, it can accept a huge list of valid options as the constructor arguments. Some of the options are platform specific that will work only on that platform. Here are some of the important option that you can pass inside the constructor; visit the Electron documentation for a complete list of options-all the options listed here are optional:

- `width`: Width of the window.
- `height`: Height of the window.
- `x`: Left offset.
- `y`: Top offset.
- `maxWidth, minWidth`: You can set these two options to set the minimum and maximum resizable width of the window.
- `maxHeight, maxHeight`: Use these options to set the minimum and maximum resizable height of the window.
- `closable`: Enable/disable the close button; not available in Linux.
- `focusable`: Whether the window can be focused or not.
- `fullscreen`: Show the window in full screen.
- `kiosk`: Enables the kiosk mode; this option is good if you are developing the application to run inside the kiosk machine.
- `title`: Title of the window.
- `icon`
- `backgroundColor`
- `vibrancy`: Add the vibrancy effect to the window on macOS. The values can be appearance-based, light, dark, titlebar, selection, menu, popover, sidebar, medium-light, or ultra-dark.
- `webPreference`: Use this to provide the settings to the web page that is rendering on this window.

Managing multiple windows

It's a very rare case that you want to split your entire application into multiple windows. This is also not recommended. With the `BrowserWindow` API, you can define the parent and child windows inside the application. You can also define modal windows using the `BrowserWindow` class. However, on Mac, these modal windows will be displayed as a sheet same as the `openFileDialog` window. The following example opens a settings page in a new `BrowserWindow`, which is created as a child of an active window:

```
const { BrowserWindow, app, ipcMain } = require('electron');
let appShell = null;
let settingsWindow = null;

function onClosed() {
   settingsWindow = null;
   mainWindow = null;
}

function createMainWindow() {
   var win = new BrowserWindow({ width: 600, height: 400 });
   win.loadURL(`file://${__dirname}/index.html`);
   win.on('closed', onClosed);

  ipcMain.on('settings', () => {
     settingsWindow = new BrowserWindow({ parent: win, width: 500, height: 500, modal: false });
     settingsWindow.loadURL(`file://${__dirname}/settings.html`);
  });
  return win;
}
app.on('window-all-closed', () => {
   if (process.platform !== 'darwin') { app.quit(); }
});

app.on('activate', () => {
   if (!mainWindow) { mainWindow = createMainWindow(); }
});

app.on('ready', () => {
   mainWindow = createMainWindow();
});
```

To set the parent window, just pass the reference to the parent window in the constructor options. The flag modal says whether the window is a modal dialog or normal window. If the modal is true, then the parent window UI will be blocked until the modal window is closed. Here, whenever the rendered web page sends an IPC message for settings, the window will be opened using the `BrowserWindow` class. You can pass a flag called `show` to not to show the window immediately after instantiating the object. For example, you can delay opening the window until the content of the window is loaded:

```
settingsWindow = new BrowserWindow({ parent: win, width: 500, height: 500, modal: false, show: false });
settingsWindow.once('ready-to-show', () => {
    settingsWindow.show();
})
settingsWindow.loadURL(`file://${__dirname}/settings.html`);
```

The `ready-to-show` event will be fired when the renderer process draws the page for the first time.

Loading POST requests

`BrowserWindow` can load local or remote content using POST requests. You can do a form post and load the response into the `BrowserWindow` in the Electron. The `loadURL` method also provides you the option to override the user agent while requesting the resource:

```
const { BrowserWindow, app } = require('electron');
let appShell = null;

function createMainWindow() {
    let win = new BrowserWindow({ width: 600, height: 400 });
    let url = require('url').format({
        protocol: 'http',
        slashes: true,
        pathname: "localhost:8080/post"
    });
    win.loadURL(url, {
        postData: [
            {
                type: 'rowData',
                bytes: Buffer.from('param1=value&param2=value')
            }
        ],
        extraHeaders: 'Content-Type: application/x-www-form-urlencoded',
        userAgent: 'Mozilla/5.0 (Macintosh; Intel Mac OS X 10_11_4) AppleWebKit/537.36 (KHTML, like Gecko) Chrome/55.0.2883.95 Safari/537.36'
```

```
    });
    return win;
}

app.on('ready', () => { mainWindow = createMainWindow(); });
```

Instead of passing the URL as a string, here we use Node.js URL module to compose the URL string, which is better always with the Electron. Here, the window is loaded from the local server but the URL that we provided is accepted as only a POST request. So, we need to pass the second argument to the `loadURL` method with the parameter values inside the `postData`. As I mentioned, you can override the user agent string using the `userAgent` property. The `loadURL` method can also be used to upload a file or blob data. The type can be `rowData`, `file`, `filesystem`, or `blob` depending upon the type of the `post` method. Use file if you want to `loadURL` that accepts the file to be uploaded on request.

Listening for APPCOMMANDs on a Windows platform

Windows machine can notify the Electron when an application command is generated. For example, when a user clicks on a browser back button or uses the keyboard to go back to the previous page, the application command will be emitted. This feature is only available on the Windows platform. The operating system will emit a string with the type of the command that is being emitted by the OS. You can get the complete list of commands available on Windows platform at https://msdn.microsoft.com/en-us/library/windows/desktop/ms646275(v=vs.85).aspx.

The command string that Windows emit is something like APPCOMMAND_HELP if you press *F1*, which is usually bound to open the help window. For `browser-backward` button press, this can be APPCOMMAND_BROWSER_BACKWARD. In Electron's browser, the window will emit the `app-command` event for all these events when running inside the Windows machine. So, you can use this event to make your application behave more like a native Windows application. The basic browser navigation commands can be attached to the Electron window, as follows:

```
// In your main process
let win = new BrowserWindow();
const homePageURL = `file://${__dirname}/index.html`;

win.on('app-command', (e, cmd) => {

    switch(cmd) {
```

```
            case 'browser-backward':
               if(win.webContents.canGoBack()) {
                 win.webContents.goBack();
               }
               break;
            case 'browser-forward':
               if(win.webContents.canGoForward()) {
                 win.webContents.goForward();
               }
               break;

             case 'browser-refresh':
                 win.webContents.reload();
               break;

            case 'browser-home':
               win.loadURL(homePageUrl);
               break;
         }
});
```

The `cmd` is the same command string that the platform emits. However, the string is transformed to lowercase, with underscores replaced by hyphens. Here, the `APPCOMMAND_BROWSER_BACKWARD` will be converted to `browser-backward`, and `APPCOMMAND_BROWSER_FORWARD` is `browser-forward`. This is helpful to provide the default operating system behaviors to the application without having much code.

Offscreen rendering

Offscreen rendering lets you render the content of the browser window into the bitmap so that it can be used anywhere. The image can be obtained from the paint event of `webContents` API:

```
const { app, BrowserWindow } = require('electron');

//Disable hardware acceleration
app.disableHardwareAcceleration();

let win;
app.once('ready', ()=> {
  win = new BrowserWindow({
     webPreferences: {
        offscreen: true
     }
  });
});
```

```
    win.loadURL(`file://${__dirname}/index.html`);
    win.webContents.on('paint', (event, dirty, image) => {
        let bitmap = image.getBitmap();
        // process the bitmap here
    });
});
```

Working with the shell

The shell module provides functionalities that are related to the native desktop integrations. You can use this module to manage the files and URLs using the default application. For example, if you want to open a file using its default application, you can use this module. You can also open the URL in the default browser. This gives a deep integration with the operating system. The API is available both in the main process and the renderer process.

For example, you can open a file in native file explorer using the showItemInFolder method of the shell:

```
const { shell } = require('electron');
// Open the file explorer
shell.showItemInFolder('/Users/Guest/Downloads');
```

This opens the Downloads folder inside the file explorer or finder on Mac. To open a file with the default application that your file is associated with, you can use openItem method of the shell:

```
shell.openItem('/Users/Guest/Downloads/file.txt');
```

To open a link in the system default browser, use the openExternal method:

```
shell.openExternal('http://www.google.com', {
   activate: true // brings the application to the foreground, only available on the mac OS
}, function() {
   console.log('Browser opened successfully');
});
```

A file can be moved to the trash using the moveItemToTrash method, as follows:

```
let deleted = shell.moveItemToTrash('/Users/Guest/Downloads/file.txt');
if(deleted) {
   console.log('File deleted successfully');
}
```

Controlling the application life cycle using app module

The app module inside the Electron controls your application's event life cycle. This also provides some utility functions that can be used with the main process. This module emits a number of events at various stages of the application's life cycle. This module is essential to initialize your application. Let's go through the some of the functionalities that this module provides, which we did not discuss yet.

Setting up the default protocol client

Handling and defining a custom protocol is simple with the Electron. However, what if you want to make your application as the default application for specific protocols. If you want to open all the `app://someurl` with the application that you are developing, the app module's `setAsDefaultProtocolClient` should be used. This can be used in your main process to register your application with a particular protocol; this method works fine on Windows and Mac:

```
// In your main process
app.setAsDefaultProtocolClient('customprotocol');

// In windows you can also pass the executable path
app.setAsDefaultProtocolClient('customprotocol' 'C:Program FilesAppapp.exe');
```

The second parameter is optional. This will make the current executable as a default application for the `customprotocol`. You should not use `'://'` when passing the protocol name. When you click on a link with your custom protocol, the current executable will be opened, and the full URL will be sent to the application as a parameter. You can unregister the executable from handling the protocol, as follows:

```
app.removeAsDefaultProtocolClient('customprotocol');
```

The `isDefaultProtocolClient` method can be used to check whether the application is the default client for a protocol, as follows:

```
app.isDefaultProtocolClient('customprotocol');
```

Managing the recent document list

You use recent files and folders on a daily basis, especially with your editors. You can get the last opened file and folder by clicking on the right button on the dock menu icon or taskbar icon. You can add the document to the recent document list programmatically using app module. Use the following code to add a path or file to your recent document list; this module is available only in the main process; you can access it through the remote object inside your renderer process:

```
const { app } = require('electron');
//...
app.addRecentDocument('/Users/Guest/Desktop/file.txt');

// In renderer process, you can access the app
const { app } = require('electron').remote;
```

Use the `clearRecentDocuments` method to clear all the recent document lists:

```
app.clearRecentDocuments();
```

Summary

In this chapter, we have discussed how to manage the browser window and application using built-in Electron API. However, we did not discuss each and every method and property available in these classes. Instead, we went through some of the common scenarios and corresponding API methods, which usually comes in real-life application development. Some of the API details will be discussed in the next chapter; we will also discuss integrating our application with the operating system. There are always some differences in the operating system that should be taken care of at development time. The next chapter will explain how you can integrate the application into the operating system.

9
Integrating with Desktop Environments

The difference in the native operating system environment is one of the key challenges when developing a cross-platform desktop application. Even though the Electron provides cross-platform APIs and functionalities without having much development efforts, this can be a barrier when you need a deeper operating system environment integration. This chapter discusses how to integrate your Electron application deep into the underlying operating system and its environments. This chapter will be discussing how to use operating system components and APIs from your Electron application. The following points will be discussed in this chapter:

- Desktop notifications and alerts
- Dock menu and taskbar integration
- Using Electron APIs to integrate with the desktop environments
- Using Node.js runtime and libraries and accessing the operating system components when Electron does not provide a native implementation for that
- Creating custom native implementation to integrate with the Electron runtime environment

This chapter discusses deeply operating system components and using those components inside the Electron, using Node.js and sometimes native code.

Introduction to desktop integration

Different operating systems are built on top of different architectures and technologies so that implementing a feature will be different in each platform, and you need to make sure that the steps or code that you are writing works perfectly with each operating system by following its rules and technologies. Let's take an example of Task menu in Windows platform and the dock menu in Mac machine. Both have almost the same functionality. In Windows, the Task menu gives some quick action menu on your application's taskbar icon. In a similar way, the dock menu in Mac provides some quick actions that can be executed by right-clicking the dock menu icon; so the user requirement in both cases is the same; they just need a quick action menu shortcut on the desktop. However, when it comes to the developer, it needs different code and approach for each platform. Electron provides a rich set of APIs that works closely with operating system environments. Not all methods are cross-platform. Also, you cannot implement the same feature on every platform in a common way, as some components are out of scope on another platform.

Due to these environment differences, you should always be careful when implementing or integrating a native feature in your Electron application. You should try to follow the following points when you want to implement a feature that closely relates to the operating system:

- Search for a built-in Electron API for the functionality that you are looking for. Always use the Electron API if it is available.
- If you are not able to find an API inside the Electron, then search inside the npm registry. However, some Node.js libraries are platform specific and work only on that platform. Then, you should also find an alternative library for all other platforms that you want to support. Finally, your code should match the platform with the library to be executed.
- If you can't find a library in npm, then the final option is to write your own native Node.js modules. Sometimes, you may have to write native Node.js add-ons to get it work, which is more complicated.

Always try to avoid writing native add-ons. This will make your application more complex and hard to maintain. Also, you may have to write separate code for each platform, which is not an easy task; that needs deep knowledge on the target platform. Let's look into each of these steps in detail in the following sections with some real-world examples. At the end of this chapter, you will be familiar with writing Node.js module that targets multiple operating systems and using it inside your Electron application. So, let's start with built-in Electron APIs that can access the operating system components.

Handling desktop notifications

Desktop notifications are useful when you want to show some notifications out of the browser window even when the application is not activated in a minimized state. Electron provides a convenient way to display the notifications with an HTML5 notification API. It uses the underlying operating system API to display and manage the notifications. The HTML5 notifications API is a W3C standard that defines an API to show the desktop notifications to the end user from a web page. As this is an HTML5 standard API, it will work only in a renderer process. However, the way that the Electron implements this API is purely native and varies according to the platform; it won't work on Windows 7 machines.

To show notifications from the main process, you need to either use IPC messaging or any third-party Node.js modules. Node-notification is a good example of such module that provides a cross-platform notification functionality. Let's take a look at how we can send the desktop notifications using the standard HTML5 notification API and also with a third-party library `node-notifier`.

Creating a notification with the HTML5 notifications API is super easy with the following code:

```
const notification = new Notification('Your Notification Title', {
    body: 'Notification content goes here'
});

// Attaching various events on the notification
notification.onclick = () => {
    console.log('Clicked on the notification');
};

notification.onshow = () => {
    console.log('Showing the notification on screen');
};

notification.onclose = () => {
    console.log('Notification closed')
};
```

The full API specification defined by the W3C is available at https://notifications.spec.whatwg.org/. Here, you can get all the possible methods and properties that can be used with the notification API. The preceding code simply creates a plain text notification. The notification API provides various events that can be hooked into the object to be delegated on different stages of the notification life cycle. Custom actions and icons can be added to the notifications by passing it through the constructor argument:

```
let notification = new Notification({
    body: 'Notification content',
    icon: 'image.png',
});
```

As I mentioned, the event handlers that the notification API provides can be useful to invoke some actions inside the renderer process. For example, in a simple mail client application, you can notify the user for an incoming mail, and when the user clicks on the notification, the mail thread can be opened.

The HTML5 notification API is very limited to the renderer process. You can't use this from the main process. Even though you can use IPC module for communication with the main process, it's not a good solution to invoke the notification API from the main process through the IPC messaging. So, we can use third-party Node.js modules that give access to the native notification API. A number of libraries are available on the npm registry. Always try to select a library that works well with all major platforms. Node-notifier is one such library that provides cross-platform system notification. This library uses notification center on macOS, `notify-osd/libnotify-bin` on Linux, and toaster for Windows 8/10 to provide the native notifications. As this is a Node.js library, you can use this from both the main and renderer processes. Install the library into your project using the following command:

```
npm install node-notifier --save
```

The cross-platform library usage is as follows:

```
// in your main process or in renderer proess
const notifier = require('node-notifier');
const path = require('path');

notifier.notify({
    title: 'You have 10 unread mail',
    message: `Lorem Ipsum is simply dummy text of the printing and typesetting industry.`,
    icon: path.join(__dirname, 'image.jpg'),
    sound: true,
    wait: true
}, (error, response) => {
```

```
});

// add click handler to notification as follows
notifier.on('click', () => {
    let window = new BrowserWindow({ width: 500, height: 500 });
    window.loadURL(`file://${__dirname}/inbox.html`);
});
```

The above code sends the same type of notification that we notified using the HTML5 notification API. You can attach the click and time-out event to the notification using 'on' method like we did in the preceding code. This library provides some platform-specific features and functionalities. The details can be found at GitHub repository (https://github.com/mikaelbr/node-notifier/blob/master/README.md). The following screenshot shows the notification that pops up after executing the preceding code:

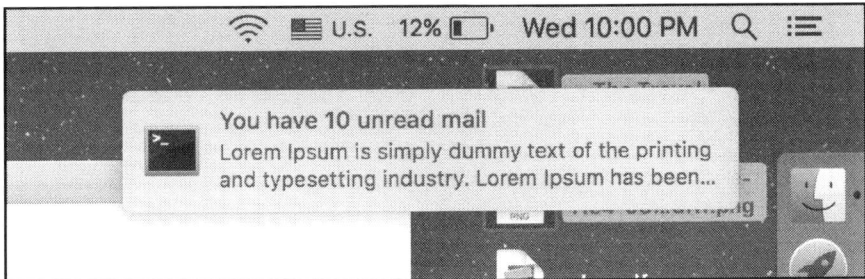

Managing task list, recent documents, and the dock menu

In Windows and macOS, you can see the recently opened documents by right-clicking on the taskbar icon or dock menu icon. The recent document list can be added to the application dock menu icon using Electron's app module. A recent list can be displayed by simply adding a file to the recent list in the app module:

```
const { app } = require('electron');
app.addRecentDocument('/User/Guest/Downloads/image.png');
```

Integrating with Desktop Environments

You can clear the recent document list using the `app.clearRecentDocuments` method. Adding a file path into the recent document list is very simple, as shown above. However, handling a user click event on the recent document list more important and difficult; it varies in different platforms. On macOS, clicking an item in the recent document list will emit an `open-file` event on app module. This event should be handled properly to open the target file in your application. The following code snippet shows you to open the file from the recent document list in MacOS:

```
const { BrowserWindow, app } = require('electron');

// prevent window being garbage collected
let mainWindow;

function onClosed() {
    mainWindow = null;
}

function createMainWindow() {
    const win = new electron.BrowserWindow({
        width: 600,
        height: 400
    });

    win.loadURL(`file://${__dirname}/index.html`);
    win.on('closed', onClosed);

    app.addRecentDocument('/Users/guest/desktop/image001.png');

    // Works only on mac
    app.on('open-file', (event, path) => {
        if (path != null) {
            let ext = path.substr(path.lastIndexOf('.'));
            if (['.png', '.jpg', '.gif', '.html', '.txt'].indexOf(ext) != -1) {
                let browserWindow = new electron.BrowserWindow({ width: 500, height: 500 });
                browserWindow.loadURL('file://' + path);
            }
        }
    });
  return win;
}

app.on('window-all-closed', () => {
  if (process.platform !== 'darwin') {
     app.quit();
  }
```

```
});

app.on('activate', () => {
  if (!mainWindow) {
     mainWindow = createMainWindow();
  }
});

app.on('ready', () => {
     mainWindow = createMainWindow();
});
```

The preceding code will give you the following output when you right-click on the dock icon. It simply adds a static image file into the recent list. When the user clicks on the menu item, the `open-file` event will be triggered. The file path will be passed to the event handler as its argument. You can use this path to do whatever you need to the file. Here, we matches the file extension with a set of file extension, and if it matches, open the file in a new browser window:

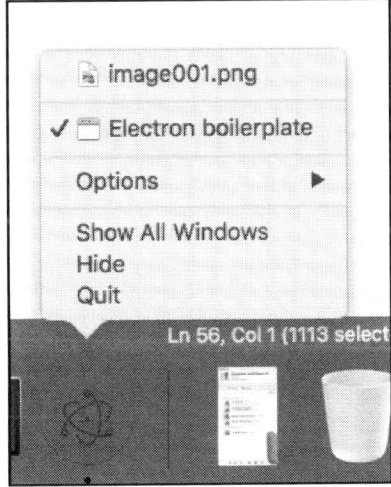

Integrating with Desktop Environments

In order to implement the click handler inside the Windows platform, you need to associate your application with a specific file type that you want to open when you click on the recent document menu, only then the click handler will work in your Windows machine. However, this cannot be done from the application code. This is all about adding registry keys into the Windows registry. It's not practical to ask the end user to do this manually for each install. So, it should be automated with your installer or setup script. You can find detailed instructions for registering an application with a specific file type in the Microsoft website at: https://msdn.microsoft.com/en-us/library/windows/desktop/ee872121(v=vs.85).aspx:

Linux Unity launcher shortcuts

Unity launchers are actually files stored in your computer with a .desktop extension. In order to add the launcher shortcut menu on a Linux machine, you need to create a proper .desktop file. The .desktop file contains configurations that describe how an application is launched and which type of application it can handle. However, unlike other platforms for Linux, we can't add any shortcut from the code itself. You can read about this configuration page on Linux main pages and for Ubuntu, you can visit https://help.ubuntu.com/community/UnityLaunchersAndDesktopFiles#Adding_shortcuts_to_a_launcher.

Here is a sample `.desktop` file that adds three shortcut menus into the Unity launcher:

```
[Desktop Entry]
Version=1.0
Type=Application
Name=ElectronApplication
GenericName=Electron Application
Comment=A sample comment
Icon=icon
Categories=AudioVideo;Audio;Player;GTK;

Exec=electronapp %U

TryExec=audacious

Terminal=false

MimeType=audio/mp3
Actions=ActionOne;ActionTwo;ActionThree

[Desktop Action ActionOne]
Name=Action-One
Exec=electronapp -t
OnlyShowIn=Unity;

[Desktop Action ActionTwo]
Name=ActionTwo
Exec=electronapp -f
OnlyShowIn=Unity;

[Desktop Action ActionThree]
Name=ActionThree
Exec=electronapp -r
OnlyShowIn=Unity;
```

Custom macOS dock menu

In macOS, you can define some custom quick actions to the dock menu using Electron API. These actions can be executed even when the application is not active on the desktop. To set your custom dock menu, use the `app.dock.setMenu` method as follows:

```
const dockMenu = Menu.buildFromTemplate([
    {
        label: 'New Window',
        click() {
```

```
                console.log('New Window')
            }
        },
        {
            label: 'New Window with option',
            submenu: [
                { label: 'Basic' },
                { label: 'Pro' }
            ]
        },
        {
            label: 'New Command....'
        }
]);

app.dock.setMenu(dockMenu)
```

The menu will be added to the dock menu, and the output should be as follows:

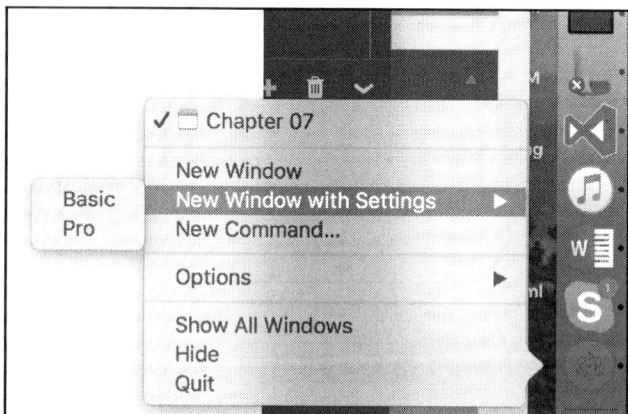

The preceding output is the same as creating the menu for the Electron application. You can create a custom menu with Menu class and attach it to the dock icon using Electron's app module. Use click property and define a handler function to handle the click events for each menu item as we did in the preceding code.

The Windows platform also provides the same feature, but we call it as user tasks. Similar to dock menu, this will be displayed with taskbar icons. You should use the `setUserTask` method of the app module to create the custom task menu in Windows. Ensure that you do not put any dynamic menu item inside the task menu.

Also, as per Microsoft recommendation, always try to put some common actions that do not have any dependency on your application state because we can't ensure that the application is running when the user clicks on the action. So, the actions should be independent of the application's state:

```
const { app } = require('electron')
app.setUserTasks([
    {
        program: process.execPath,
        arguments: '-newWindow',
        iconPath: process.execPath,
        iconIndex: 0,
        title: 'New Window',
        description: 'Create a new window'
    },
    {
        program: process.execPath,
        arguments: '-openSettings',
        iconPath: process.execPath,
        iconIndex: 0,
        title: 'Open settings',
        description: 'Open the settings window'
    }
])
```

Here, we don't have the option to attach a click handler directly into the menu in Windows. Instead, we need to pass the command-line arguments to the application that should be handled properly to execute that action. The command-line arguments passed from the task menu should be handled in your main process, as follows:

```
const { app } = require('electron');
const argv = require('yargs').argv;

function createElectronShell() {
  if(argv.newWindow) {
    let window = new BrowserWindow({ width: 500, height: 500 });
    window.loadURL(`file://${__dirname}/index.html`);
  }

  if(argv.newSettingsWindow) {
```

```
        let window = new BrowserWindow({ width: 500, height: 500 });
        window.loadURL(`file://${__dirname}/settings.html`);
    }
}

app.on('ready', createElectronShell);
```

We use `yargs` a third-party library that makes it easier to manage the command-line arguments in the node application. You can get all the arguments inside the `argv` object. If the argument is present, then do what is shown in the preceding code. The menu will be shown even if the application is not running on a Windows platform. As I mentioned above, the actions should not depend on the application state, as we are not sure whether the application is running when the user clicks on the menu item. To remove all the menu items in the task menu, use an empty array in the `setUserTasks` method:

```
app.setUserTasks([]);
```

Thumbnail toolbars

From Windows 7 onward, the platform provides a feature called thumbnail toolbars. You don't have to switch between the windows if you are busy with other applications. Thumbnail toolbar allows you to interact with a pinned site without opening it first. You can add custom command buttons, image, and video into the thumbnail toolbar.

The following code adds two command buttons into the thumbnail toolbar:

```
const { BrowserWindow } = require('electron');
const path = require('path');

let win = new BrowserWindow({
    width: 800,
    height: 600
})

win.setThumbarButtons([
    {
        tooltip: 'button1',
        icon: path.join(__dirname, 'button1.png'),
        click () { console.log('button1 clicked') }
    },
    {
        tooltip: 'button2',
        icon: path.join(__dirname, 'button2.png'),
```

```
      flags: ['enabled', 'dismissonclick'],
      click () { console.log('button2 clicked.') }
    }
  ])
```

Managing display properties

The preceding section described using a built-in Electron API to hook into the some of the operating system components. However, what if the Electron does not provide an API to implement your requirement. You should search for a corresponding npm module in the npm registry. In this section, let's check how we can control the display properties of a machine from your Electron application. In a real-world scenario, it's very rare to have this type of requirement. However, this will give you a detailed description about dealing with machine components. The operating system itself provides a lot of utility functions that can be used to interact with crucial internal components. These utilities can be executed via a terminal or command-line prompt.

If an operating system provides a utility program and the application user have access to it, then you can easily control that utility using Node.js shell. Let's take a look at the display properties example here. The main challenge with this example is each operating systems has different ways to manage the native hardware and OS components. Also, each platform uses different ways to implement the same functionality, which will not work on another platform. So, you need to implement the functionality for each platform that you are targeting to support. Here, let's start with the Windows platform.

Windows command line provides a command-line utility that can be used to control the power system settings. You can configure computer's hibernate and standby modes. To get more details about `powercfg` utility, visit https://technet.microsoft.com/en-us/library/cc748940(v=ws.10).aspx.

Integrating with Desktop Environments

Running the `powercfg -q` command will give you the following output in you command-line prompt:

This list down each and every power setting and its GUID. In this example, we need to get these GUIDs in order to manipulate power settings. Create a new JavaScript file called `power-config.js` and add the following method to it. Here, we are just going to deal with the display brightness. The `powercfg` tools are quite powerful to deal with a lot of things in the power settings:

```
function adjustBrightnessWindows(brightness, callback) {
    let guid;
    let subGroup;
    let powerSettings;
}
```

Node.js' `exec` method can be used here to execute the `powercfg` command from our application. This method will give you the output of the command in a buffer, and the end users can consume it as they want. Once the output is finished, the callback function will be called with the desired result. Add the following line to the preceding method:

```
exec('powercfg -q', (error, stdout, stderror) => {
    if(!error) {
        let regExp = /([a-z-0-9]+)sD+$/;
        let splitOutput = stdout.split('rn');
        guid = regExp.exec(splitOutput[0])[1];

        for (var i = 0; i < splitOutput.length; i++) {
            if(splitOutput[i].match(/(Display)$/)) {
```

```
                    subgroup = regExp.exec(splitOutput[i])[1];
            }
            else if(splitOutput[i].match(/(Displaysbrightness)$/)) {
                //The powerSetting is derived from the output named Display
                powerSetting = regExp.exec(splitOutput[i])[1];
            }
        }
    }
});
```

The preceding code loops each line of the output received from the `powercfg` command and extracts the GUID, power settings, and subgroup of each item from the output. Once we have the GUID and other information for the display properties, we can adjust the values according to that. Once we have all these values, you can use the following command to adjust the brightness of your machine:

powercfg -SetAcValueIndex GUID subgroup powerSetting brightness

This command will set the display brightness to the passed value when the power is plugged in. Let's convert this command into the Node.js code:

```
let command = `powercfg -SetAcValueIndex ${GUID} ${subgroup} ${powerSetting} ${brightness}`;

exec(command,function(err,out,stderror) {
    if(err) throw err;
});
```

Next, add the same brightness settings for DC Power plan settings. The command is almost the same, but the argument that we need to pass has some changes:

```
let dcCommand = `powercfg -SetDcValueIndex ${guid} ${subgroup} ${powerSetting} ${brightness}`;

exec(dcCommand,function(err,out,stderror) {
    if(err) throw err;
});
```

Here, the code is same, and we execute Windows shell command using the node exec function. The changed values are not yet persisted as the current system setting. We need to do it manually using the following code:

```
// Set the modified power plan as the current system plan
exec('powercfg -S' + ' ' + GUID, function(err, out, stderror) {
    if(err) throw err;
    if(callback)
```

Integrating with Desktop Environments

```
            callback();
        return true;
    });
```

That's it for setting the display properties in the Windows platform. There are some other ways to manipulate the Windows platform's native properties. You can use something like we have done in this using standard platform utilities. You can create custom native node add-ons using C++. Also, on Windows, you can use the .NET runtime environment features using the Node.js library, Edge.js. The final code for the Windows platform should be as follows:

```
function windows(brightness, callback) {
    let GUID;
    let subgroup;
    let powerSetting;

    exec('powercfg -q', function(error, stdout, stderr) {
        if(!error) {
            let regExp = /([a-z-0-9]+)sD+$/;
            let splitOutput = stdout.split('rn');
            GUID = regExp.exec(splitOutput[0])[1];

            for(let i = 0; i<splitOutput.length; i++) {
                if(splitOutput[i].match(/(Display)$/)) {
                    subgroup = regExp.exec(splitOutput[i])[1];
                } else if(splitOutput[i].match(/(Displaysbrightness)$/))
                {
                    powerSetting = regExp.exec(splitOutput[i])[1];
                }
            }
        }

        let command = `powercfg -SetAcValueIndex ${GUID} ${subgroup} ${powerSetting} ${brightness}`;
        exec(command, function(err, out, stderror) {
            if(err) throw err;
            let dcCommand = `powercfg -SetDcValueIndex ${GUID} ${subgroup} ${powerSetting} ${brightness}`;
            exec(dcCommand, function(err, stdout, stderr) {
                if(err) throw err;
                exec('powercfg -S' + ' ' + GUID, function(err, out,
                stderror) {
                    if(err) throw err;
                    if(callback) callback();
                  return true;
                });
            });
        });
    });
```

```
    } else{
       throw error;
    }
  });
}
```

The `powercfg` utility provides a number of other features. You can use this utility in the same manner that we have used above. Next, let's add the same functionality to target the Linux machine. As we are implementing a custom functionality that does not support natively by the Electron, we need to implement it for each platform that we are going to target.

Add the following function to the code to manipulate the display properties in the Linux platform:

```
function linux(brightness, callback) {
 // Enumerate the backlight devices...
     fs.readdir('/sys/class/backlight', function(err, brightnessDevices) {
        if(err) {
             console.error('Error while listing brightness devices. Maybe you need superuser privileges to run this script?');
             throw err;
        }

     let devicePath = '/sys/class/backlight/' + brightnessDevices[0];
     // Read the maximum for the first device
     fs.readFile(devicePath + '/max_brightness', function(err, maxBrightness) {
        maxBrightness = parseInt(maxBrightness, 10);
        if(err) {
             console.error('Error while reading maximum brightness. Maybe you need superuser privileges to run this script?');
             throw err;
        }

     // Turn percent into the actual value we need
     let brightnessValue = Math.floor(brightness / 100 * maxBrightness);

     // Write out new value
      fs.createWriteStream(devicePath + '/brightness')
        .on('end', callback)
        .write(new Buffer(brightnessValue.toString()));
   });
  });
}
```

Integrating with Desktop Environments

Screen brightness is tricky to control. The brightness of the screen backlight is adjusted by setting the power level of the backlight LEDs or cathode. The power level can be often controlled using the ACPI kernel module for video. An interface to this module is provided via the folder is `sysfs` at `sys/class/backlight`. In a Linux machine, most of the system configurations can be changed using filesystem module of Node.js. As the platform provides the configurations in simple files with admin rights, you need to read the current configuration and write it back with the new values.

In this example, we read the backlight configuration from the `/sys/class/backlight` directory using the Node.js `fs` module and write the new value in the same manner.

For macOS, let's use a third-party npm module called `osx-brightness`. Add it to the project using npm:

```
npm install --save osx-brightness
```

This is a small library that provides access to the display brightness properties. You can change the current settings value with the following code:

```
const osxBrightness = require('osx-brightness');
function mac() {
   osxBrightness.set(0.75).then(() => {
     console.log('Changed brightness to 75%');
   });
}
```

The preceding code increases the display brightness by 75 percent. Now, we have the code for three major platforms for the same feature. Let's combine it all together and plug it into the Electron renderer process.

Add the following method to the file and export it to be accessed from other node modules, as follows:

```
const os = require('os');

function adjustBrightness(brightness, callback) {
    switch (os.platform()) {
        case 'darwin':
           mac(brightness/100, callback);
           break;
        case 'linux':
           linux(brightness, callback);
           break;
        case 'win32':
           windows(brightness, callback);
           break;
```

```
            default:
                throw new Error('OS is not recognized or is supported');
                break;
        }
    }

    module.exports = adjustBrightness;
```

This simply recognizes the current operating system and executes corresponding methods. The next step is to attach this method to the renderer process. The module can be imported into the renderer process or the rendered page using standard Node.js require method. As we have the Node.js context available inside the web page and this code is purely based on the Node.js APIs, you can execute this from both main process and renderer process.

Add a slider field into the HTML page, and add the change event to the field that will change the display brightness; the HTML looks as follows:

```
<!DOCTYPE html />
<html>
<head>
  <title>Electron power config manager</title>
  <script type="text/javascript">
    const powerConfig = require('./power-config');
    window.onload = function() {
      let slider = document.getElementById('slider');
      slider.onchange = (e) => {
        powerConfig(slider.value, () => {
          console.log('Brightness changed to ' + slider.value);
        });
      };
    }
  </script>
</head>
<body>

<label for="slider">Change the brightness</label>
<input type="range" id="slider" />

</body>
</html>
```

The display brightness can be adjusted by moving the input range. In this section, we discussed manipulating native operating system components from an Electron application. We haven't discussed anything special about the Electron. Instead, we went through the practical example of operating system integration. The similar methodology can be used if you need to implement any additional features or functionality in your Electron application.

Dealing with tray icons

Electron has a built-in class called `Tray`, that can be used to add custom icon and menu to the notification area. Each platform is having different look and feels for this tray icon. However, this is quite useful to attach some quick action to the application. For instance, the tray icon on macOS should look as shown the following screenshot:

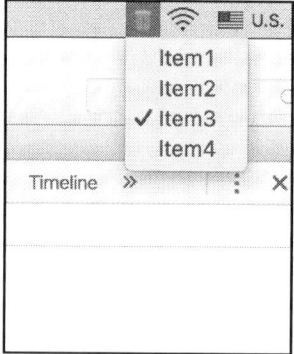

In Linux and Windows, it looks different. However, the same `Tray` class can be used to create tray icon for all major platforms. Creating a tray icon is simple with the `Tray` class. The class should be instantiated after the app module emits the ready event. The following code creates a tray icon and adds some quick menu items into the tray icon context menu:

```
const { app, BrowserWindow, Tray, Menu } = require('electron');

let appShell;
let tray;

app.on('ready', () => {
    appShell = new BrowserWindow({ width: 800, height: 600 });
    appShell.loadURL(appUrl);
    appShell.on('closed', () => { appShell = null; });
    tray = new Tray('/Users/Guest/Workspace/icon.png');
    const contextMenu = Menu.buildFromTemplate([
```

```
         {
            label: 'Show window',
            click: function () {
               appShell.show();
            }
         },
         {
            label: 'Hide Window',
            click: function () {
               appShell.hide();
            }
         },
         { label: 'Quick action' },
         {
            label: 'Exit',
            accelerator: 'Command+Q'
         }
      ]);
      tray.setToolTip('This is my application.');
      tray.setContextMenu(contextMenu);
});
```

This creates a custom tray icon with context menu in the notification area of your operating system.

Managing application logs

For better production support, logging is an important part. We can not use the console for logging messages on production environments. Instead, we can use file stream to save the log output. If you are a Windows user, you may have worked with Windows event log viewer where you can see all the log messages produced by the different applications. This section describes how we can use the Windows event viewer to manage the various logs from the Electron application.

Integrating with Desktop Environments

The event viewer in Windows looks like the following image:

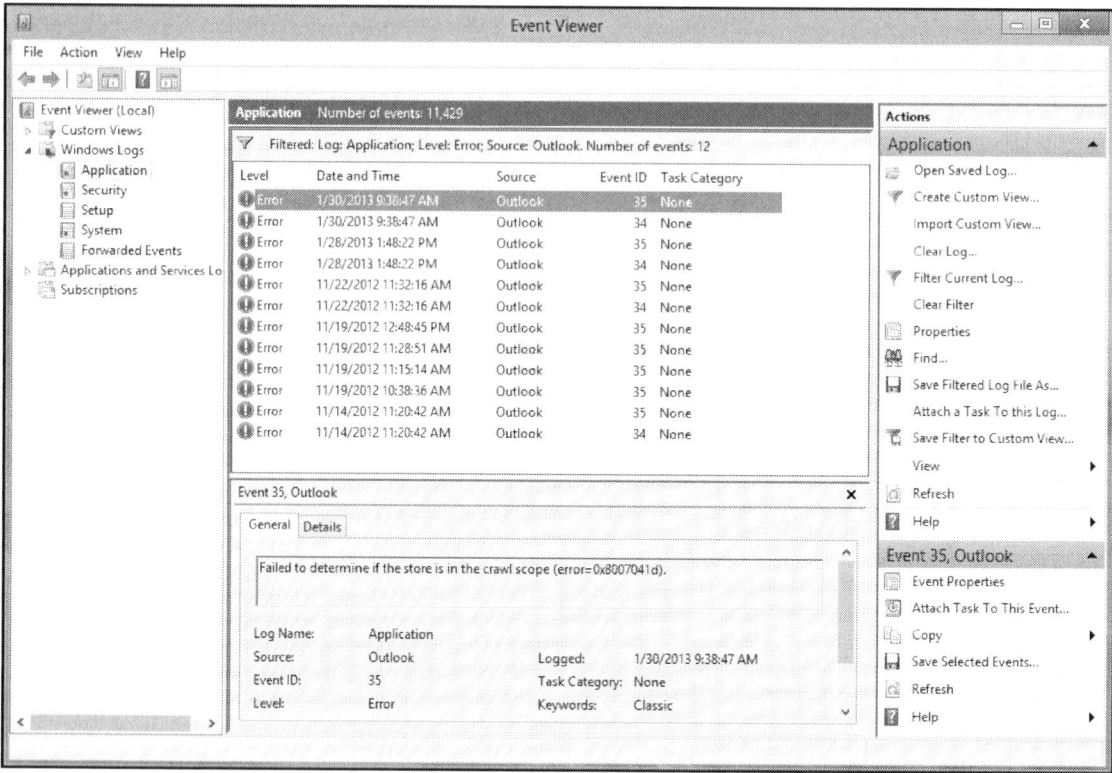

This utility is very useful to provide exception and warning information about the program to the end user. Let's look at how we can add some message to the event viewer from our Electron application. There is a third-party node module available called `node-windows` to interact with the event viewer. This library provides some other useful features, such as event logging, windows service integrations, and so on. Install the library using npm into the project, as follows:

```
npm install --save node-windows
```

For a better usage, let's create a wrapper class around this library so that other platforms can be added easily without affecting the actual application code. Create a new module called event-logger.js and add the following code to it:

```
const os = require('os');
const { EventLogger } = require('node-windows');

var log = new EventLogger('Electron application');

module.exports = {

  info(msg) {
    if (os.platform == 'win32') {
      log.info(mg);
    }
  },

  error(msg) {
    if (os.platform == 'win32') {
      log.error(mg);
    }
  },

  warn(msg) {
    if (os.platform == 'win32') {
      log.warn(mg);
    }
  }

};
```

The preceding code simply creates three methods for various logging levels. We created a separate module because each platform has its own implementation for logging. In this way, you can add more platform to this code without breaking your running application code. To use this code in your renderer process, or the main process, import the module and use it as a standard JavaScript module. The following code shows how you can use this code:

```html
<!DOCTYPE html>
<html>

<head>
 <meta charset="UTF-8">
 <base href="/">
 <title> Electron Event Logger</title>
 <meta name="viewport" content="width=device-width, initial-scale=1">
 <script type="text/javascript">
   const logger = require('./event-logger');
   window.onload = () => {
     document.getElementById('info').addEventListener('click', () => {
     logger.log('This is a log message');
   });
     document.getElementById('warn').addEventListener('click', () => {
     logger.log('This is a warning message');
   });
     document.getElementById('error').addEventListener('click', () => {
     logger.log('This is a error message');
   });
 };
 </script>
</head>

<body>
    <button id="info">Info</button>
    <button id="warn">Warn</button>
    <button id="error">Error</button>
</body>

</html>
```

This will add the log messages to the Windows event viewer. The output should be as follows:

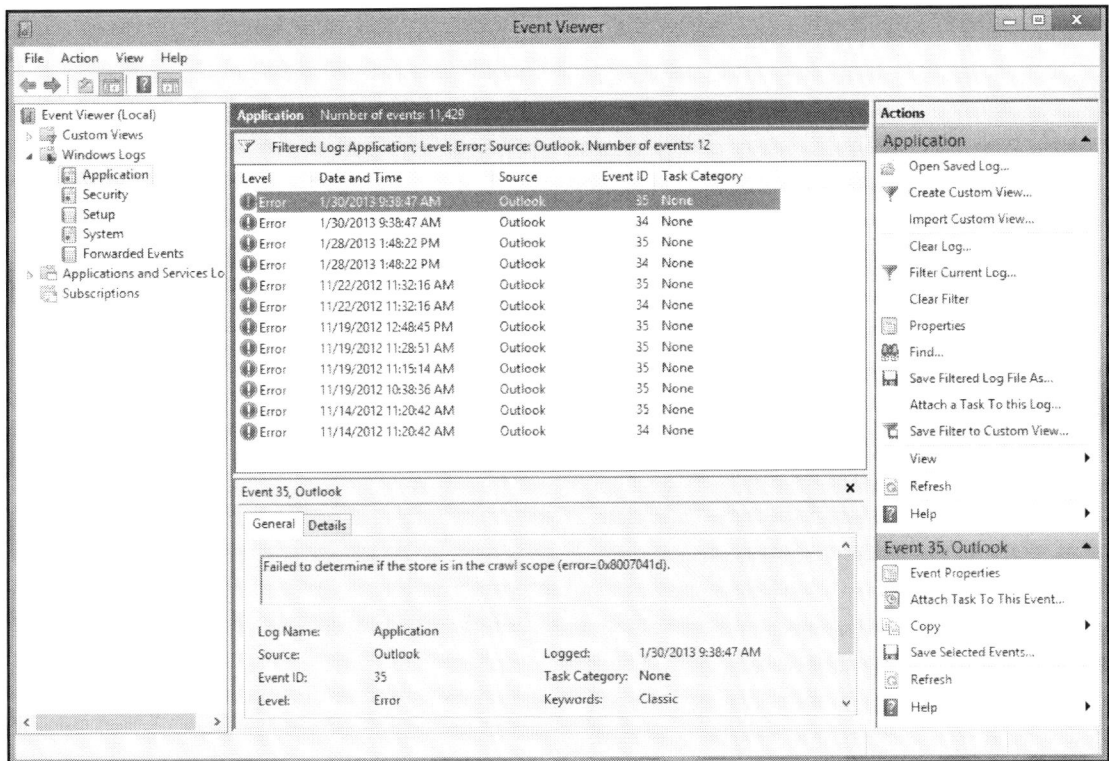

Running Electron application as Windows service

In Windows or Linux, the application can be operated in the background, which is similar in concept of UNIX daemons. In this section, let's look at how we can run an Electron application or a Node.js server as a Windows server or UNIX daemons. There are some CLI tools already available in Node.js world, such as pm2 or forever, which gives the same functionality for node servers. These programs run the node server as background service in Windows or daemons in Linux.

Integrating with Desktop Environments

For each platform, we need to write separate code to run the application in the background as service. To create a Windows service, the same `node-windows` library can be used. Let's create a small Windows service that runs in the background on Windows platform. Background services can be invoked using CLI tools, such as pm2, forever, winser, or may be some other similar Node.js modules. In this section, let's look at how we can start a Node.js server as Windows service and integrate it into the Electron application. In Windows machine, a running service can be monitored in Windows service manager application. The following example is an Electron application that can create a web server and run it as a Windows service. You can think of this application as a small web server manager that can manage a running web server as Windows service.

Create a simple Node.js server with the following code; you need to install the express js as npm dependency into your application:

```
npm install --save express
```

Add the code into `server.js` as follows:

```
const express = require('express');
const app = express();

app.get('/', (req, res) => {
   res.send('<h1>Server is up and running on port 8080</h1>');
});

app.get('*', (req, res) => {
   res.send('<p>Server is running on port 8080</p>');
});

app.listen(8080, () => {
   console.log('The server is running in port 8080');
});
```

This is a simple express server with a single route defined. There is no more complicated code in this server implementation. You can test this server using the following command:

```
node server.js
```

Let's create an interface to start this server as Windows server and Linux daemon. Add the following code into the `main.js`--that is your main process; define a menu with following code that starts and stop the Node.js server as a Windows service:

```
'use strict';
const { app, BrowserWindow, Tray, Menu } = require('electron');
const { Service } = require('node-windows');
const path = require('path');
```

```
let appShell;
let appUrl = 'file://' + __dirname + '/index.html';
let service;

function createElectronShell() {
 appShell = new BrowserWindow({ width: 800, height: 600 });
 appShell.loadURL(appUrl);
 appShell.on('closed', () => { appShell = null; });

 const template = [
    {
      label: 'Service',
      submenu: [
      {
        label: 'Start service',
        click() {
          createService();
        }
      },
      {
        label: 'Stop service',
        click() {
          stopService();
        }
      }
    ]
   }
 ];
 const menu = Menu.buildFromTemplate(template)
 Menu.setApplicationMenu(menu);
}

app.on('ready', createElectronShell);
app.on('window-all-closed', () => {
   if (process.platform !== 'darwin')
      app.quit();
   stopService();
});

app.on('activate', () => {
   if (appShell == null)
      createElectronShell();
});

function createService() {
 if (!service) {
    service = new Service({
      name: 'Node JS Server',
```

Integrating with Desktop Environments

```
        description: 'A simple node js server',
        script: path.join(__dirname, 'server.js'),
        env: {
          name: 'HOME',
          value: process.env['USERPROFILE']
        }
    });
    service.on('install', () => {
      service.start();
    });
    service.install();
  }
  else {
    service.start();
  }
}

function stopService() {
  if (service) {
    service.stop();
  }
}
```

This will work only on a Windows machine. Once you click to start the service menu, the Windows service will be started and can be monitored using Windows service manager window:

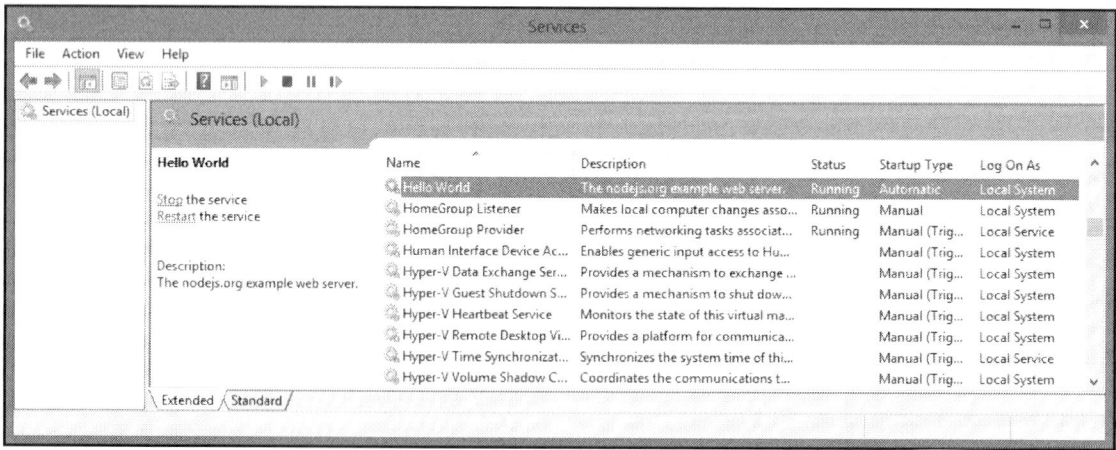

If you have worked with PHPMyAdmin in Windows, you would have noted that the service can be started from the Windows tray. In a similar way, an Electron application can be used to invoke a node server or node application from your Windows tray icon or from an Electron window.

The node-windows library can also be used to list down and manage the currently running processes on a Windows machine. A simple example of managing currently running operating system tasks is as follows in an Electron application:

```
<html>
<head>
    <script type="text/javascript">
        const wincmd = require('node-windows');

        window.onload = function () {
            wincmd.list((svc) => {
              let html = '';
              svc.forEach(task => {
                html += '<tr><td>' + task.ImageName + '</td><td><button onclick="killProcess(' + task.PID + ')">Kill Process</button></td></tr>';
              });
              document.getElementById('app').innerHTML = '<table>' + html + '</table>';
           });
      };

     function killProcess(pid) {
         wincmd.kill(pid, function () {
             console.log('Process Killed');
         });
     }
    </script>
</head>

<body>
    <div id="app">
    </div>
</body>

</html>
```

Running Electron application as Linux daemons

The `node-windows` library can only work on a Windows machine. This is just one of the libraries available in the npm registry. You can use any of the available process manager libraries to make your application a background service. In Linux machine, this can be achieved in several ways. Let's use the `node-linux` library to run the node script as background from your Electron application. Install the dependency from the npm registry:

```
npm install --save node-linux
```

We can use the same server script as an example. Once the dependency is installed, the script can be started as service with the following code:

```
const { Service } = require('node-linux');
 service = new Service({
     name: 'Node JS Server',
     description: 'A simple node js server',
     script: path.join(__dirname, 'server.js'),
     env: {
       name: 'HOME',
       value: process.env['USERPROFILE']
     }
});
service.on('install', () => {
  service.start();
});

service.install();
```

The code is similar to the code snippet that we discussed in the preceding section. Also, you don't have to use this library. You can even use the shell script or batch file to start a node script as a service.

There is an alternative version of this library available for Mac called `node-mac` that can be used to create and manage background services. The code is similar, but importing the library is different, depending on your platform. Use `node-windows`, `node-linux`, or `node-mac` based on the target operating system. Mac background services can be monitored in activity monitor:

Universal Windows platform

With Windows 8, there is a new type of the application executable on Windows platform called universal Windows application that can work universally on Windows platform. Electron provides strong guidelines to convert the application to universal Windows platform. There is an open source project called `node-rt`, which leverage us to use the WinRT APIs inside the Node.js project. So, combining the Electron UWP guidelines with node-RT API that enables us to create a perfect universal Windows applications.

In this section, let's take a look at how we can make our Electron application as the universal Windows application. The universal Windows platform has a new format called `.appx`. This format enables you much more powerful Windows APIs, such as push notifications, Cortana, and so on. The first step you need to do is to convert your Win32 `.exe` file into the `.appx` format. Microsoft developed a tool that compiles Electron app as a `.appx` package.

Windows 10 anniversary update is able to run Win32 `.exe` binaries as the new universal Windows application package. To convert or compile an existing Electron application into the `.appx` package, the following requirements should be in your toolbox:

- Windows 10 anniversary update
- Windows 10 SDK
- Node.js (version 4 and above)

Developing with WinRT

At the core of the Electron application is Node.js that can interact with the native code with native add-ons. With the help of dynamically linked shared object written in C or C++ code, you can closely work with native operating system environments. In Windows 8 and above, the underlying operating system environment API is called Windows Runtime APIs or WinRT. There is an open source project available called NodeRT that uses WinRT's descriptive metadata files and automatically generates native add-ons for each WinRT namespace. So, in our Electron application, this allows us to replace the native C++ add-ons with JavaScript code.

For example, you can import a WinRT namespace using standard `require` function. The following code imports the namespace `windows.system.userprofile` into the Node.js context:

```
const { LockScreen } = require('windows.system.userprofile');
```

Download the NodeRT from https://github.com/NodeRT/NodeRT/releases and extract it into the directory. Open the solution inside visual studio and build it into the executable files. As this is a native node add-on module, you need to build it against your native operating system. Install the `node-gyp` using npm:

```
npm install -g node-gyp
```

Once you build the executable for NodeRT, you need to generate native node modules that you want to use inside your application using the executable files inside the NodeRT project.

Launch the UI tool by running `NodeRTUI.exe`:

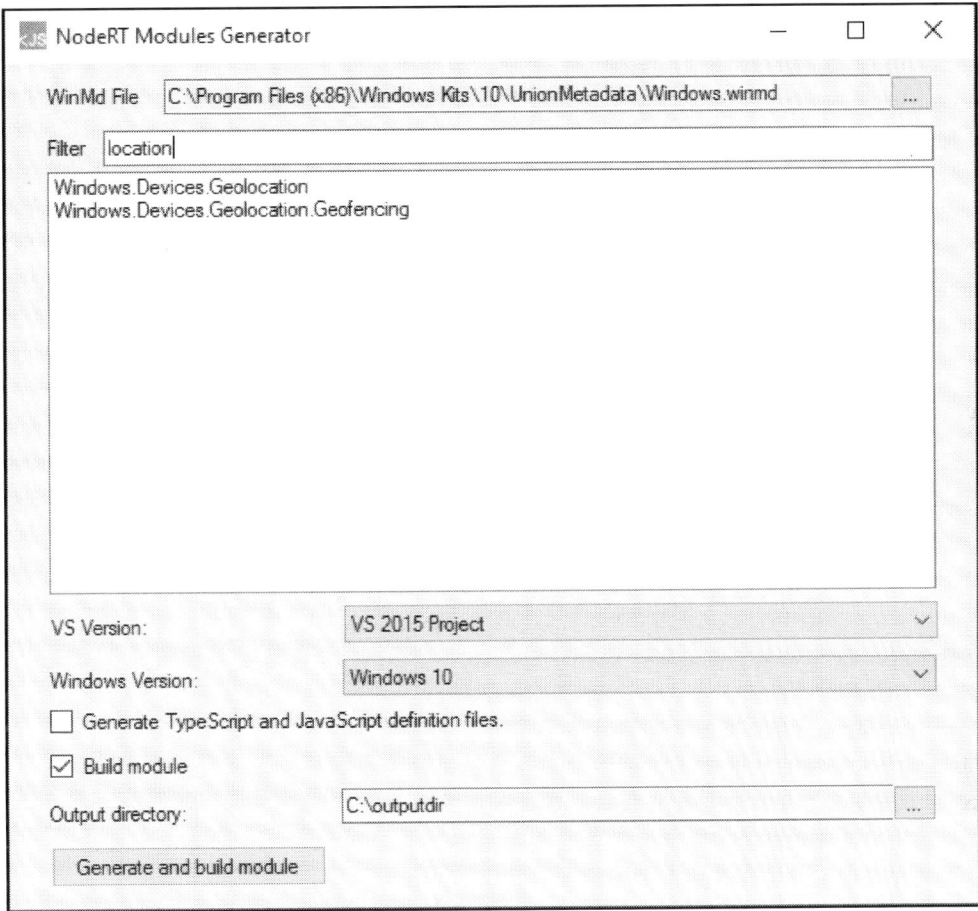

Choose a `.winmd` file to generate the NodeRT module. You can choose among Windows 8, Windows 8.1, and Windows 10 SDK. Choose a namespace to generate the list of the namespace. Choose the output directory and build the module.

Once you generate the NodeRT module, you need to build the module against the Electron. That is similar to building native node add-ons against Electron binaries. Install `node-gyp` globally using npm:

```
npm install -g node-gyp
```

Integrating with Desktop Environments

Open the command-line prompt and navigate to the generated NodeRT module folder. Type the following command to build the module against Electron binaries:

```
node-gyp rebuild --target=1.3.1 --arch=x64 --dist-url=https://atom.io/download/atom-shell
```

Ensure that you used the correct Electron module in the target option. Here, we used 1.3.1. Once you finish the build, copy the folder into your project's `node_modules` folder. Then, you can use it in the same way as other Node.js modules inside your Electron application.

Using notification API

In the previous section, we have checked how we can prepare WinRT module inside the Electron application by converting it into the NodeRT modules using the NodeRT GUI tool. NodeRT also provides command-line utilities to do the same things. In this section, let's look at how we can use a WinRT API inside the Electron application with an example. We had discussed desktop notification when discussing the Electron API. The WinRT API also provides a notification API that can be used inside Windows platform to send the desktop notification to the end user.

In order to show a desktop notification through a WinRT API, you need to have a shortcut with an app-id. For more information, visit Microsoft official WinRT documentation found at http://msdn.microsoft.com/en-us/library/windows/desktop/hh802762. You can do this easily with Node.js using the node-win-shortcut module with the following code to install the dependency:

```
npm install node-win-shortcut
```

Use the following code to create the shortcut:

```
var win_shortcut = require('node-win-shortcut');
win_shortcut.createShortcut(process.execPath, 'node', 'node_app_id');
```

You can use the following code to create the notification using WinRT API:

```
// Show a windows notification from node.js using NodeRT modules
var util = require('util');

var xml = require('windows.data.xml.dom');
var notifications = require('windows.ui.notifications');

var msgTemplate = `
  <toast>
      <visual>
```

```
            <binding template="ToastImageAndText02" branding="none">'
               <image id="1" src=""/>
               <text id="1">${title}</text>
               <text id="2">${text}</text>
            </binding>
        </visual>
</toast>`;

// use here an app id that was used for creating a shortcut
var appId = 'node_app_id';

// A Helper function for showing notifications
function showNotification(title, text, onActivation, onDismissal) {

 var toastXml = new xml.XmlDocument();
 toastXml.loadXml(msgTemplate);
 var toast = new notifications.ToastNotification(toastXml);

 toast.on("activated", function (sender, eventArgs) {
   onActiviation();
 });

 toast.on("dismissed", function () {
   onDismissal();
 });

notifications.ToastNotificationManager.createToastNotifier(appId).show(toas
t);
}

showNotification('Hello NodeRT!', 'Please click here', function() {
 console.info('got event: toast activated!');
 process.exit(0);
}, function() {
 console.info('got event: toast dismissed!');
 process.exit(0);
});

// wait for user interaction.
setTimeout(function() {
 console.info('no event was fired');
}, 30000);
```

This example first requires two WinRT APIs using standard require function. This should be converted and copied to a NodeRT module using the steps that we had discussed in the preceding chapter. Importing a namespace is same as importing standard Node.js module:

```
var notifications = require('windows.ui.notifications');
```

It then creates a toast UI using standard XML format provided by the Microsoft WinRT platform. This is processed using a XmlDocument class to create the notification and display it to the end user. This can be used both in the renderer process and the main process, as it runs separately from the Electron shell API.

However, as we discussed before, you need to package the Electron .exe into the .appx format to use the full power WinRT API. We will be discussing this in the last chapter with packaging and distribute the application.

You can use any of the WinRT APIs with the Electron. However, you cannot get JavaScript documentation or example with the official documentation. The docs describe the example in C or C++. However, you can easily convert the C++ code into a JavaScript code using same classes and namespaces. For example, you can set the lock screen image using WinRT API, as follows; this example uses C++ code:

```
using namespace Windows::Storage;
using namespace Windows::System::UserProfile;

create_task(myFolder->GetFileAsync("image.jpg")
  .then([this](StorageFile^ imageFile) {
     if (imageFile != nullptr) {
        LockScreen::SetImageFileAsync(imageFile)
     }
  }
}
```

If you go through the documentation, the examples provide you with C++ code. This can be rewritten into the JavaScript using NodeRT, as follows:

```
const {KnownFolders} = require('windows.storage')
const {LockScreen} = require('windows.system.userprofile')

myFolder.getFileAsync('image.jpg', (err, file) => {
  LockScreen.setImageFileAsync(file, (err) => { })
})
```

Both code snippets are the same; the only difference is the language and its syntax and semantics. So, if you are getting a C++ code, you can easily convert it into a JavaScript code in a similar way. You should always take care while generating NodeRT modules using the GUI tool like we discussed before.

Packaging for Windows store in appx format

To use the universal Windows platform APIs inside the Electron application, you need to launch the Electron exe inside the appx model. From Windows 10-anniversary update, it's possible to run the good old Win32 exe files as the universal Windows application. That leverage us to use several Windows 10 or universal Windows platform APIs, such as Cortana, communication with other applications, live tiles, notifications, and so on. Converting the exe into appx package is a compile-time process and should be when you build the application.

Install the `electron-windows-store` CLI:

```
npm install -g electron-windows-store
```

Before running the CLI, first, you need to set up 'Windows Desktop App Converter'. You can download it from https://www.microsoft.com/en-us/download/details.aspx?id=51691. The installation instructions can be found with the download button.

Package the application using `electron-packager` or with any other similar tools. We will be discussing the packaging in detail in the last chapter. The output of packaged application roughly should like the following:

```
├── Ghost.exe
├── LICENSE
├── content_resources_200_percent.pak
├── content_shell.pak
├── d3dcompiler_47.dll
├── ffmpeg.dll
├── icudtl.dat
├── libEGL.dll
├── libGLESv2.dll
├── locales
│   ├── am.pak
│   ├── ar.pak
│   ├── [...]
├── msvcp120.dll
├── msvcr120.dll
├── natives_blob.bin
├── node.dll
```

```
├── pdf.dll
├── resources
│   ├── app
│   └── atom.asar
├── snapshot_blob.bin
├── squirrel.exe
├── ui_resources_200_percent.pak
├── vccorlib120.dll
└── xinput1_3.dll
```

Open the PowerShell command prompt as an administrator user and run the `electron-windows-store` utility with required parameters:

```
electron-windows-store
  --input-directory C:electronapp
  --output-directory C:outputelectronapp
  --flatten true `
  --package-version 1.0.0.0
  --package-name electronapp
  --container-virtualization
```

This will flatten your `node_modules` folder, and the final output will be generated in an `app.zip` file. That's it! You have converted your Electron application into a Window appx package. You can now use any universal Windows platform APIs in your electron application.

Summary

This chapter discussed integrating Electron application with operating system environments. There are several ways to integrate an Electron application with operating system APIs. The first section was about using built-in Electron APIs, and we discussed some of the useful Electron APIs that can be used to plug into the operating system API. We then discussed controlling the underlying hardware using some third-party npm module. The example was about controlling display properties in all major platforms. The last section was about converting an Electron application into a universal Windows application. Now, you know how to control the operating system component or underlying hardware from your Electron application.

The next chapter will be about using web standards inside your Electron application. We will be discussing modern web standards and how to use them inside your Electron application.

10
Dealing with Web Standards

Modern browsers are very fast at implementing the web standard defined by W3C. As the Electron aligns with the latest version of the chromium, most of these features are available in Electron also. Even though we have native capabilities with Electron, these features are useful and more productive than the native or custom approach. For example, when your application requests a remote resource or your pages and assets are hosted on a remote server, using a service worker is better than implementing a custom resource caching mechanism. In this chapter, we will be looking into using these technologies and features in our Electron applications. This will give you a brief idea about increasing the productivity using the built-in web standard features that are available in the chromium or Electron shell.

These are the standard APIs that are well known for web application development. Here we are not targeting to discuss the details of the API, but we will be discussing the usage and benefits of using these features along with your Electron application with the desktop environment as the platform target. The following points will be discussed in this chapter:

- Using service workers and its APIs in an Electron application
- Using local storage and index DB to store your data locally in the shell

Service workers

The service workers are pretty new technology and not all browsers provide support for it. However, this will be a common API that is available in all the major browsers as the browser vendors have already started implementing the API. It's super useful for some type of desktop application that is built on top of the remote content. The service workers basically let you have a programmable proxy for network requests at the higher level. This leverages us to trump the normal browser caching rules. It is built to bring the real native experience to the web. However, we are already native when developing an Electron application, so why do we need to use service worker again to bring the native experience? Not all type of applications needs to use the service workers. Also, you won't be implementing the service worker on the client side as it's a feature that should be implemented on the server side. It's fit to be used when your application is accessing a remote content that can be static resources or dynamic data with API requests.

You need to manually implement the client caching mechanism and build a custom proxy for your network request for better performance and native-like experience when not using a service worker. With the service worker, these resources can be cached and can enable the background sync event; you can have push notifications from your server without having additional efforts on the client side. It's supported out of the box with Electron shell.

What is a service worker?

Basically, a service worker is a script that runs in the background separated from your web page. It has nothing to do with your web page user interface. However, it provides you the ability to send push notifications, background sync, programmatically manage the response caching, and manage network request and response by acting as a proxy. In future, it will support features such as periodic sync and geofencing. It's a JavaScript worker running in a separate thread than your user interface, so you cannot access the DOM directly from a service worker and vice versa. Instead, you need to send the message to the main thread using the `postMessage` method.

The service worker life cycle

The service worker life cycle is completely different from your web page life cycle. It starts when the remote web page installs the service worker script into the browser.

The activation step will follow the installation process where you can manage your old caches if any changes in the server are detected through the version number. Once it's activated, the service worker will start controlling the web pages under its scope. If any of the files fail to install the cache, the installation process will not be successful and the service worker won't be activated properly. The service worker will be in two states after it has been activated. Either the service worker will be terminated to save the memory or it will handle the fetch and message events that occur when a network request or message is made from your page. The following diagram shows the life cycle of a typical service worker:

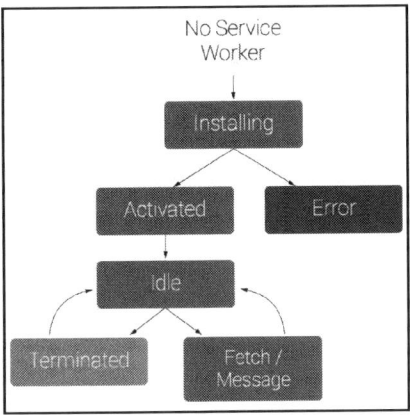

Browser support is growing for service workers. Still, not all the browsers are supporting the service workers. Google Chrome supports service worker from the early stage itself so that the Electron applications have the Service Worker support out of the box.

Managing the service workers in Electron

Before we get into the examples, let's take a look at how the service worker can be used along with the Electron application. In Chrome browser, you can check whether a service worker is enabled for a page by navigating to chrome://inspect/#service-workers. Also, the Chrome developer tools have a tab named Application, which can be used to inspect the service workers, including the cached files and resources.

Dealing with Web Standards

With Electron, you can open the inspector programmatically by calling the `inspectServiceWorker` method of the `webContent` API:

```
const { BrowserWindow, app } = require('electron');

let appShell;
function createElectronShell() {
    appShell = new BrowserWindow({ width: 800, height: 600 });
    appShell.loadURL(appUrl);
    appShell.on('closed', () => { appShell = null; });

    // Add this two line of code
    const contents = appShell.webContents;
    contents.inspectServiceWorker();
}

app.on('ready', createElectronShell);
```

This will open the service worker inspector like the following image:

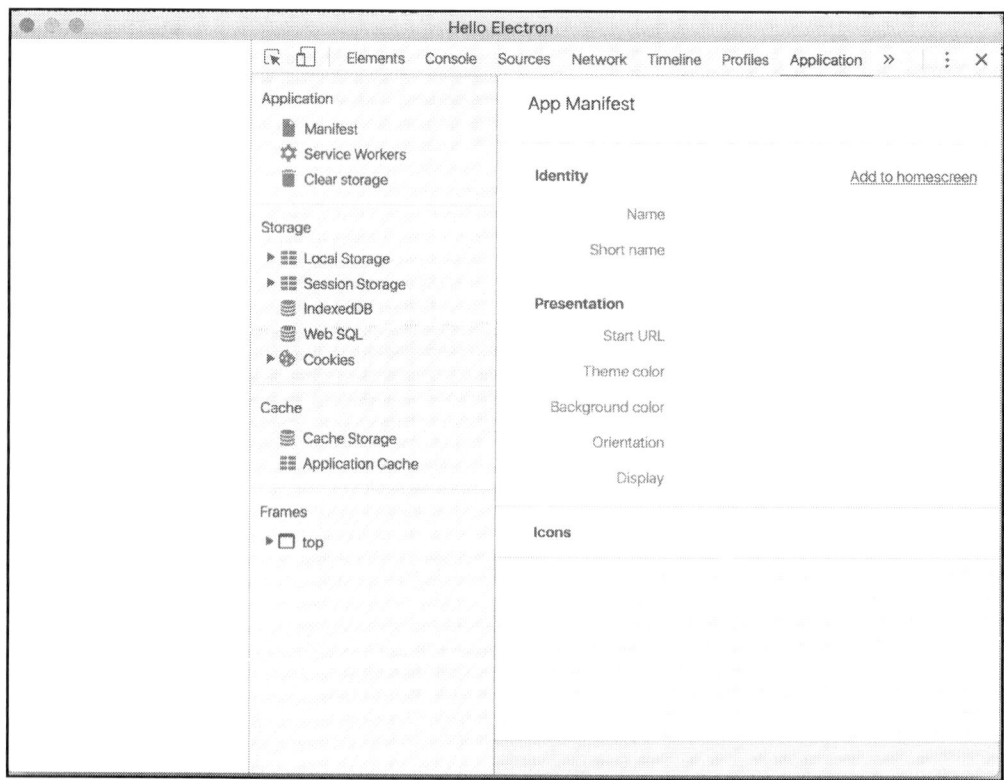

You can use the `hasServiceWorker` method to check whether any service worker is registered. The code is as follows:

```
browserWindow.webContents.hasServiceWorker();
```

A service worker can be uninstalled programmatically, as follows:

```
browserWindow.webContents.unregisterServiceWorker();
```

These methods are built into the Electron shell by default. One thing you need to take care about service worker is that the content should be served through a `https` protocol, which means the connection to the remote host should be secured using the certificate. Let's check a practical example. The following example checks how we can cache the remote content using the service worker API. We will be also discussing some other interesting service worker features, such as background sync and push notifications. Let's do these things for an Electron application.

The basic requirement for a service worker is that the connection to the remote host should be secured. So, we will create a simple `https` server using Node.js for testing purposes. Then, our Electron client will connect to this server, and we can play with the service worker features in the Electron.

Creating HTTPS server

The Node.js has a variety of options to create a server. There are a number of frameworks available to create a web server, from the basic HTTP module to the complex MVC frameworks like Sails.js. For demo purposes, we can create a simple web server using the popular Node.js web framework, called Express.js. Initialize a node project using the `npm init` command and install the dependencies with the following command:

```
npm install --save express path cookie-parser body-parser
```

Create a directory structure that's similar to the following. It's a simple server that demonstrates the caching mechanism. We don't want to get into the details of the express server programming here in chapter:

```
|- api
   |-- index.js
|- assets
   |- favicon.ico
   |- images
   |- css
      |- style.css
   |- scripts
```

Dealing with Web Standards

```
    |- script.js
|- views
    |- index.html
|- server.js
|- package.json
```

This is a simple boilerplate structure so that we can test how we can cache the assets, HTML files, and the API response to the Electron client. The `server.js` is responsible for creating and running an express server. Create the `server.js` file with the following code:

```
'use strict';

const path = require('path');
const express = require('express');
const bodyParser = require('body-parser');
const cookieParser = require('cookie-parser');

const app = express();
const ROOT = path.resolve(__dirname);

app.set('port', process.env.PORT || 3000);
app.set('views', path.join(ROOT, 'views'));
app.set('view engine', 'html');

app.use(cookieParser('Electron Service Worker'));
app.use(bodyParser.json());

app.use('/assets', express.static(path.join(__dirname, 'assets'), { maxAge: 30 }));

app.use('/', (request, response) => {
  console.log('Rendering views/index.html as home page');
  response.render('index', {});
});

app.listen(app.get('port'), () => {
  console.log(`Listening on: http://localhost:${server.address().port}`);
});
```

Create the `index.html` in the views folder with the following content. This file will be rendered as the home page when accessing the server:

```
<!DOCTYPE html />
<html>
  <head>
    <link type="text/css" rel="stylesheet" href="/assets/css/style.css" />
  </head>
  <body>
    <h1>Server is up and running</h1>
    <script type="text/javascript" src="/assets/scripts/script.js"></script>
  </body>
</html>
```

The basic server is ready. Run the server using the node `server.js` command from your project directory. You can get the server running on `localhost:3000`. This is a simple HTTP server that is not secured using the certificate. To enable the service worker, we need to run this server over TLS. So, let's enable the TLS by creating a self-signed certification for demo purposes.

Generate a certificate if you don't have one already. Use the following command to generate the certificate in your project folder:

```
openssl req -x509 -newkey rsa:2048 -keyout key.pem -out cert.pem -days 365
```

We have generated a self-signed certificate for 365 days. Let's add this certificate to the express server. Change the `server.js` code, as follows:

```
'use strict';

const fs = require('fs');
const path = require('path');
const crypto = require('crypto');
const express = require('express');
const bodyParser = require('body-parser');
const cookieParser = require('cookie-parser');

const app = express();
const ROOT = path.resolve(__dirname);

app.set('port', process.env.PORT || 3000);
app.set('views', path.join(ROOT, 'views'));
app.set('view engine', 'html');

app.use(cookieParser('Electron Service Worker'));
```

Dealing with Web Standards

```
app.use(bodyParser.json());

app.use('/assets', express.static(path.join(__dirname, 'assets'), { maxAge: 30 }));

app.use('/', (request, response) => {
  console.log('Rendering views/index.html as home page');
  response.render('index', {});
});

const options = {
   key: fs.readFileSync('key.pem'),
   cert: fs.readFileSync('cert.pem')
};

require('spdy')
    .createServer(options, app)
    .listen(app.get('port'), () => {
         console.log(`Listening on:http://localhost:${server.address().port}`);
    });
```

The code here is the same as the preceding code except that it is secured with the certificate. You can find spdy in the last line when creating the server and listening to the port. The spdy enables us to create HTTP2.0/SPDY servers in Node.js. HTTP2 gives more control over the response and is better for caching the response in the client. HTTP2 is a vast area that is out of the scope of this book. There are a lot of articles and videos already available about creating HTTP2 server in almost all the technologies. Using HTTP2 in server gives much more powerful features, such as better resource caching and server-side push. You can see a red colored certificate icon once you run the above code using the following command:

```
node server.js
```

Adding a JSON service

Now we have enabled the TLS on the server, which is enough to install the service worker in a client. Let's add an API route before adding the service worker so that we can check how we can cache the static resources, such as stylesheets and script files, and also dynamic API responses. Create a new file, called api.js, with the following content:

```
'use strict';

module.exports = function (request, response) {
  const data = [
      { id: 1, name: 'Verdie Gulgowski' },
```

```
            { id: 2, name: 'Dr. Markus Davis' },
            { id: 3, name: 'Mr. Retha Abernathy' },
            { id: 4, name: 'Macey Dickinson' },
            { id: 5, name: 'Kane Daniel III' }
        ];

        response.json(data);
};
```

Add the route to the server to access the API data by adding the following code to the `server.js` file:

```
const api = require('./api/index');
//...

app.use('/assets', express.static(path.join(__dirname, 'assets'), { maxAge: 30 }));

// Add the following line
app.get('/api', api);
```

You can access the API at `http://localhost:3000/api` from your browser.

Creating the service worker

Now the service worker can be added to the server code. Let's create a service worker skeleton by adding a script file into the scripts folder and naming it as `sw.js`. Add the following content into it:

```
'use strict';

const version = '1';

self.oninstall = event => event.waitUntil(self.skipWaiting());
self.onactivate = event => event.waitUntil(self.clients.claim());
self.onfetch = event => event.respondWith(fetch(event.request));
```

Dealing with Web Standards

You should install the service worker in your page. Open your `index.html` file and add the code into the bottom section of the HTML file:

```
<script typ="text/javascript">
  navigator.serviceWorker.register('/assets/sw.js', { scope: '/' })
          .then(function (reg) {
              // registration worked
              console.log('Registration succeeded. Scope is ' + reg.scope);
          }).catch(function (error) {
              // registration failed
              console.log('Registration failed with ' + error);
          });

</script>
```

When you run the application in the browser, you can see the service worker script with the gear icon on the left-hand side in network tab inside the Chrome developer tools. Reload the page again; you can see that the network requests are sending twice: one to the service worker and another to the actual server. This means that all your network requests will be passing through the service worker. The service worker can decide whether the request should be passed to the server to return the locally cached resource as the response to the request.

Next, add the resources that we need to cache in the local client; in our case, it's Electron shell. Declare an array of files and resources at the top of the service worker script. Open the `sw.js` file and add the following code to it:

```
const assets = [
    '/assets/css/style.css',
    '/assets/favicon.ico',
    '/assets/scripts/script.js'
];
```

These assets should be downloaded when browser installs the service worker. The `onInstall` life cycle callback will be called and the assets will be downloaded at this time. Change the `onInstall` method that we wrote earlier as follows:

```
self.oninstall = event => event.waitUntil(async function () {
    const cache = await caches.open('static');
    await caches.addAll(ASSETS);
    return self.skipWaiting();
});
```

This will download all the files listed in the ASSETS array again and will cache the files into the browser. Once it's downloaded, you can see the caches downloaded for this web page in the application tab of the Chrome developer tools:

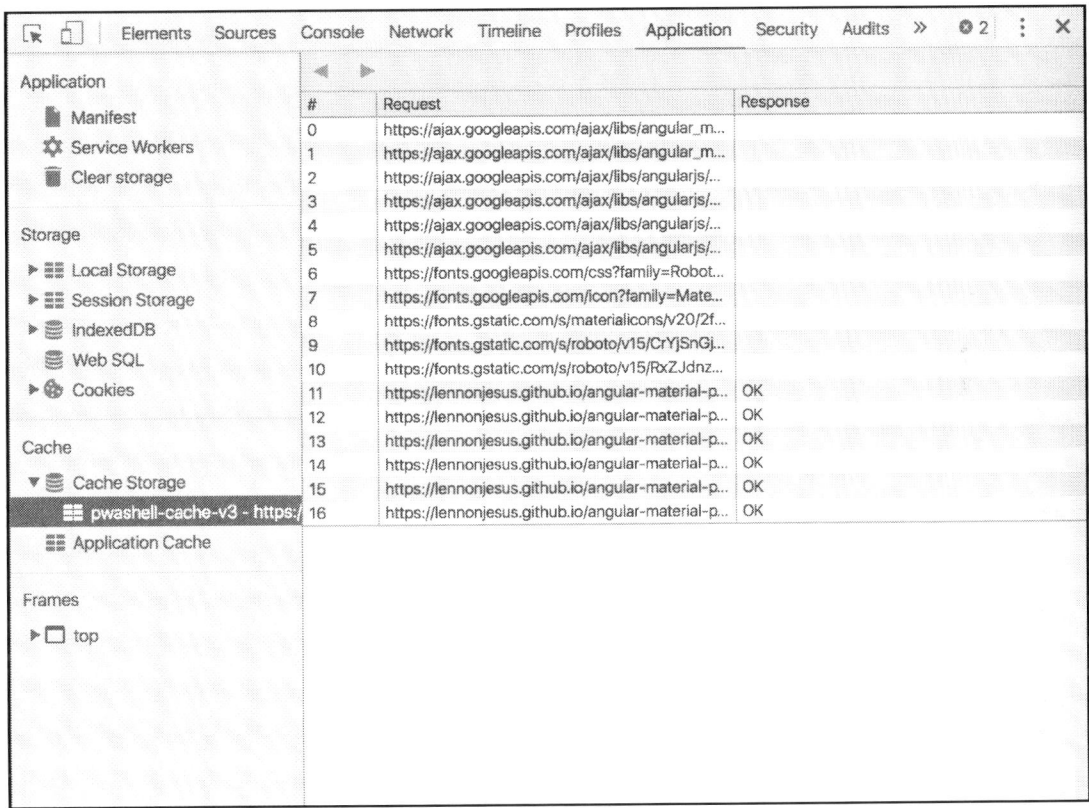

Let's intercept the fetch event happening inside the service worker scope and filter it if the resource is available inside the cache. The `onfetch` callback can be used to filter the fetch resources. All the network requests will first hit the service worker `onfetch` method; then, the actual network request will be initiated if needed. Update the `self.onfetch` method in service worker with the following code:

```
self.onfetch = event => {
  event.respondWith(
    caches.match(event.request).then(function (response) {
      return response || fetch(event.request);
    })
  );
}
```

This is a simple script that executes for each network request happening in the service worker scope. This function matches the passed request against the cached resource URLs. If any match is found, the request will be blocked and the content will be delivered from the cache. If the resource is not found in the cache, the request will be passed to the target host and will continue to work as normal. That's all that's needed for caching the resources using service worker.

Without service worker, you need to take care of all the procedures that need to store a file locally inside the browser. Here, we just need to take care of the list of the files that should be cached and need to create some logic to serve the resources from the cache. You don't have to code anything in your Electron application to enable service worker as it is supported out of the box. However, the manual implementation should be done on the client side. This means that, in our case, the Electron application needs more efforts and can be buggy.

Managing the cache version

The issue with this implementation is that cache will never be updated if the cached resources in the server are changed. So, we need to manage the cached files along with the cache version. When we have some changes in the cached resources on the server, we just need to update the version in the service worker script so that the next time the user loads the page, the service worker will check the installed version against the current version of the worker and update the cache if any changes detected in the server.

Update the `onInstall` method with the following code; just add the version to the installation process and install the specified version of caches into the browser or Electron shell:

```
const VERSION = 'v1';
const ASSETS = [
  //....
]

self.oninstall = event => event.waitUntil(
    const cache = await caches.open(VERSION);
    await caches.addAll(ASSETS);
    return self.skipWaiting();
);
```

The code here is the same as the earlier `onInstall` method, except that the cache name is changed. The change is because we cannot use a static name for the cache when we need to update the cache on server change. Instead, we use the version name of the current assets here.

Next, change `onfetch` to include the caches only from the current cache version. Update the `onfetch` life cycle event with the following code:

```
self.onfetch = event => event.respondWith(
    caches.match(event.request).then(function(resp) {
        return resp || fetch(event.request).then(function(response) {
            caches.open(VERSION).then(function(cache) {
                cache.put(event.request, response.clone());
            });
            return response;
        });
    }).catch(function() {
        console.log('Error: ');
    });
);
```

This matches each request against the cached resources and delivers it in response if it found it inside the cache, else the network request will be initiated. Once the response is received from the server, the resource will be cached into the local browser so that the resources are served from the local cache the next time.

We need to invalidate the previous cache when the new version of the resource is released. We can invalidate the previous cache on the activated life cycle hook. You can add the event listener for the activated event and do the following:

```
this.addEventListener('activate', function(event) {
  var cacheWhitelist = ['v2'];

  event.waitUntil(
    caches.keys().then(function(keyList) {
      return Promise.all(keyList.map(function(key) {
        if (cacheWhitelist.indexOf(key) === -1) {
          return caches.delete(key);
        }
      }));
    })
  );
});
```

The activate event will be triggered right after the install process has been completed. Here, we match the old versions of current caches against the whitelisted cache versions. Then, we delete the old caches using the `caches.delete()` method.

It's very easy to implement the caching using service workers as compared to other custom implementations. As we discussed earlier, service worker also provides some other features that are very useful when developing a real-time application. For example, the push notification, which is very important in real-world applications. We had discussed desktop notification in the last chapter; let's combine the push notification along with the desktop notification to provide better user experience.

Customizing the notification

The notification API provides a number of configuration options to customize the look and feel of the notification. You can also define the custom actions that enable users to execute some quick actions from the notification itself. Custom actions can be added to the notification just by passing the action array in to the showNotification method:

```
const title = 'Actions Notification';
const options = {
  actions: [
    {
      action: 'coffee-action',
      title: 'Coffee',
      icon: '/images/demos/action-1-128x128.png'
    },
    {
      action: 'doughnut-action',
      title: 'Doughnut',
      icon: '/images/demos/action-2-128x128.png'
    }
  ]
};

options.body = `This notification can displays action button `;

registration.showNotification(title, options);
```

This will show the action button in the notification, similar to the following image:

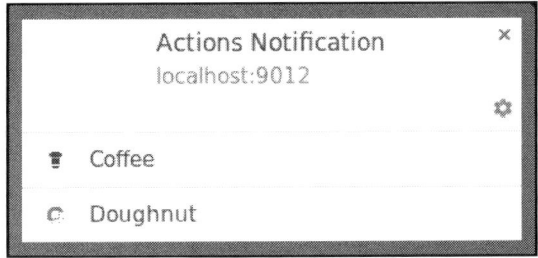

To handle the actions inside the notification, you need to handle the notification click event. The action will be passed as a property to the event parameter:

```
self.addEventListener('notificationclick', function(event) {
  const clickedNotification = event.notification;
  clickedNotification.close();

  const promiseChain = somePromise();
  event.waitUntil(promiseChain);
});
```

As I mentioned, the actions can be handled in this notification click event as the action name is passed to the event as the property in the event parameter:

```
self.addEventListener('notificationclick', function(event) {
  if (!event.action) {
    console.log('This is a normal notification click.');
    return;
  }

  switch (event.action) {
    case 'coffee-action':
      console.log('Clicked on coffee action');
      break;
    case 'doughnut-action':
      console.log('Clicked on doughnut action');
      break;
  }
});
```

Multiple notifications can be grouped using the `tag` option. When a new notification for the same tag is added, the old notification with the same tag will be replaced with the new notification:

```
const title = 'Notification title';
const options = {
    body: 'Notification body',
    tag: 'message-group-1'
};
registration.showNotification(title, options);

// get the tag on the event handler.
```

Storing database locally

We had checked using the relational database directly from your Electron application when discussing with Node.js integration in Chapter 6, *Using Node.js with Electron*. However, that scenario is suitable mostly for the complex type of data operations. When you just need to store some configuration or app settings per user, you can use standard HTML5 storage APIs. There are several options available for storing inside the Electron shell itself using HTML5 technologies. `IndexDB`, local storage, and `WebSQL` are some of the examples that can be used for this purpose. You can use these technologies directly, like you can use them inside the web application.

In this section, let's try using HTML5-based storage mechanism in the Electron application. However, here I recommend using a JavaScript database instead of using the standard web technologies. `PouchDB` is a JavaScript database inspired by Apache `CouchDB` that is designed to work well in browsers. The interesting part is that it gives a common wrapper around most of the available web storage mechanisms. You can specify the adapter that should be used to store the data. The supported adapters include `indexedDB`, `WebSQL`, `HTTP`, `LevelDB`, and `SQLLite`.

`PouchDB` is a JavaScript library that can be installed from npm. Install the `PouchDB` from npm, as follows:

npm install pouchdb

Import the module into the context and initialize the database with the following code:

```
const PouchDb = require('pouchdb');
var db = new PouchDB('database.db', { adapter: 'idb' });
```

The adapter can be any type of supported storage target, such as WebSQL and SQLite. You can easily switch the storage type when you use these type of libraries instead of directly using the local browser APIs.

Visit `https://pouchdb.com/` for more information about PouchDB. If you would like to use low-level browser APIs, such as `LocaleStorage` or `IndexDB`, visit the MDN or refer to any other official docs (`https://www.w3.org/TR/IndexedDB/`) to get more details about those technologies. Electron supports most of these APIs, so there's no need to make any extra effort.

Summary

In this chapter, we discussed using standard web technologies inside the Electron application. The first section was about using service worker to enable the resource caching and providing the offline experience when accessing remote content. The next part was about implementing the push notification with service worker inside the Electron application. Finally, we checked how we can store the data inside the shell/browser itself using the standard HTML5 APIs. Instead of directly using the low-level API, we used a custom library so that the storage target can be easily migrated.

The next chapter will cover testing the Electron application. We will also be discussing how to test a web application as the Electron's user interface is built with web technologies.

11
Testing Electron Application

Testing the code is an important step when developing an application. The testing process should be carried out carefully to ensure the quality of the application. There are a number of automated testing tools available in the industry, which enhance the software stability and quality by catching more errors before the software reaches the end user. Especially with JavaScript, the choices are more. In this chapter, we will be discussing how to test an Electron application. If you are new to JavaScript testing, the first part of this chapter will give you a brief introduction to JavaScript testing, which is essential to test your application. The following points will be discussed in this chapter:

- Introduction to JavaScript testing
- Testing the Electron application with Spectron
- Exploring the Spectron API

The chapter covers, mostly, a testing library called Spectron based on Chrome driver and WebDriverIO. Spectron can work with any other testing framework that you are using for your other JavaScript applications. So, we will check how we can integrate Spectron with these frameworks.

Introduction to JavaScript testing

Testing an application is a complicated process similar to development. It should validate the application against the possible bugs and errors and should check whether the code produces the targeted results properly. Different types of testing methodologies need to be carried out while developing an application from unit testing to integration testing. Testing the very basic unit of your code can be carried out using unit testing frameworks. Let's check how this works in common for JavaScript applications. Testing a JavaScript function with unit testing frameworks is very simple. For example, let's test a simple JavaScript function using the popular JavaScript testing framework, Mocha.

Mocha is a very popular testing framework. It has a number of good features and browser support that need an entire book to be explained. So, let's just look into a simple example with Mocha that is enough to get an idea. To read more about Mocha, visit https://mochajs.org/. Like most of the JavaScript testing frameworks, Mocha is also based on Node.js. You can install Mocha using npm, in your terminal, as follows:

```
npm install mocha --save-dev
```

Now add a small function to your JavaScript file. For a demo purpose, the following function calculates the sum of the arrays passed as arguments. The function is very simple, and we know how the function should behave when passing an array of numbers to it. This behavior should be validated. Also, the error values and exceptional behaviors should be validated as part of the testing. Add the following code to your JavaScript file:

```
module.exports = function calculateSum(arr) {
    let sum = 0;
    if(!arr instanceof Array) {
        throw new Error('The parameter should be an array');
    }
    arr.forEach(item => {
        if(typeof item != 'number') {
            throw new Error('The values in array should be number');
        }
        sum += item;
    });
    return sum;
}
```

Chapter 11

The code simply iterates over the array and calculates the sum of the array into a variable that is the return value for the function. Create a folder, called spec, in your project, and add a file with filename.spec.js. You can also place the file with your actual code. If you are new to JavaScript testing, it's about validating the code against some specific input and output. Let's pass a static array with [1, 3, 5, 7] values into the function. The function should return 16 as the sum. Also, the function should throw an error if we pass non-array values to the function. Also, if the data type is not the number for any of the array items, the method should throw an error. The following code handles these three scenarios:

```
var assert = require('assert');
var calculateSum = require('./calculateSum');

describe('Sum', function() {
  describe('#calculateSum()', function() {
    it('should return sum of the array elements', function() {
      assert.equal(16, calculateSum([1,3,5,7]));
    });
  });
});
```

Mocha allows you to use any assertion libraries that you wish to use. The preceding code example uses Node's built-in assert library. You can use your favorite assertion libraries, such as should.js, chai, or assert.js. Let's add one more validation on the parameter type by passing an invalid parameter so that exception cases can be validated with the test cases. Add the following code to your test cases:

```
describe('#calculateSum()', function() {

    it('should return sum of the array elements', function() {
        assert.equal(16, calculateSum([1,3,5,7]));
    });

    it('should throw an exception after matching the parameter type', function() {
        assert.thrown(
          calculatesum('String value'),
          /The parameter should be an array/,
          'Did not throw the expected exception'
        );
    })

    it('should throw an exception after matching the array item', function() {
        asset.thrown(
          calculateSum([1, 2, 3, 'S']),
          /The values in array should be number/,
```

```
            'Did not throw the exception'
        );
    });
});
```

Three scenarios are validated in the preceding code. One valid result and two other exception cases. In order to run this test case, use the `mocha` command from your working directory, as follows:

```
mocha tests/sum.test.js
```

If you have installed the Mocha locally, then use the relative path to the local `node_module` folder. You should be getting the following output once you run the tests in your console:

```
$ ./node_modules/mocha/bin/mocha

Sum
  #calculateSum()
✓ should return sum of the array elements

1 passing (7ms)
```

Introduction to Spectron

Spectron is a testing library based on the Chrome driver and WebDriverIO, which targets Electron applications. Spectron can work with any testing framework. We will be using Mocha and Chai to explore the Spectron APIs here. Add Spectron to the project using a package manager, such as npm or yarn:

```
npm install --save-dev spectron
```

To run the Spectron tests, you need to install Mocha or any other testing framework. Spectron can easily invoke your Electron application and execute the UI and functionality with the help of Chrome driver and WebDriverIO. A very simple Spectron script is as follows:

```
const assert = require('assert');
const { Application } = require('spectron');

describe('Application launch', () => {
    this.timeout(10000);

    beforeEach(() => {
        this.app = new Application({
```

```
            path: '/Applications/AppName/Contents/MacOS/App'
        });
        return this.app.start();
    });

    afterEach(() => {
        if(this.app && this.app.isRunning()) {
            return this.app.stop();
        }
    });

    it('Shows an initial window', () => {
        return this.app.client.getWindowCount().then((count) => {
            assert.equal(count, 1);
        });
    });
});
```

The `Application` class from the Spectron API can be used to invoke an Electron application. You need to pass the application's executable path through the options in the argument. The class will be returning the exported Electron application instance that can be used to start the application using the `start` method. Once the application is executed, the instance object can be used to assert the values. For example, the preceding code checks the current window count present in your desktop and asserts the value of the static count. Spectron uses WebDriverIO and exposes the client property on the created application instance. The details of the WebDriverIO client API can be found at http://webdriver.io/api.html.

You are supposed to have the main process script as follows to run the preceding example:

```
const { app, BrowserWindow } = require('electron');

let appShell;
const appUrl = 'file://' + __dirname + '/index.html';

function createElectronShell() {
    appShell = new BrowserWindow({ width: 800, height: 600 });
    appShell.loadURL(appUrl);
    appShell.on('closed', () => { appShell = null; });
    // appShell.webContents.openDevTools();
}

app.on('ready', createElectronShell);
app.on('window-all-closed', () => {
    if (process.platform !== 'darwin')
        app.quit();
```

```
});

app.on('activate', () => {
    if (appShell == null)
    createElectronShell();
});
```

Usually, the test cases will be in the test folder or may be along with the source code. Whatever the cases, it's inside your project folder. So, in your test case `beforeEach` method, the `Application` class can be initialized with the local `main.js` file and no need to pass the absolute path to the `Application` object parameter option. Change the `beforeEach` hook in your test case as follows to invoke your current project in the test case. You are supposed to have the Electron package installed locally in your project:

```
beforeEach(() => {
    this.app = new Application({
        path: './node_modules/.bin/electron',
        args: ['main.js']
    });
    return this.app.start();
});
```

Here, you just pass the Electron executable inside your `node_modules`. The application object accepts another option, called `args`, which can be used to pass the command-line arguments. You can pass the chromium command-line switches to the Electron by adding it to the `args` array. Here, we passed the main filename, and it should be the first argument in the `args` array so that the Electron will start executing that file. Run the test case with Mocha using the following command from your terminal:

mocha tests/spectron.test.js

You should be getting the following output with a success message in your terminal once you run the test:

```
bash-3.2$ mocha tests/test.js

application launch
  ✓ shows an initial window

1 passing (2s)
```

The preceding code checks the current window count, and only one Electron window is expected to be present in the screen to make the test cases to be successful. So that adding a developer tool into the `main.js` script will cause the test case to fail. We have already commented that in the `main.js` script file in the preceding code snippet. Uncomment that line and run the test again. The test case should fail, and you will get an error, as follows:

```
bash-3.2$ mocha tests/test.js

  application launch
    1) shows an initial window


  0 passing (3s)
  1 failing

  1) application launch shows an initial window:

      AssertionError: 2 == 1
      + expected - actual

      -2
      +1
```

Accessing the Electron API

The Spectron API allows the Electron and chromium APIs to be available to your test cases. The Electron property on the application instance is the gateway to your Electron API from your test cases. Let's look at how we can test Electron's clipboard API using Spectron. The details of the clipboard API were discussed in the last chapter. Let's create a test case for validating the clipboard functionality:

```
var Application = require('spectron').Application
var assert = require('assert')

const SAMPLE_TEXT = "This is a sample text";

describe('application launch', function () {
   this.timeout(10000)

   beforeEach(function () {
      this.app = new Application({
         path: './node_modules/.bin/electron',
         args: ['main.js']
      });
      return this.app.start();
   });
```

```
    afterEach(function () {
       if (this.app && this.app.isRunning()) {
          return this.app.stop()
       }
    });

    it('shows an initial window', function () {
        let { clipboard } = this.app.electron;
        clipboard.writeText(SAMPLE_TEXT);
        return clipboard.readText().then(clipboardText => {
          assert.equal(SAMPLE_TEXT, clipboardText);
        });
    });
})
```

BeforeEach and AfterEach are the life cycle hooks for the test that can be used to initialize and clean up the process. The beforeEach method will be executed before your test cases start to execute. It's the best place to initialize any resources that your test needs. In our case, we initialized the Electron application and Spectron in this block so that it will be available for all the code blocks in the test case. In a similar way, the afterEach method will be executed when all your code blocks are executed in a test case. This can be used to stop your Electron application and clean up any data and resources used in the test case. The preceding code is not a real test case as it's only validating the built-in Electron API. The code just writes some text to the clipboard using Electron's clipboard API and reads it back with the same API.

Testing DOM tree

When testing an application, functional unit testing is not enough to ensure the quality of the application. Sometimes you need to mock the browser behavior in your test cases. However, Spectron is not a unit testing framework. For that purpose, Mocha and Chai are enough. Spectron is more about testing your Electron application as you are doing it manually. One of the most important things when testing a web application or an Electron application is to validate your DOM tree state. You may have to programmatically invoke certain events or manipulate the DOM tree based on some input. Selenium-based testing tools allow you to run your application in a browser and invoke the testing from your testing code. Here, with the help of WebDriverIO, Spectron leverages us to access the DOM element. You can use the client property of Spectron or the webContents API of the Electron to access your DOM from the test cases.

Let's look at how we can manipulate and test the DOM elements and their state from your Spectron test cases. For a simple version, the client property of the Application class can be used to manipulate or retrieve the DOM tree. For example, to get the `innerText` of an HTML element from the renderer process can be done as follows:

```
it('Banner should have value', function () {
    const bannerText = 'Electron is up and running';
    this.app.client.getText('#banner').then((value) => {
       assert.equal(value, bannerText);
    });
});
```

This assumes that the rendered web page is having a div or any element with ID banner and the inner text as specified in a `bannerText` variable. The client property exposed to the application instance is coming from the WebDriverIO. You can get full APIs provided by the WebDriverIO at `http://webdriver.io/api.html`.

This client property leverages us to mock the user behavior in an HTML page programmatically. Most of the user actions can be done using this API. Let's look at a small example on how to use this for a sample app. Create a sample `Todo` application. Here's a sample HTML file with scripts. The example just contains a text field and a list of todos. When the user clicks on the button, the text field value should be inserted into the list:

```
<!DOCTYPE html>
<html>

<head>
   <meta charset="UTF-8">
   <base href="/">
   <title>Electron App</title>
   <meta name="viewport" content="width=device-width, initial-scale=1">

   <script>
     let index = 0;
     function addTodo() {
        let todoInput = document.getElementById('todotxt');
        createTodo(todoInput.value);
        todoInput.value = "";
     }
     function createTodo(text) {
        let listCt = document.getElementById('todolist');
        let el = document.createElement('li');
        el.innerHTML = text;
        listCt.appendChild(el);
     }
   </script>
```

```
</head>

<body>
 <div id="banner">Electron is up and running</div>
 <input type="text" id="todotxt" />
 <button id="addbtn" onclick="addTodo()">Add</button>
 <ul id="todolist">
 </ul>
</body>

</html>
```

The code is very basic and does not follow any practice. However, it's enough to test the DOM using Spectron. Add the test case to your test.js file with the following code:

```
it('should add new todo', function () {
 let app = this.app;
 let client = app.client;
 let element = client.element;
 return element('#todotxt').setValue('SampleInput')
.then(function () {
    client.getValue('#todotxt').then(function (data) {
       element('#addbtn').click().then(function () {
          client.elements('#todolist li').then(function (d) {
             assert.equal(1, d.value.length);
          })
       })
    })
 });
});
```

The WebDriverIO functions are always asynchronous. So, you need to either use the promise or async functions to get the real output. Here, we query the DOM and add a static text into the text field. We then programmatically click on the button to add the Todo into the UL element. Finally, the node count inside the ul element should be matched, and it should be one as we added only one item.

Exploring Spectron API

Spectron provides us with a simple but powerful API that leverages us to handle the various aspect of an Electron application from your test cases. You can manipulate almost each and every point of the Electron application from your test cases using the Spectron API. The preceding section already gave you a brief idea about a Spectron test case. In this section, let's explore the Spectron API in detail. As I said, it's a very simple API, and you should integrate Spectron with some other testing framework for real-world use cases.

Creating an Electron application instance is the first step in testing, and it should be done when initializing the test case. When testing with Mocha the Electron application instance should be created in the `beforeEach` callback. The Application class accepts a configuration option as the parameter that can be used to configure your Electron shell application for your test cases. The path is a required option for the Application that indicates the executable path. You need to pass the absolute path to your application. If you need to invoke the Electron from your current working directory with your main script, you need to use the Electron command with the main script filename as the first item in the `args` array:

```
let application = new Application({
    path: './node_modules/.bin/electron', // OR just electron
    args: ['main.js']
});
```

You can use the `args` to pass some command-line arguments to the Electron executable. It can be chrome command-line switches that Electron supports or any other custom command-line arguments that you need to pass to the application. Basically, the `args` is an array or arguments that you need to pass:

```
let application = new Application({
    path: './node_modules/.bin/electron', // OR just electron
    args: ['main.js', 'enable-logging']
});
```

Here are the some of the options that you can pass to the Application constructor:

```
let application = new Application({
    path: './node_modules/.bin/electron', // OR just electron
    args: ['main.js', 'enable-logging'],
    cwd: path.join(__dirname, '..'),// current working directory
    env: { //Custom environment variables
      var1: 'Value'
    },
    host: 'localhost',
    port: 9515,
```

```
    nodePath: '/User/node/',
    requireName: 'require'
});
```

Not all the options are listed here. You can pass the custom environment variables in the `env` object so that your code can be accessed those variables in using the `process.env` of the node. The host and port are the host and port of the Chrome driver process.

The Electron helpers provided by Spectron need to access the Electron API. So, if you have disabled the node integration in your application, you will need to expose the `require` function to Spectron in your code. You can do this by adding the following code to the application code first:

```
if(process.env.NODE_ENV == 'test') {
    window.electronRequire = require;
}
```

Then, in your Spectron application constructor, you need to use this variable, as follows:

```
let application = new Application({
    path: './node_modules/.bin/electron', // OR just electron
    args: ['main.js', 'enable-logging'],
    requireName: 'electronRequire' // add this line
});
```

You need to set the `NODE_ENV` variable before running the test:

```
NODE_ENV=test mocha tests/test.js
```

The application instance exposes some properties and methods that give access to the underlying Electron application and its window. The Electron property, which we had already discussed before, is equivalent to the following:

```
// In your Spectron test case
var application = new Application({
    path: '....'
});
var electron = application.electron;

// The above line is equivalent to
var electron = require('electron');
```

This property can be used as the gateway to the Electron API. You can access the Electron API through this property.

The current browser window object can be accessed using the `browserWindow` object. The property is an alias for the following code method call:

```
require('electron').remote.getCurrentWindow();
```

This will return a `BrowserWindow` object. The full access to the `BrowserWindow` API is available on this property. For example, check whether the window is visible or not using the `BrowserWindow` method, as follows:

```
var application = new Application({...})
var isWindowVisible = application.browserWindow.isVisible();
console.log('Visible - ' + isWindowVisible);
```

Accessing the webContents API

The `webContents` API can be accessed through the `webContents` property. This property will give you the `webContents` for the current window and will contain all the API. The following code matches the window title in the test case:

```
const { Application } = require('spectron');
const assert = require('assert')

describe('application launch', function () {
   this.timeout(10000);

   beforeEach(function () {
      this.app = new Application({
        path: './node_modules/.bin/electron',
        args: ['main.js']
      });
      return this.app.start();
   });

   afterEach(function () {
      if (this.app && this.app.isRunning()) {
        return this.app.stop()
      }
   });

   it('It should match the window title', function () {
     this.app.webContents.getTitle().then(function (data) {
        assert.equal(data, 'Application Title');
     });
   });
});
```

[275]

In this way, you can have the full access to the `webContents` API through the application object instance.

Accessing the process object

Accessing process object is essential when developing the Electron application and when testing the developed code. As you know, the Electron has two type of processes in the application: the main process and the renderer process. The Spectron's `mainProcess` and `rendererProcess` properties can give you access to the process object. For example, the environment variables from any of the Electron's processes should be done as follows:

```
// Accessing the main process arguments
app.mainProcess.argv().then(function (argv) {
 console.log('main process args: ' + argv)
})
```

In a similar way, the renderer process environment variables can be accessed as follows:

```
app.rendererProcess.env().then(function (env) {
   console.log('renderer process env variables: ' + env)
})
```

Accessing the renderer process logs

The console logs cannot be accessed from your test case. The application will be automatically closed after running your test cases; so, if you need to check any log messages, Spectron provides a method to watch all your console messages. The `getRenderProcessLogs` method on the client property can be used to get all of your logs from the Chrome developer tools console. The method should be used as follows:

```
app.client.getRenderProcessLogs().then(function (logs) {
   logs.forEach(function (log) {
      console.log(log.message)
      console.log(log.source)
      console.log(log.level)
   });
});
```

Using ESNext in test cases

Mocha does not support ESNext features. You may have to use babel to use the latest ECMAScript features in your test cases. However, there is another testing framework, called AVA, which gives you the ability to use the latest JavaScript language features out of the box in your test cases. Why do we need to use this? It's because most of the Spectron APIs return the JavaScript promise. If you look at the preceding code, you may note the long list of callbacks and promise chains just to get a simple output, especially when we need to access the Electron and client API. With ES2017, this can be avoided using async functions. Also, there are a number of useful features that reduce our effort and code available in the new ECMAScript. You can even use Mocha with Babel transpiler to get the same features in your current test cases. As Spectron supports any testing frameworks, let's check how we can use AVA framework to test our Electron application.

First, import the dependencies in your test case code:

```
import test from 'ava';
import { Application } from 'spectron';
```

You can use the ES6 import statement with this framework. Add the initialization code using the `beforeEach` life cycle callback:

```
test.beforeEach(async t => {
    t.context.app = new Application({
      path: '/Applications/MyApp.app/Contents/MacOS/MyApp'
    });

    await t.context.app.start();
});
```

The code is similar to Mocha, but it uses an async function instead of promises. Next, add the `afterEach` callback for cleaning up the resources:

```
test.afterEach.always(async t => {
    await t.context.app.stop();
});
```

Add the actual test to the file by adding the following code:

```
test(async t => {
  const app = t.context.app;
  await app.client.waitUntilWindowLoaded();

  const win = app.browserWindow;
  t.is(await app.client.getWindowCount(), 1);
```

```
    t.false(await win.isMinimized());
    t.false(await win.isDevToolsOpened());
    t.true(await win.isVisible());
    t.true(await win.isFocused());

    const {width, height} = await win.getBounds();
    t.true(width > 0);
    t.true(height > 0);
});
```

The code itself briefs us about the type of checking that it's executing in each line. The test method is the key point to enter into a test case. That's what accepts an async function as the parameter. The `app.client.waitUntiWindowLoad` asks the test case to wait until the Electron loads its window before executing the next line. Once it is loaded, then the `browserWindow` object can be accessed and used to test the features and functionalities. The `t.is` method is similar to `assert.equal` that we used with Mocha. The `currentCount` should be equal to one in our test case. You should be able to understand the rest of the line as the code itself describes what functionality is being tested.

To run the test case, install the framework using npm into your global npm cache:

```
npm install -g ava
```

The `ava` command can be used to run the tests. The command is the same as Mocha that we used in the preceding section.

Using Chai as Promised

Using Chai and Chai as Promised pairs well with WebDriverIO and, hence, with Spectron. Using these together allows you to chain the assertions together and have fewer callback blocks. This is another option for using the Spectron test cases. Install the libraries using npm:

```
npm install --save-dev chai
npm install --save-dev chai-as-promised
```

The same preceding code can be rewritten using Chai, as follows. Let's check it part by part. Initialize the skeleton of the test case, as follows:

```
var Application = require('spectron').Application;
var chai = require('chai');
var chaiAsPromised = require('chai-as-promised');
var path = require('path');

chai.should();
chai.use(chaiAsPromised);

describe('application launch', function() {
   this.timeout(10000);

   beforeEach(function() {
       this.app = new Application({
           path: './node_modules/.bin/electron',
           args: ['main.js']
       });
       return this.app.start();
   });

   beforeEach(function () {
      chaiAsPromised.transferPromiseness = this.app.transferPromiseness
   });

    afterEach(function() {
       if(this.app && this.app.isRunning()) {
           return this.app.stop();
       }
    });
});
```

Add the real test case. Here, most of the methods return promise so that you can chain all your actions one by one. For example, you can wait for the window to be loaded and validate the current window count with Chai as Promised, as follows:

```
return this.app.client.waitUntilWindowLoaded()
 .getWindowCount().should.eventually.equal(1)
```

Here's the sample code using Chai and Chai as Promised that integrates with the Electron code:

```
it('opens a window', function () {
 return this.app.client.waitUntilWindowLoaded()
 .getWindowCount().should.eventually.equal(1)
 .browserWindow.isMinimized().should.eventually.be.false
 .browserWindow.isDevToolsOpened().should.eventually.be.false
 .browserWindow.isVisible().should.eventually.be.true
 .browserWindow.isFocused().should.eventually.be.true
.browserWindow.getBounds().should.eventually.have.property('width').and.be.
above(0)
.browserWindow.getBounds().should.eventually.have.property('height').and.be
.above(0)
 })
```

Summary

Testing an Electron application is the same as testing any other JavaScript application code. You can have various levels of testing in your application from simple unit testing to a comprehensive testing using Spectron. This chapter discussed testing an Electron application with Spectron. We checked how we can integrate the Spectron along with other testing frameworks. The syntax should be very familiar to you if have worked with the JavaScript testing frameworks. Spectron is based on `ChromeDriver` and WebDriverIO so that it will be an added advantage if you look into these tools.

The next chapter will look at packaging the Electron application for production. The chapter will look at creating installers, continuous integration, and the automatic updates that an application needs for production quality.

12
Packaging and Distributing the Application

The earlier chapters discussed how to develop an Electron application. However, that code can't be delivered to the end user. It should be packaged properly in order to deliver the application to the end user. It's a completely different task from developing the application. Usually, we use a different set of tools and libraries to package and deliver the application to the end user. In this chapter, we will look at how we can package the application for production use. We need to take care of a number of checklists when packaging the application. The following points will be discussed in this chapter:

- Building and packaging the Electron application
- Using Electron builder to package the application
- Automating the build process
- Creating the installers
- Implementing the code signing for Windows and Mac
- Publishing the artifacts
- Continuous integration
- Configuring the auto update

This chapter will also discuss some other aspects of the production workflow, such as preparing for uploading the application into the various app stores, configuring the automatic application updates, and so on. This will give you a clear idea about delivering a desktop application on production for different platforms.

Building and packaging the Electron application

Packaging an Electron application can be done in various ways. There are different tools available to do the packaging for you. It can also be done manually. Before checking the tools that automate the Electron application packaging, let's check how we can package the application manually so that you will get a detailed idea about the internals of the Electron packaging process, which is essential even when you are using the automated tools.

Distributing an Electron application is simple when comparing desktop applications that are developed using other technologies. The prebuilt binaries that can be used to distribute the application are available for download. This prebuilt binary is also shipped with the npm module that you have already installed as part of your application development. You can find this inside your `node_modules/electron/dist` folder. For the time being, download the same or copy the folder to your disk and extract it if downloaded from the Internet. It can be downloaded from the GitHub repository: https://github.com/electron/electron/releases. The binaries are available for most of the platforms and architectures. Download the binary for the platform that you are going to target. Actually, the prebuilt binary itself is a packaged application with minimal code that contains a simple HTML with JavaScript code inside it. The application can be executed directly so that the default application will be rendered on the shell. To package your Electron application, rename your Electron application folder as the app and place it in the resource directory of Electron prebuilt:

```
locales
resources
blink_image_resources_200_percent.pak
content_resources_200_percent.pak
content_shell.pak
d3dcompiler_47.dll
electron
ffmpeg.dll
icudtl.dat
libEGL.dll
libGLESv2.dll
LICENSE
LICENSES.chromium
natives_blob.bin
node.dll
snapshot_blob.bin
ui_resources_200_percent.pak
version
views_resources_200_percent.pak
xinput1_3.dll
```

The typical structure of Electron prebuilt for Windows is shown in the preceding screenshot. There will be slight differences in this structure on other platforms. You can find a default `_app.asar` file inside the resources directory, which is the default application shipping with the prebuilt Electron. Replace your application folder with this asar archive, and you are ready to distribute your application after making your app into a zip archive or any other compressed format.

For example, if we are having a simple application with only three files--the `package.json`, `index.html`, and the `main.js` file--then the structure after copying the app to the prebuilt binary should be as follows:

```
|- locales
|- resources
    |- app
        |- index.html
        |- package.json
        |- main.js
```

The application can be run by executing the `electron.app` on Mac and `electron.exe` on Windows platform. The Electron shell will start your application immediately after executing the executable. You can use this as your output bundle that can be distributed to the end user.

Packaging the Electron into asar archive

The preceding part just copied your Electron application, and the files were simply placed under the Electron prebuilt resources directory. This will expose the source to the end user. Users can just navigate to the `resources` folder to get the real source code of the application. Electron provides a simple archiving format called asar that can be used to package the source code into a zip like a file format. Asar is a simple archive format created for Electron apps. With asar, it still can be extracted into the actual code structure. However, it gives some way to archive all your source code into a single file, which hides the source code from the user. Once the asar is created, you then need to place the file into the resources directory and rename the file into `app.asar` so that the Electron shell can detect the application automatically.

On Windows and Linux, the structure should be as follows after copying the asar archive:

```
Electron Prebuilt
|- locales
  |- resources
      |- app.asar
```

Generating the asar archive

The asar archive is a simply tar-like format that concatenates all the files into a single file. The Electron can read the files from the asar archive and execute it without unpacking the whole file. To generate the asar file, you need to use the asar utility, which is a node-based tool and is available through the npm. Install the utility using npm into your global `npm` cache, as follows:

```
npm install -g asar
```

It should be available in your path once you install it. You can execute it using the `asar` command from your terminal. Navigate to your project folder, and execute the following command from your terminal to generate an asar archive for your application:

```
asar pack app-name app.asar
```

You can then copy the asar file into the Electron prebuilt distributable to distribute your application as we discussed earlier. Basically, an asar file is an uncompressed archive. This means that you can access the files and the contents of the asar archive from outside the archive file using Node API or Electron API. For example, loading an HTML file into the Electron shell (`BrowserWindow`) from outside the asar file can be done as follows:

```
const { BrowserWindow } = require('electron');
let win = new BrowserWindow({ width: 800, height: 600 });
win.loadURL('file:///path/to/app.asar/static/index.html');
```

Here, you can note that we are accessing the HTML file inside the asar archive using the file protocol with the path to the physical location of the file inside the asar archive. In a similar way, you can use Node's `fs` module to read the content of the asar file. However, it's a read-only format, so you cannot write or modify the files inside the asar archives. If you need to get the list of the files inside an asar file, the list command can be used. The asar list with the asar filename as the argument can give you the list of the files and folder packed inside that archive file.

You can read a file inside the asar archive using your Node.js code using the following code:

```
const fs = require('fs');
fs.readFileSync('/path/to/app.asar/files/text.txt');
```

The path string should specify the file path inside the asar archive concatenated with the asar path inside your project, as shown in the preceding example. When using it inside the Node.js code, you can think of it as a normal directory. You can use the standard require function and import the JavaScript module inside your application from the asar, as follows:

```
var jsModule = require('/path/to/app.asar/js/module.js');
```

So, the asar can be treated as a read-only directory from your Node.js project. You can use all the file operations from the archive, as you are working with a normal directory.

Packaging and Distributing the Application

Rebranding the application

The Electron prebuilt binary comes with the Electron icon and its own branding. You will need to rebrand the Electron binary after bundling the application into your own brand and theme. This includes changing the executable icon, application metadata, platform registration information for the application, and so on.

You need to use different tools for each platform to rebrand the executable. Also, the steps to edit the executables will be platform specific, and you should follow unique steps for each platform to rebrand the binary-for example, when the application is in an .exe format and you need to use the exe editor like rcedit or any other .exe resource editor tools. You can get more information about rcedit on GitHub repository at https://github.com/electron/rcedit/releases. rcedit is a command-line tool that can be used to edit the resource file inside the .exe files. Let's see how we can use this tool and also about rebranding the Electron application for Mac, Linux, and Windows platforms.

On MacOS, the executable is named as electron.app; you can simply rename it to whatever name you want to. You also need to rename the CFBundleDisplayName, CFBundleIdentifier, and CFBundleName fields in the following files:

- Electron.app/Contents/Info.plistElectron.app/Contents/Frameworks/Electron Helper.app/Contents/Info.plist
- Electron.app/Contents/Frameworks/Electron Helper.app/Contents/Info.plist

You can also rename the helper app to avoid showing the Electron Helper in the activity monitor. Ensure that you have renamed the helper app's executable filename.

The structure of the renamed app would be like the following on Mac OS:

```
MyApp.app/Contents
├── Info.plist
├── MacOS/
│   └── MyApp
└── Frameworks/
    ├── MyApp Helper EH.app
    │   ├── Info.plist
    │   └── MacOS/
    │       └── MyApp Helper EH
    ├── MyApp Helper NP.app
    │   ├── Info.plist
    │   └── MacOS/
    │       └── MyApp Helper NP
```

```
└── MyApp Helper.app
    ├── Info.plist
    └── MacOS/
        └── MyApp Helper
```

On the Linux machine, simply rename the executable of the application and it will reflect everywhere when you run the application.

For Windows platform, as we discussed you can use `rcedit`. The rcedit executable is available at https://github.com/electron/rcedit/releases. You can download the exe file and use it from the command line. Make it available in your PATH or copy the exe into the project. This can be used as a command-line tool, or you can use it with your task runners. The executable icon can be changed using `rcedit` through the following command:

```
rcedit "electron.exe" --set-icon "path-to-ico"
```

The rcedit is an executable file. So that the actual command may have to change according to the command line prompt. For example, if you are using windows command line prompt, you can try either use rcedit command directly or with "./rcedit.exe". When using PowerShell command prompt or similar command line prompts, change the path notations accordingly.

The icon file should be in the `.ico` format and provide the exact path information to the file as in the preceding command. In a similar way, the product and file version can be changed using the following command:

```
rcedit "electron.exe" --set-file-version "10.7"
rcedit "electron.exe" --set-product-version "10.7"
```

Using Electron builder

The `electron-builder` is a complete solution for packaging and distributing the Electron application on Mac, Windows, and Linux platforms. It provides a number of options that can automate the build process. It's recommended to use this tool instead of packaging your application manually, and this is well suited with your task runners. It provides some useful features out of the box that includes npm package management, code signing, auto update the application, numerous target formats, build version management, publishing the artifacts, and so on.

In order to use the electron-builder, the configuration should be done in your application source code itself. This is a single-time process, which will save your time later when you build the application. The configuration should be done in your application's package.json file. The electron-builder provides a wide variety of options to customize your packaging process. Let's check how we can use this tool to package your Electron application.

The first step is to provide the right package information to your application. The package.json should be defined with a proper name, version, description, author name, and e-mail. The next step is to provide the build configuration inside the package.json file. As I mentioned, the electron-builder provides a wide variety of options. You can get more details about all available options on the GitHub page at: https://github.com/electron-userland/electron-builder/wiki/Options.

Add the following code to your package.json file. We will discuss the details of these options shortly in this chapter:

```
"build": {
    "appId": "electron.app.id",
    "mac": {
       "category": "com.company.app.type"
     }
 }
```

Create a directory called build in the root of your project and save the assets for the executable into that folder. Copy a background.png (for Mac OS dmg background), icons.icns (Mac OS app icons), and icon.ico (For Windows exe icon) to that folder.

The Linux icon set will be generated automatically based the Mac OS icns file. If you need to specify the files for Linux platform, you just need to copy the files into the build/icons directory. The filename must contain the size of the icon 32x32.

Add the script key to your package.json, as follows:

```
"scripts": {
"pack": "build --dir",
"dist": "build"
}
```

Then, you can run the npm dist to pack your application for the distribution. We will discuss more on electron-builder in the upcoming sections.

Automating the build process

What we have done in the preceding section is to build the Electron application manually by copying the Electron prebuilt binaries. That is not a practical solution when working on a real-world application. It should be integrated with your task runners or build scripts. Even though the `electron-builder` provides a way to run the packaging from your command line, that is not enough especially when you use the continuous integration systems. In this section, let's automate the build process programmatically. In the first section, let's look at how we can do the packaging that we did manually in the first section programmatically. After that, let's integrate the Electron prebuilt into the task runner and automate the same process.

You can find the Electron prebuilt distributable binaries in your application's Electron dependency. Expand the `node_modules` folder, and search for your `electron` folder. The distributable binary can be found under the `dist` folder. This is the same binary that we downloaded in the previous section. Suppose, we are having the following structure for the application and we want to build it programmatically:

```
|- node_modules
|- dist
|- build
|- tools
   |- build.js
|- src
   |- main.js
   |- index.html
|- package.json
```

Here, the `dist` folder will be the final distributable output after packaging the application. The `tools` folder should contain your build scripts that can be used to execute the bundling process. Create the application that you want to package. We need to have some node libraries to be installed in order to manipulate the files and folders inside the project. Install the following node libraries. If you are already familiar with node and node libraries you can use any other libraries that do the job for you. It's just a sample of how to do the packaging programmatically. There can be multiple ways and options available to do the same thing. Install the following libraries using npm:

```
npm install fs-jetpack asar rcedit --save-dev
```

Using node's native `fs` module is the too low level you need more efforts to do get it done. Here, instead of `fs` module, we use `fs-jetpack` module that provides a high-level API on top of the Node.js native `fs` library. We use this library for the smooth manipulation of the files and folders. First, let's target for Windows platform. Most of the methods used for Windows can be used in other platforms, too. Only some of the platform-specific things needed to be rewritten for that specific platform. Add the following code into the `build.js` file:

```
var childProcess = require('child_process');
var asar = require('asar');
var jetpack = require('fs-jetpack');

var projectDir;
var buildDir;
var manifest;
var appDir;

function init() {
    return new Promise((resolve, reject) => {
        // Project directory is the root of the application
        projectDir = jetpack;
        // Build directory is our destination where the final build will be placed
        buildDir = projectDir.dir('./dist', { empty: true });
        // angular application directory
        appDir = projectDir.dir('./src');
        // angular application's package.json file
        manifest = appDir.read('./package.json', 'json');
        // resolving the promise
        resolve();
    });
}
```

The preceding code just initializes the script by initializing the variables that should be used throughout the build process. The variable `jetpack` will provide you a singleton object of the `jetpack` library, which represents the current working directory. Based on the current working directory, we then configure our output directory in the above folder.

The next step is to copy the `electron-prebuilt` folder into the `dist` folder-as I mentioned earlier-the Electron distributable binaries at the `/node_modules/electron-prebuilt/dist` folder. Copy it using the code into the `dist` folder. Add the following function to your build script:

```
function copyElectron() {
    return projectDir
        .copyAsync(
            './node_modules/electron-prebuilt/dist',
            buildDir.path(), { overwrite: true }
        );
}
```

The distributable folder contains a `default_app.asar` file, which contains the actual Electron application inside the resources folder. This file needs to be replaced with our Electron application. As a first step, clean up the resources folder from the Electron distributable bundle that we copied into the dist folder using the preceding code. Use the following code to do the same:

```
function cleanupRuntime() {
    return buildDir.removeAsync('resources/default_app');
}
```

As we discussed, we won't copy the actual source code into the distributable package. Even though it will work with an Electron executable, we need to create an asar file before copying the source code into the resources folder so that the source code can be more secure at the user end. Add the following code to create an asar package:

```
function createAsar() {
    return new Promise((resolve, reject) => {
asar.createPackage(appDir.path(),
buildDir.path('resources/app.asar'), function () {
        resolve();
    });
   });
}
```

This combines all your source code into the single asar archive and put it into the resource folder of your Electron distributable folder.

Packaging and Distributing the Application

The `dist` folder is now ready to distribute to the end user. Next step is to rebrand the executable and its resources. For Windows, the `rcedit` tool can be used to edit the executable and its resources. We have used it in the preceding section as a command-line tool. Here, let's use it programmatically to edit the resource files of the `electron.exe` and rebrand it with your own assets. Add the following code into the build script:

```
function updateResources() {
    var deferred = Q.defer();

    // Copy your icon from resource folder into build folder.
    projectDir.copy('resources/windows/icon.ico', buildDir.path('icon.ico'));

    // Replace Electron icon for your own.
    var rcedit = require('rcedit');
    rcedit(buildDir.path('electron.exe'), {
        'icon': projectDir.path('resources/windows/icon.ico'),
        'version-string': {
            'ProductName': manifest.name,
            'FileDescription': manifest.description,
        }
    }, function (err) {
        if (!err) {
            deferred.resolve();
        }
    });
    return deferred.promise;
}
```

Now, the executable resource files are rebranded using our own custom resource files. The preceding method just works only on Windows platform. The executable filename(here for Windows it's exe) is still `electron.exe`. Rename the file with your application's manifest name with the following code:

```
//Rename the electron exe
function rename() {
    return buildDir.renameAsync('electron.exe', manifest.name + '.exe');
}
```

Now, let's zip the output directory so that it can be easily distributed as a single zip file. You can use any other available Node.js zip libraries for this purpose. Let's install one such library using the following command in the project:

```
npm install --save-dev archiver
```

Add the following method to the build script:

```
var file_system = require('fs');
var archiver = require('archiver');

function zipPackage() {
  return new Promise((resolve, reject) =>{
    var output = file_system.createWriteStream(manifest.name + '.zip');
    var archive = archiver('zip');
    output.on('close', function () {
      console.log(archive.pointer() + ' total bytes');
      console.log('archiver has been finalized and the output file
      descriptor has
      closed.');
    });
    archive.on('error', function(err){
      throw err;
    });
    archive.pipe(output);
    archive.bulk([
      { expand: true, cwd: 'source', src: ['**'], dest: 'source'}
    ]);
    archive.finalize();
    resolve();
  });
}
```

The preceding code uses archiver library to zip the folder. The output will be generated with your application's package manifest name. This can be distributed to your end user. Add the following code into the script to execute all these methods together for a complete build process:

```
function build() {
  return init()
         .then(copyElectron)
         .then(cleanupRuntime)
         .then(createAsar)
         .then(updateResources)
         .then(rename)
         .then(zipPackage);
}
module.exports = { build: build };
```

Packaging and Distributing the Application

Creating the native installer

The native installers are important to distribute the application to the users. This will automate the installation process of an application so that users don't need to worry about setting up the application for the first use. There are some tools already available for creating the installer, such as Wix and NSIS. For Windows, you can use one of these tools to generate your installers. Here, we use NSIS, which is designed to be small and suitable for internet distribution. With NSIS, you can create such installers that are capable of doing everything that is needed to set up your software. When you use the `electron-builder`, `electron-packager`, or any other Electron build tool, this process will be an automatic process that the tool will do for you. Here, let's check first how we can do this manually so that you can get a clear detail about how the installers are being created for the Electron application.

The NSIS needs to be scripted in a special scripting language called NSIS script; you can more obtain details about this at `http://nsis.sourceforge.net/Simple_tutorials`. Here, create an NSIS script file called `windows.nsis` inside the tools directory. Add the following content into it to initialize the script:

```
!include LogicLib.nsh
!include nsDialogs.nsh

; --------------------------------
; Variables
; --------------------------------

!define dest "{{dest}}"
!define src "{{src}}"
!define name "{{name}}"
!define productName "{{productName}}"
!define version "{{version}}"
!define icon "{{icon}}"
!define banner "{{banner}}"

!define exec "{{productName}}.exe"

!define regkey "Software${productName}"
!define uninstkey
"SoftwareMicrosoftWindowsCurrentVersionUninstall${productName}"

!define uninstaller "uninstall.exe"
```

Chapter 12

The preceding code just defines some variables for the later usage. First two lines import the core libraries into the context. We initialized the variables using some template placeholder that will be replaced by real values from the build script. The line starts with the semi-column indicating a comment. We also defined two registry keys in the last two lines of the preceding code. The last line is the name of the uninstaller file that will be placed along with the application installer. Add the following code into the script to start the installation process:

```
;  -------------------------------
;  Installation
;  -------------------------------

SetCompressor lzma

Name "${productName}"
Icon "${icon}"
OutFile "${dest}"
InstallDir "$PROGRAMFILES${productName}"
InstallDirRegKey HKLM "${regkey}" ""

CRCCheck on
SilentInstall normal

XPStyle on
ShowInstDetails nevershow
AutoCloseWindow false
WindowIcon off

Caption "${productName} Setup"

; Don't add sub-captions to title bar
SubCaption 3 " "
SubCaption 4 " "

Page custom welcome
Page instfiles

Var Image
Var ImageHandle
```

[295]

The preceding code initializes the actual installation process that initializes the install folders and output directory. Add the following code into the script:

```
Function .onInit
      ; Extract banner image for welcome page
      InitPluginsDir
      ReserveFile "${banner}"
      File /oname=$PLUGINSDIRbanner.bmp "${banner}"
FunctionEnd
```

Define a custom welcome page with the following code in the NSIS script:

```
; Custom welcome page
Function welcome
    nsDialogs::Create 1018

    ${NSD_CreateLabel} 185 1u 210 100% "Welcome to ${productName} version ${version} installer.$r$n$r$nClick install to begin."

    ${NSD_CreateBitmap} 0 0 170 210 ""
    Pop $Image
    ${NSD_SetImage} $Image $PLUGINSDIRbanner.bmp $ImageHandle

    nsDialogs::Show

    ${NSD_FreeImage} $ImageHandle

FunctionEnd
```

Add the actual installation declaration steps to the code. The following code adds some entries to the Windows operating system registry and includes all the directories inside the build folder. Add the following code:

```
; Installation declarations
Section "Install"

    WriteRegStr HKLM "${regkey}" "Install_Dir" "$INSTDIR"
    WriteRegStr HKLM "${uninstkey}" "DisplayName" "${productName}"
    WriteRegStr HKLM "${uninstkey}" "DisplayIcon" '"$INSTDIRicon.ico"'
    WriteRegStr HKLM "${uninstkey}" "UninstallString" '"$INSTDIR${uninstaller}"'

    ; Remove all application files copied by previous installation
    RMDir /r "$INSTDIR"

    SetOutPath $INSTDIR
```

```
; Include all files from /build directory
File /r "${src}*"

; Create start menu shortcut
CreateShortCut "$SMPROGRAMS${productName}.lnk" "$INSTDIR${exec}"
"" "$INSTDIRicon.ico"

WriteUninstaller "${uninstaller}"

SectionEnd
```

The first four lines of the preceding code write the registry keys to the windows registry. It then copies the source code files into the installer and writes the shortcut and uninstaller at the last two lines. This is enough for creating the installer. However, we should have some way to uninstall the application. So, add the following code into the script; this will give you an uninstaller generated along with the installer:

```
; -------------------------------
; Uninstaller
; -------------------------------

ShowUninstDetails nevershow

UninstallCaption "Uninstall ${productName}"
UninstallText "Don't like ${productName} anymore? Hit uninstall
button."
UninstallIcon "${icon}"

UninstPage custom un.confirm un.confirmOnLeave
UninstPage instfiles

Var RemoveAppDataCheckbox
Var RemoveAppDataCheckbox_State

; Custom uninstall confirm page
Function un.confirm

    nsDialogs::Create 1018

    ${NSD_CreateLabel} 1u 1u 100% 24u "If you really want to remove
    ${productName} from your computer press uninstall button."

    ${NSD_CreateCheckbox} 1u 35u 100% 10u "Remove also my
    ${productName} personal data"
    Pop $RemoveAppDataCheckbox

    nsDialogs::Show
```

```
    FunctionEnd

    Function un.confirmOnLeave

        ; Save checkbox state on page leave
        ${NSD_GetState} $RemoveAppDataCheckbox
        $RemoveAppDataCheckbox_State

    FunctionEnd

    ; Uninstall declarations
    Section "Uninstall"

        DeleteRegKey HKLM "${uninstkey}"
        DeleteRegKey HKLM "${regkey}"

        Delete "$SMPROGRAMS${productName}.lnk"

        ; Remove whole directory from Program Files
        RMDir /r "$INSTDIR"

        ; Remove also appData directory generated by your app if user
        checked this option
        ${If} $RemoveAppDataCheckbox_State == ${BST_CHECKED}
            RMDir /r "$LOCALAPPDATA${name}"
        ${EndIf}

    SectionEnd
```

You can execute this script using NSIS utility. However, let's do it programmatically instead of doing it manually. Add the `createInstaller` method as follows; this method replaces the tags with real values that we used inside the NSIS script:

```
function createInstaller() {
    return Promise.resolve();
}
```

First, let's replace the string tags used inside the script with real values. Add the following code to the `createInstaller` method:

```
function createInstaller() {
    function replace(str, patterns) {
        Object.keys(patterns).forEach(function (pattern) {
            console.log(pattern)
              var matcher = new RegExp('{{' + pattern + '}}', 'g');
            str = str.replace(matcher, patterns[pattern]);
        });
        return str;
    }

    var installScript = projectDir.read('resources/windows/installer.nsi');

    installScript = replace(installScript, {
        name: manifest.name,
        productName: manifest.name,
        version: manifest.version,
        src: buildDir.path(),
        dest: projectDir.path(),
        icon: buildDir.path('icon.ico'),
        setupIcon: buildDir.path('icon.ico'),
        banner: projectDir.path('resources/windows/banner.bmp'),
    });
    buildDir.write('installer.nsi', installScript);

    return new Promise(....);
}
```

Next, add the following code to execute the NSIS script and create the installer:

```
function createInstaller() {
    ....
    return new Promise((resolve, reject) => {
        var nsis = childProcess.spawn('makensis', [buildDir.path('installer.nsi')], {
            stdio: 'inherit'
        });

        nsis.on('error', function (err) {
            if (err.message === 'spawn makensis ENOENT') {
                throw "Can't find NSIS. Are you sure you've installed it and"
                + " added to PATH environment variable?";
            } else {
                throw err;
```

[299]

```
        }
    });

    nsis.on('close', function () {
        resolve();
    });
  });
}
```

The preceding code executes the `makensis` command that will create the installer from the NSIS script. Next, update the build function to execute the `createInstaller` function as part of the build. Update the build function as follows:

```
function buildWindows() {
  return init()
    .then(copyElectron)
    .then(cleanupRuntime)
    .then(createAsar)
    .then(updateResources)
    .then(rename)
    .then(createInstaller);
}
```

This build function will work only with the Windows platform. Some of the code that we used here is not compatible with Linux and Mac. So, we need to target the Windows platform when executing the build function. Add the following code to the build script; this checks the current platform and executes the corresponding build function for that platform:

```
var os = require('os');
switch(os.platform()) {
   case 'darwin':
      // here execute build method for Mac OS
      break;
   case 'linux':
      // execue for linux
      break;
   case 'win32':
      buildWindows();
      break;
}
```

The preceding process was a little bit complicated. However, you have full control over the build process. This requires some amount of effort and time to do the work for you. We have already discussed that there are some tools are available to do the packaging of an Electron application. The `electron-builder` and `electron-packager` are two popular tools that can be used to package the application. We have already discussed `electron-builder` in the preceding sections. Let check how we can use these tool in detail in the next section.

The entire code that we discussed here can be replaced just with configuration when using the `electron-builder`. The configuration should be done inside the `package.json` file. Install the `electron-builder` using the following command if you don't have it already:

```
npm install -g electron-builder
```

The tool provides a command-line interface that can be executed via a `build` command from your terminal, which will be available globally if you have installed it into your global npm cache. Here, as we installed the `npm` library as dev dependency, the `build` command can be found at the `node_modules/.bin/build` file. Run the `node_modules/.bin/build --help` command to get all the available options.

Once you have configured the `package.json` for building the application, you can run the build using `build` command. Add the following configuration to your `package.json` file:

```
"build": {
   "productName": "ELectronApplication",
   "appId": "org.develar.ElectronReact",
   "category": "public.app-category.tools",
   "dmg": {
      "contents": [
         {
            "x": 410,
            "y": 150,
            "type": "link",
            "path": "/Applications"
         },
         {
            "x": 130,
            "y": 150,
            "type": "file"
         }
      ]
   },
   "files": [
      "dist/",
      "node_modules/",
```

```
            "app.html",
            "main.js",
            "main.js.map",
            "package.json"
    ],
    "win": {
        "target": "nsis"
    },
    "linux": {
        "target": [
            "deb",
            "AppImage"
        ]
    },
    "directories": {
        "buildResources": "resources",
          "output": "release"
      }
    }
```

The productId, appId, and category is important especially when you work with the app stores. It provides numerous build targets. Here, for example, we have configured Mac-, Windows-, and Linux-based target formats. The following build targets are supported with `electron-builder`; you can easily customize the build according to your requirements:

- All platforms: 7z, zip, tar.xz, tar.lz, tar.gz, tar.bz2, and dir (unpacked directory).
- macOS: dmg, pkg, and mas.
- Linux: AppImage, snap, debian package (deb), rpm, freebsd, pacman, p5p, and apk.
- Windows: nsis (Installer), nsis-web (Web installer), portable (portable app without installation), AppX (Windows Store), and Squirrel.Windows.

You can customize the files to be included in the build by providing it in the files array. Copy all your icons and icns files into the resources folder that will be used as a build resource folder. We have already configured it inside the directories section. You can package the application using `build` command from your project directory. However, a better way is to add the `build` command to the scripts section of the `package.json` file:

```
{
  ....
  "scripts" : {
      "dist": "build"
   }
}
```

Execute the build by running the following command:

```
npm run dist
```

Programmatic Usage

Electron-builder also provides a programmatic API to deal with your application packaging. The configuration should be passed to the build function as follows in your build script:

```
"use strict"

const builder = require("electron-builder")
const Platform = builder.Platform

// Promise is returned
builder.build({
  targets: Platform.MAC.createTarget(),
  config: {
   "//": "build options, see https://goo.gl/ZhRfla"
  }
})
.then(() => {
  // handle result
})
.catch((error) => {
  // handle error
})
```

Publishing the artifacts

The `electron-builder` provides multiple ways to publish your artifacts. The following methods are supported:

- GitHub release
- Amazon S3
- Bintray

Like always, it can be done either via command line or using the configuration inside the `package.json`. The following command can be used to publish the artifacts:

```
build --publish "always"
```

To publish a prerelease you can use `--prerelease` in the same command, as follows:

```
build --publish "always" --prerelease
```

You can also draft an unreleased version using the draft flag, as follows:

```
build --publish "always"  --draft
```

The publish tag can accept four tags as the value. These are related to the GitHub release tags. You should be familiar with these concepts if you have ever worked with GitHub releases. The following values are accepted for the publish flag:

- **onTbagOrDraft**: This is the recommended workflow for the tool. To do this, you need to tag a new version release inside the GitHub. The tag version should be set to the version of your application inside the `package.json` file and prefix with v. Push some commit to the repo so that the CI will be building new artifacts. Once you are done, publish the application and the GitHub will tag the latest release for you.
- **onTag:** The release will be drafted when the new tag is pushed to the GitHub.
- **always:** The artifacts will be published always.

The GitHub information is already detected from your `package.json` or from the `.git/config`. If you need to override the default publish options for GitHub, you can provide it inside the configuration options that is inside your `package.json`, as follows:

```
{
 ...
 "build": {
 "publish": [{
    "provider": "github",
    "owner": "user",
    "repo": "repo-name"
   }],
   ...
  }
}
```

Auto updating the application

Auto updating the application is important when you want to push the new changes to the user. If you have worked with the Visual studio code or similar applications, you can note that each month the application getting updated automatically without breaking your existing application installation. You need to configure the CI for automatic deployment. Follow the preceding section to automate the publishing your artifacts.

To configure the auto update, install the `electron-updater` package first to the project using the npm package manager:

```
npm install --save-dev electron-updater
```

Next, configure the publish as we discussed before. Once you configure the publish option, you can import the `autoUpdater` from `electron-updater`, which will do the work for you. Let's look at the code sample with the `electron-updater`. The Electron already provides a built-in class called `autoUpdater.`. Actually, the `electron-updater` package is built on top of the Electrons' `autoUpdater` class, which provides more functionalities to the developer. You can use the Electron's built-in class, but you need to set up the release server to work with the auto update.

With a built-in `autoUpdator` class, you need to set the release server URL using the following code:

```
autoUpdater.setFeedURL(url)
```

Checking for an update programmatically can be done using the `autoUpdater.checkForUpdates()` method. Whenever a new update is available, the `autoUpdater` will emit `update-available` method and the Electron will download the update automatically. As the native Electron `autoUpdater` is of low level, let's use the `electron-updater` package. The API itself almost same as the native `autoUpdator` class including the class names and function names. Here is a sample implementation done using `electron-update`. The coding should be done for the main process:

```
const {app, BrowserWindow, Menu, protocol, ipcMain} = require('electron');
const log = require('electron-log');
const {autoUpdater} = require("electron-updater");

autoUpdater.logger = log;
autoUpdater.logger.transports.file.level = 'info';
log.info('App starting...');

let template = []
if (process.platform === 'darwin') {
```

```
    // OS X
    const name = app.getName();
    template.unshift({
      label: name,
      submenu: [
        {
          label: 'About ' + name,
          role: 'about'
        },
        {
          label: 'Quit',
          accelerator: 'Command+Q',
          click() { app.quit(); }
        },
      ]
    })
}

let win;

function sendStatusToWindow(text) {
  log.info(text);
  win.webContents.send('message', text);
}
function createDefaultWindow() {
  win = new BrowserWindow();
  win.webContents.openDevTools();
  win.on('closed', () => {
    win = null;
  });
  win.loadURL(`file://${__dirname}/version.html#v${app.getVersion()}`);
  return win;
}
autoUpdater.on('checking-for-update', () => {
  sendStatusToWindow('Checking for update...');
})
autoUpdater.on('update-available', (ev, info) => {
  sendStatusToWindow('Update available.');
})
autoUpdater.on('update-not-available', (ev, info) => {
  sendStatusToWindow('Update not available.');
})
autoUpdater.on('error', (ev, err) => {
  sendStatusToWindow('Error in auto-updater.');
})
autoUpdater.on('download-progress', (ev, progressObj) => {
  sendStatusToWindow('Download progress...');
})
```

```
autoUpdater.on('update-downloaded', (ev, info) => {
  sendStatusToWindow('Update downloaded; will install in 5 seconds');
});
app.on('ready', function() {
  // Create the Menu
  const menu = Menu.buildFromTemplate(template);
  Menu.setApplicationMenu(menu);

  createDefaultWindow();
});
app.on('window-all-closed', () => {
  app.quit();
});

//-------------------------------------------------------------------
// Auto updates
//
// For details about these events, see the Wiki:
//
https://github.com/electron-userland/electron-builder/wiki/Auto-Update#events
//
// The app doesn't need to listen to any events except `update-downloaded`
//
// Uncomment any of the below events to listen for them. Also,
// look in the previous section to see them being used.
//-------------------------------------------------------------------
// autoUpdater.on('checking-for-update', () => {
// })
// autoUpdater.on('update-available', (ev, info) => {
// })
// autoUpdater.on('update-not-available', (ev, info) => {
// })
// autoUpdater.on('error', (ev, err) => {
// })
autoUpdater.on('download-progress', (ev, progressObj) => {
})
autoUpdater.on('update-downloaded', (ev, info) => {
  // Wait 5 seconds, then quit and install
  // In your application, you don't need to wait 5 seconds.
  // You could call autoUpdater.quitAndInstall(); immediately
  setTimeout(function() {
    autoUpdater.quitAndInstall();
  }, 5000)
})
```

```
app.on('ready', function() {
  autoUpdater.checkForUpdates();
});
```

You don't need to use all these events for configuring the update. Only the update-downloaded event is needed to do our work. The `autoUpdater.quitAndInall` method will quit the application and install the new updates.

Submitting to the App Store

Once you have the application packaged, you need to submit it to various app stores. In this section, let's look on how to do this for windows app store and Mac app store.

Windows App Store submission guide

With Windows 8, Microsoft introduced a new type of executable, which is called the appx format. Microsoft has developed a tool that compiles Electron app into the appx package. Install the `electron-windows-store` package to convert the Electron app into the appx format:

```
npm install -g electron-windows-store
```

Once you finish the installation, follow the steps described below in order to package your application for Windows App Store:

1. Package your Electron application with `electron-packager` or using the method that we discussed in the earlier section.
2. Open the powershell and run the `electron-windows-store` command with required parameters. Ensure that you do not include the unwanted `node_modules` folders. Use the command with the following parameters:

```
electron-windows-store --input-directory C:appname --output-directory C:outputappname --flatten true --package-version 1.0.0.0 --package-name appname
```

Once executed, the tool starts to work. It accepts your Electron app as an input, flattening the node_modules. Then, it archives your application as `app.zip`. Using an installer and a Windows Container, the tool creates an expanded AppX package, including the Windows Application Manifest (`AppXManifest.xml`) as well as the virtual filesystem and the virtual registry inside your output folder.

Once the expanded AppX files are created, the tool uses the Windows App Packager (`MakeAppx.exe`) to create a single-file AppX package from those files on disk. Finally, the tool can be used to create a trusted certificate on your computer to sign the new AppX package. With the signed AppX package, the CLI can also automatically install the package on your machine.

In order to run the package, the users need to have Windows 10 with its anniversary update. As it's a packaged application, the app store need to have manual approve to get it approved and to deliver the application to its end user. You can start submitting the application to the Windows store by navigating to https://developer.microsoft.com/en-us/windows/projects/campaigns/desktop-bridge.

Mac App Store submission guide

You need to enroll Apple developer program to submit the application to the mac app store. You need to get the certificate from Apple to sign your app. First, you need to add the team id to the `info.plist` file. Add the following code into it:

```xml
<plist version="1.0">
  <dict>
    ...
    <key>ElectronTeamID</key>
    <string>TEAM_ID</string>
  </dict>
</plist>
```

Then, prepare the following file with the content:

```
child.plist:

<?xml version="1.0" encoding="UTF-8"?>
<!DOCTYPE plist PUBLIC "-//Apple//DTD PLIST 1.0//EN"
"http://www.apple.com/DTDs/PropertyList-1.0.dtd">
<plist version="1.0">
  <dict>
    <key>com.apple.security.app-sandbox</key>
    <true/>
    <key>com.apple.security.inherit</key>
    <true/>
  </dict>
</plist>

parent.plist:

<?xml version="1.0" encoding="UTF-8"?>
```

```xml
<!DOCTYPE plist PUBLIC "-//Apple//DTD PLIST 1.0//EN"
"http://www.apple.com/DTDs/PropertyList-1.0.dtd">
<plist version="1.0">
  <dict>
    <key>com.apple.security.app-sandbox</key>
    <true/>
    <key>com.apple.security.application-groups</key>
    <string>TEAM_ID.your.bundle.id</string>
  </dict>
</plist>
```

You have to replace `TEAM_ID` with your team ID, and replace `your.bundle.id` with the bundle ID of your app.

Then, sign your app with the following script:

```bash
#!/bin/bash

# Name of your app.
APP="YourApp"
# The path of your app to sign.
APP_PATH="/path/to/YourApp.app"
# The path to the location you want to put the signed package.
RESULT_PATH="~/Desktop/$APP.pkg"
# The name of certificates you requested.
APP_KEY="3rd Party Mac Developer Application: Company Name (APPIDENTITY)"
INSTALLER_KEY="3rd Party Mac Developer Installer: Company Name (APPIDENTITY)"
# The path of your plist files.
CHILD_PLIST="/path/to/child.plist"
PARENT_PLIST="/path/to/parent.plist"

FRAMEWORKS_PATH="$APP_PATH/Contents/Frameworks"

codesign -s "$APP_KEY" -f --entitlements "$CHILD_PLIST"
"$FRAMEWORKS_PATH/Electron Framework.framework/Versions/A/Electron
Framework"
codesign -s "$APP_KEY" -f --entitlements "$CHILD_PLIST"
"$FRAMEWORKS_PATH/Electron
Framework.framework/Versions/A/Libraries/libffmpeg.dylib"
codesign -s "$APP_KEY" -f --entitlements "$CHILD_PLIST"
"$FRAMEWORKS_PATH/Electron
Framework.framework/Versions/A/Libraries/libnode.dylib"
codesign -s "$APP_KEY" -f --entitlements "$CHILD_PLIST"
"$FRAMEWORKS_PATH/Electron Framework.framework"
codesign -s "$APP_KEY" -f --entitlements "$CHILD_PLIST"
"$FRAMEWORKS_PATH/$APP Helper.app/Contents/MacOS/$APP Helper"
```

```
codesign -s "$APP_KEY" -f --entitlements "$CHILD_PLIST"
"$FRAMEWORKS_PATH/$APP Helper.app/"
codesign -s "$APP_KEY" -f --entitlements "$CHILD_PLIST"
"$FRAMEWORKS_PATH/$APP Helper EH.app/Contents/MacOS/$APP Helper EH"
codesign -s "$APP_KEY" -f --entitlements "$CHILD_PLIST"
"$FRAMEWORKS_PATH/$APP Helper EH.app/"
codesign -s "$APP_KEY" -f --entitlements "$CHILD_PLIST"
"$FRAMEWORKS_PATH/$APP Helper NP.app/Contents/MacOS/$APP Helper NP"
codesign -s "$APP_KEY" -f --entitlements "$CHILD_PLIST"
"$FRAMEWORKS_PATH/$APP Helper NP.app/"
codesign -s "$APP_KEY" -f --entitlements "$CHILD_PLIST"
"$APP_PATH/Contents/MacOS/$APP"
codesign -s "$APP_KEY" -f --entitlements "$PARENT_PLIST" "$APP_PATH"

productbuild --component "$APP_PATH" /Applications --sign "$INSTALLER_KEY"
"$RESULT_PATH"
```

Native modules used in your app also need to be signed. If you are using `electron-osx-sign`, ensure that you include the path to the built binaries in the argument list:

```
electron-osx-sign YourApp.app
YourApp.app/Contents/Resources/app/node_modules/nativemodule/build/release/
nativemodule
```

After these steps, you can upload your application and request for approval through the Apple store.

Continuous Integration

The Electron can be plugged into **Continuous Integration** (**CI**) systems. It will be better to use the CI system for the continuous delivery of your application. You need to register your GitHub account or any other source control account with the CI systems if you are using one of the following CI systems that we are going to discuss. These tools are free for open source projects. It will be good to use Travis CI for testing the Linux and Mac and Appveyor for the Windows because of its native platform support. You need to configure the CI by logging into this website and attach your GitHub repo into the CI server. Then, you need to add the .travis.yml file and appveyor.yml file into the root of your project. You can define the steps to be done by CI server in these files. Add the following content to your .travis.yml file:

```
language: javascript

before_script:
 - chmod +x ./scripts/travis-build.sh
```

Packaging and Distributing the Application

```
script:
  - ./scripts/travis-build.sh
```

The `travis-build.sh` file will be executed every time you commit the changes to your source code repo. You can define anything with your `.sh` file that you want to execute. Here is the sample code for the `travis-build.sh` file:

```
git clone https://github.com/creationix/nvm.git /tmp/.nvmsource
/tmp/.nvm/nvm.sh
nvm install "$NODE_VERSION"
nvm use --delete-prefix "$NODE_VERSION"
if [[ "$TRAVIS_OS_NAME" == "linux" ]]; then
export DISPLAY=:99.0
sh -e /etc/init.d/xvfb start sleep 3fi
node --version
npm --version
npm install
npm test & npm run e2e
```

This installs the proper version of the node, then executes your test after installing the node modules. The `appveoyer.yml` can be used to test your windows version using CI server automatically. Use the following code in your `apvoyer.yml` file, and your server can execute it for you for all your commits:

```
cache:
  - node_modules -> package.json

install:
  - ps: Install-Product node $env:nodejs_version
  - npm install npm
  - .node_modules.bin npm install

build_script:
  - npm run build

test_script:
  - node --version
  - .node_modules.bin npm --version
  - .node_modules.bin npm
```

Summary

Packaging and deployment is an essential step in the development process. The configuration and the build script should be written at the time of the development itself. This chapter briefed about the packaging and deployment process for an Electron application. We had already discussed the rest of the development workflow process in the previous chapters. With the modern tools, such as Electron builder, it's super easy to package an application for all major platforms. This cannot be achieved with traditional desktop application development methods in other languages. This is the time to replace the traditional desktop application for your business application. Especially with the rise of Angular and React, the JavaScript development has crossed its border. So, it's quite worth on using this kind of technologies, which saves a lot of development efforts.

Index

A

Angular 2 service
  reference 83
Angular router
  configuring 85
Angular routing
  reference 85
Angular service
  creating 83
app linter 68
App Store
  Mac app store, submission guide 309
  reference, for Windows 309
  submission guide 308
  submitting to 308
application life cycle, controlling with app module
  about 204
  default protocol client, setting up 204
  recent document list, managing 205
application logs
  managing 227, 228, 230, 231
applications, Electron showcase page
  reference 13
applications, Electron
  Nyla's n1 14
  Pixate 15
  Slack 14
  WordPress.com 15
asar archive
  Electron, packaging into 284
  generating 284, 285
Awesome Electron
  about 130
  reference 13, 130

B

bars 112
browser window customization
  about 198
  listening for APPCOMMANDs, on Windows platform 201
  multiple windows, managing 199, 200
  offscreen rendering 202
  POST requests, loading 200
build process
  App Store, submitting to 308
  application, auto updating 305
  artifacts, publishing 303, 304
  automating 289, 290
  Continuous Integration (CI) 311, 312
  native installers, creating 294, 298
  programmatic usage 303
button
  creating, React desktop used 123

C

cache version
  managing 256, 257, 258
Chai as Promised
  using 278, 279
Chrome Developer Tools extensions
  adding 65, 66
  loading 66, 68
chromium embedded framework (CEF) 9
clipboard
  working with 174
compiler options
  reference 148
Continuous Integration (CI) 311, 312
cookies 161
crash reports

submitting, to server 77, 78
CRUD operation 137
custom macOS dock menu 215, 217
custom protocols
  defining 158

D

data stores
  database service, creating 134, 135, 139
  dependencies, installing 134
  managing 132
  Node MySQL driver, used 133
database service
  creating 134, 135, 139
database
  storing 260, 261
debugging, Visual Studio Code
  about 61
  application, monitoring with Devtron 68, 69
  Chrome Developer Tools extensions, adding 65, 66
  crash reports, submitting to server 77, 78
  desktop, capturing Electron API used 78, 79
  development workflow, leveraging 71
  Electron behavior, controlling environment variables used 76
  keyboard shortcuts, adding to application 74
  launch configuration, setting up 62
  power state changes, monitoring 77
  renderer processes 64
  task runners, integrating 70
dependencies
  installing 134
desktop applications
  need for 8, 9
desktop integration 208
desktop notifications
  handling 209, 210
desktop
  capturing, Electron API used 78, 79
development workflow
  hot module replacement, adding 72
  leveraging 71
  webpack dev server, integrating into Electron shell 73

Devtron
  about 60
  application, monitoring 68, 69
  features 68
display properties
  managing 219, 220, 224, 226
display
  managing 176, 177
dock menu
  managing 211, 212, 214
draggable regions 109

E

Electron API
  accessing 269, 270
  desktop, capturing 78, 79
Electron application
  browser/main process 28
  building 282, 284
  communication between renderer and browser 29
  debugging 60
  Electron builder, using 287, 288
  main process, debugging 61
  packaging 282, 284
  packaging, into asar archive 284
  rebranding 286
  reference 282
  renderer process 28
  running 20, 21
  running, as Linux daemons 236
  running, as Windows service 231, 232, 235
  writing 17, 19
Electron behavior
  controlling, environment variables used 76
Electron builder
  reference 288
  using 288
electron-devtools-installer 65
Electron
  about 10
  applications 14
  benefits 10, 11
  existing skill set, leveraging 11
  history 9

installing 16
multi process architecture 27
oAuth authentication, implementing with 101, 104
sandbox security model, removing 11
unlimited access, to Node.js/NPM 12
used, for building hello world application 15
users 13, 14
working 26, 28
environment variables
  reference 76
  used, for controlling Electron behavior 76
ES2015
  using, with Electron 147
ESNext
  using, in test cases 277
extended Node.js process 196

F

Facebook API
  logging in 87
  profile component, creating 98, 99
  user profile, obtaining 91, 97
Facebook application
  reference, for creating 82
  setting up 82
Facebook developer portal
  reference 87
Facebook Graph API
  about 82
Facebook SDK
  configuring 83
frameless window 108

G

generic dialog boxes 172
GitHub style sheet, markdown files
  reference 24
GraphQL explorer
  about 91
  reference 91

H

hardware
  accessing 142
  native add-on, creating 144, 147
hello world application
  building, Electron used 15
HomeBrew
  reference 15
hot module replacement
  adding 72
HTML5 notification API 210
HTTPS server
  creating 249

I

inter-process communication, with IPC module
  about 152
  callbacks, passing to main process 157
  IPCMain 154, 156
  IPCRenderer 152, 153, 154
  variables, sharing between modules 158
IPC monitor 69
IPCMain module 154, 156
IPCRenderer module 152, 153, 154

J

JavaScript testing 264
JSON service
  adding 252, 253

K

keyboard shortcuts
  adding, to application 74

L

launch configuration
  setting up 62, 63, 64
Linux daemons
  Electron application, running as 236
Linux Unity launcher shortcuts 214, 215
list view 128

M

Mac app store
  submission guide 309
marked parser
  reference 22
mini-breakpad-server
  reference 77
Mocha
  reference 264
multi process architecture, Electron
  browser 27
  modules 27
  renderer 27

N

native add-on
  creating 144, 147
  nan 144
  node-gyp 144
native installer
  creating 294, 298
native system dialogs
  about 169, 172
  generic dialog boxes 172
NavPane component 127, 128
network
  emulating, session API used 165
networking, from main process
  about 179, 180
  web requests, managing 181
Node MySQL driver
  using 133
Node.js process
  reference 196
Node.js
  about 7
  installation, ways 15, 16
  reference 15
  using, inside web pages 21, 22, 23, 25
NodeRT
  download link 238
NodeSource
  reference 16
notification API
  reference 210
  using 240, 242
NSIS script
  reference 294
Nuclide 13
Nyla's n1
  about 14
  reference 14

O

oAuth authentication
  implementing, with Electron 101, 104
operating system APIs
  accessing 12

P

Photon components
  about 111
  bars 112
Photon kit
  about 108
  application, laying out 108, 109
  draggable regions 109
  frameless window 108, 109
  Navs 113
  reference 108
  table class 114
  Toolbar & Actions 112, 113
Pixate 15
PouchDB
  reference 261
power changes
  monitoring 177
power sleep mode
  managing 176, 177
power state changes
  monitoring 77
powercfg utility
  reference 219
process object
  accessing 276
protocol 158
push notifications
  customizing 258, 259, 260

database, storing 260, 261

R

React desktop
  about 122
  list view 128
  NavPane component 127
  reference 130
  Segmented Control 125
  used, for creating button 123
  user interface, building with 116, 117, 121
  windows 124
recent documents
  managing 211, 212, 214
renderer process
  debugging 64

S

SegmentedControl component 125
service worker
  about 246
  cache version, managing 256, 257, 258
  creating 253, 254, 256
  HTTPS server, creating 249
  JSON service, adding 252, 253
  life cycle 246, 247
  managing, in Electron 247, 249
session API
  file download, managing 167
  permission requests, intercepting 166
  used, for emulating network 165
session module
  about 163
  content download, intercepting 164, 165
sessions 161
shell module
  working with 203
sidebar 111
Slack 14
socorro
  reference 77
Spectron
  about 266, 267
  API, exploring 273, 274
  DOM tree, testing 270
  Electron API, accessing 269, 270
  process object, accessing 276
  renderer process logs, accessing 276
  webContents API, accessing 275

T

tab component
  creating 100
task list
  managing 211, 212, 214
task runners
  integrating, with VS code 70
thumbnail toolbars 218
tray icons
  dealing with 226
TypeScript
  using, with Electron 147

U

Universal Windows platform 237
user interface
  creating, with React desktop 116, 117, 121

V

Visual Studio Code
  debugging with 61
  launch configuration, setting up 63, 64
  task runners, integrating 70

W

web page, managing with webContents
  about 186
  device viewport, emulating inside web view 190, 191
  guest content, embedding with WebView tag 194, 196
  page navigation, managing 187
  page snapshot, capturing 189
  web pages, printing 191, 193
  web pages, saving 191, 194
  web view requests, authenticating 188
web pages
  Node.js, using inside 21, 22, 23, 25

webContents API
  accessing 275
WebDriverIO client API
  reference 267
WebDriverIO
  reference 271
Windows 10 anniversary update 238
Windows service
  Electron application, running as 231, 232, 235
Windows store
  packaging for, in appx format 243
WinRT
  about 238
  developing with 238, 239
  reference 240
WordPress
  reference 15

Printed in Great Britain
by Amazon